British Theatre between the Wars, 1918–1939

Histories of British theatre between 1918 and 1939 have tended to
marginalise the commercial and mainstream in favour of the literary or
the politically motivated. This volume brings together a collection of
essays that reflect both a far more complex theatre world than this
strategy has allowed for, and recent scholarship on mainstream and
alternative theatres in the 1920s and 1930s. Combining the popular with
the commercial, the book includes accounts of the craze for thriller and
detective plays and musical comedy and revue, alongside analyses of
historical pageantry and the development of politicised productions of
Shakespeare. With assessments of the representation of gender and
sexuality in the theatre, this volume not only unveils hitherto neglected
theatre practices but also places them in the context of a society
undergoing rapid social and cultural change. It will appeal to advanced
undergraduates and postgraduates and scholars interested in twentieth-
century British theatre.

CLIVE BARKER has had a long career combining practical work and
academic teaching. His ideas on actor training were published as *Theatre
Games* in 1977. He is co-editor of *New Theatre Quarterly* published by
Cambridge University Press.

MAGGIE B. GALE is Senior Lecturer in Drama and Theatre Arts at the
University of Birmingham. She is the author of *West End Women:
Women on the London Stage 1918–1962* (1996) and joint editor with Viv
Gardner of *Women, Theatre and Performance: New Histories, New
Historiographies* (2000).

CAMBRIDGE STUDIES IN MODERN THEATRE

Volumes for Cambridge Studies in Modern Theatre explore the political, social and cultural functions of theatre while also paying careful attention to detailed performance analysis. The focus of the series is on political approaches to the modern theatre with attention also being paid to theatres of earlier periods and their influence on contemporary drama. Topics in the series are chosen to investigate this relationship and include both playwrights (their aims and intentions set against the effects of their work) and process (with emphasis on rehearsal and production methods, the political structure within theatre companies, and their choice of audiences or performance venues). Further topics will include devised theatre, agitprop, community theatre, para-theatre and performance art. In all cases the series will be alive to the special cultural and political factors operating in the theatres examined.

Books published

Brian Crow with Chris Banfield, *An introduction to post-colonial theatre*

Mario DiCenzo, *The politics of alternative theatre in Britain, 1968–1990:7:84 (Scotland)*

Jo Riley, *Chinese theatre and the actor in performance*

Jonathan Kalb, *The theatre of Heiner Müller*

Richard Boon and Jane Plastow, eds., *Theatre matters: performance and culture on the world stage*

Claude Schumacher, ed., *Staging the Holocaust: the Shoah in drama and performance*

Philip Roberts, *The Royal Court Theatre and the modern stage*

Nicholas Grene, *The politics of Irish drama: plays in context from Boucicault to Friel*

Anatoly Smeliansky, *The Russian theatre after Stalin*

Clive Barker and Maggie B. Gale, eds., *British Theatre between the Wars, 1918–1939*

British Theatre between the Wars 1918–1939

edited by
Clive Barker and Maggie B. Gale

CAMBRIDGE
UNIVERSITY PRESS

PUBLISHED BY THE PRESS SYNDICATE OF THE UNIVERSITY OF CAMBRIDGE

The Pitt Building, Trumpington Street, Cambridge, United Kingdom

CAMBRIDGE UNIVERSITY PRESS

The Edinburgh Building, Cambridge CB2 2RU, UK

40 West 20th Street, New York, NY 10011-4211, USA

10 Stamford Road, Oakleigh, VIC 3166, Australia

Ruiz de Alarcón 13, 28014 Madrid, Spain

Dock House, The Waterfront, Cape Town 8001, South Africa

http://www.cambridge.org

First published 2000

Printed in the United Kingdom at the University Press, Cambridge

Typeface 9.25/14 pt Trump Mediaeval and Schadow BT, in *QuarkXPress*™ [SE]

A catalogue record for this book is available from the British Library

ISBN 0 521 62407 x hardback

Contents

List of illustrations   *page* vii
Notes on contributors   viii

Introduction   *1*
MAGGIE B. GALE

1   Theatre and society: the Edwardian legacy, the First World War and
the inter-war years   *4*
CLIVE BARKER

2   Body parts: the success of the thriller in the inter-war years   *38*
JOHN STOKES

3   When men were men and women were women   *63*
JOHN DEENEY

4   Girl crazy: musicals and revue between the wars   *88*
JAMES ROSS MOORE

5   Errant nymphs: women and the inter-war theatre   *113*
MAGGIE B. GALE

6   Blood on the bright young things: Shakespeare in the 1930s   *135*
TONY HOWARD

7   The religion of socialism or a pleasant Sunday afternoon?: The ILP
Arts Guild   *162*
ROS MERKIN

8   Delving the levels of memory and dressing up in the past   *190*
MICK WALLIS

Contents

9 The ghosts of war: stage ghosts and time slips as a response to war *215*
CLIVE BARKER

Index *244*

Illustrations

1. Dr Henry Lakington tortures Phyllis before Drummond: Sir Gerald du Maurier, Mr Gilbert Hare and Miss Olwen Roose. From *Bulldog Drummond*. Reproduced in *The Sketch*, 22 February 1922. *43*
   [Feb. 1922. By permission of The British Library]
2. Downing the villains: Sir Gerald du Maurier as the hero of 'Sapper's' Melodrama. Reproduced in *The Sketch*, 22 February 1922. *44*
   [Feb. 1922. By permission of The British Library]
3. Jessica Tandy and Joyce Bland in *Children in Uniform*, the Duchess Theatre (1932). Reproduced courtesy of The Mander and Mitchenson Theatre Archive, Kent, England. *64*
4. *The Gate Revue* (1939). Reproduced courtesy of The Mander and Mitchenson Theatre Archive, Kent, England. *108*
5. Auriol Lee's production of Aimée and Philip Stuart's *Nine Till Six* (1930). Reproduced courtesy of The Mander and Mitchenson Theatre Archive, Kent, England. *130*

6 and 7. *Pageant of Bradstone* (Mary Kelly, 1929). Reproduced by kind permission of Margery Kelly. As the squire's daughter, Mary Kelly could draw on the financial and persuasive resources of her father as well as her own popularity to mount this quite substantial pageant in the hamlet directly neighbouring her native Kelly in Devon. Most of the performers are from local tenant farmer families. *202–3*

Notes on contributors

CLIVE BARKER has had a long career combining practical work and academic teaching. His ideas on actor training were published as *Theatre Games* (1977). He is co-editor of *New Theatre Quarterly* (Cambridge University Press).

JOHN DEENEY is Lecturer in Theatre Studies at the University of Ulster at Coleraine. He is editor of *Writing Live: an Investigation of the Relationship between Writing and Live Art* (1998). Deeney's most recent work is on censorship and 'other' sexualities in British Theatre between the two world wars and on new contemporary British playwrights.

MAGGIE B. GALE is Senior Lecturer in Drama and Theatre Arts at the University of Birmingham. She is author of *West End Women: Women on the London Stage 1918–1962* (1996), and is joint series editor with Viv Gardner of the Women, Theatre and Performance series for Manchester University Press.

TONY HOWARD is Senior Lecturer in English and Comparative Literature at Warwick University. He has published widely on Shakespearean stage, film and television production and on East European theatre. Howard is currently writing a transhistorical, transcultural study of female Hamlets.

ROS MERKIN is Senior Lecturer in the Department of Drama at Liverpool John Moore's University. She is the editor of *Popular Theatre?* (1996) and has published articles on the Independent Labour Party and the Arts Guild. Her current research is in the area of musical theatre.

JAMES ROSS MOORE was chair of the Department of English,

Literature and Journalism at Mt. San Antonio College in California. He has recently published and presented broadcasts for the BBC on the British careers of Cole Porter, George and Ira Gershwin and André Charlot. He is currently engaged in writing a biography of Charlot.

JOHN STOKES is Professor of Modern British Literature in the Department of English at King's College, London. His most recent book is *Oscar Wilde: Myths, Miracles and Imitations* (Cambridge University Press, 1996). He has written widely on nineteenth-century French actresses, on nineteenth- and twentieth-century theatre, and reviews for the *The Times Literary Supplement* and other journals.

MICK WALLIS is Reader in Drama at the University of Loughborough. He is presently engaged in a national survey of historical pageants in Britain. Other research interests include theatre pedagogy, British Leftist theatre, cultural performance, queer theory and politics.

Introduction

MAGGIE B. GALE

The social and economic shifts which followed in the wake of the First World War are perceived as having greatly affected British society but not necessarily British theatre. Inter-war theatre has traditionally been seen as conservative and as somehow failing to reflect the cultural upheavals which surrounded it. Typical assessments of the theatre between the wars suggest that, with certain exceptions, it pandered to escapism and commercialism. This volume aims to undermine such assertions by providing closer readings of certain theatres of the age and by suggesting that the relationship between theatre, politics and social change was far more complex than a superficial survey of 'key' writers or 'key' production companies might suggest.

Clive Barker's opening chapter re-assesses the impact of the immediate pre-war years and of the war years themselves. Barker stresses that theatre did not, in fact, suddenly change because of the First World War but that changes in policy and production, changes in for whom theatre was being made and why, are rooted in the pre-war years. John Stokes and John Deeney both examine the impact of the immediate post-war years on the way in which images of masculinity and gender were negotiated on the stage. Stokes, in his exploration of the thriller genre and its regular charismatic performers, looks at the relationship between theatricality, violence, sexuality and audience reception. Deeney, on the other hand, explores the interconnected nature of expressions of sexuality and censorship, both formal and informal. James Ross Moore and Maggie B. Gale both offer survey chapters as a way into opening up vast areas of inter-war British theatre which continue to be underrated – either because of their performative contexts or because of the ways in which current frameworks of analysis could be said to validate marginal rather than commercially 'successful' theatre practices. Moore provides a trajectory from the revues and musical comedies of the 1920s through to the more overtly politicised intimate revues of the late inter-war period. Gale offers an overview of the variety of ways in which women contributed to the theatre of the age, and locates the critics' concerns about the overwhelming 'feminisation' of theatre in the 1920s within the context of increased levels of female participation in theatre, and the cultural and historical centrality of questions about women's social roles. Tony Howard offers an analytical survey of the meaning and significance of Shakespeare in production for inter-war audiences, drawing close parallels between political contexts and theatrical interpretations of a variety of Shakespearian plays.

All the chapters in this volume place an emphasis on the importance of changes in the social make-up of theatre audiences between the two world wars. Theatre became a popular pastime, and this is reflected in the two penultimate chapters where the significance of amateur companies and amateur productions is investigated. Ros Merkin looks at the ways in which the Independent Labour Party encouraged the use of drama and theatre as a way of discoursing socialist ideas and practice in a social as opposed to a professional context. Mick Wallis extends the analysis of amateur practice through an examination of the relation between pageantry, history and community. The final chapter, by Clive Barker, provides an overview of the ways in which national reaction to the two world wars – one having happened, the other clearly on the horizon by the mid- to late-1930s – produced an avoidance of direct representations of the First World War and the politics of war on stage until the late 1920s. He asserts that the prevalence of 'ghost' plays and 'time' plays is evidence of the limited but complex ways in which a commercially based theatre dealt with both the horrors of the First World War and cultural anxiety about the war which was yet to happen.

This volume does not offer coverage of, for example, the enormous developments in Irish theatre or in the regional theatres of the age. Neither does it attempt to cover every key playwright or indeed every significant theatrical movement of the day. Rather, *British Theatre between the Wars* has been written with the intention of opening up areas of debate about a period of British theatre which hitherto has been largely neglected by contemporary critics and theatre historians.

1 Theatre and society: the Edwardian legacy, the First World War and the inter-war years

CLIVE BARKER

This chapter traces social change which came about as a result of the First World War, in terms of its relationship to both pre- and post-war society and developments in theatre as an industry. British society had been moving towards shifts in class make-up and cultural production before 1914, but those shifts were accelerated by the devastating effects of the war. The inter-war years saw, among other things, a growth in mass communications – especially the popularity of radio and cinema – the influx of Americanised culture, the strength of labour militancy culminating in the betrayal of the General Strike of 1926, economic instability, the full franchise for women in 1928, the opening up of educational opportunities and the seeming dissolution of the aristocracy. Much of this change is rooted in the immediate pre-war years, just as much inter-war theatre, separated by the limitations of processes of periodisation, finds connections and roots in theatre before the First World War.

Before the First World War

Camillo Pellizzi, Professor of Italian at the University of London, in 1935 published a translation of an original Italian work of 1932: *The English Drama: The Last Great Phase*.[1] Tracing the growth in power of the middle classes from the time of the Reformation to what he perceived as an hiatus, as the third decade of the twentieth century gave way to the fourth, he generously attributed to the British middle-class character a drive to self-judgement and consequent moral improvement. The malaise, which Pellizzi sees as a positive feature of members of middle-class society '(which) in the hour of their victory, began to feel the need of seeing themselves as they really were, in order to judge themselves . . .', provokes, in his opinion, the great flowering of late-middle-class culture, and few would deny that the plays of Shaw, Granville Barker, St John Hankin, Elizabeth Baker, Cicely Hamilton, John Galsworthy and Harold Chapin, among a number of others, show a considerable improvement in content, dramatic skill and sophistication over what had preceded them in the previous century. Many would argue that play-writing reached a standard that would not be surpassed in the decades which followed it.

Pellizzi's journey through the history of the middle class and its art is full of insights and has the great virtue of maintaining the connection between society and the drama. He has a partisan adherence to the values of the middle class and he wrote, looking back upon halcyon days, in a period of great confusion which equally mystified older and younger generations. Esmé Wingfield-Stratton, patriotic historian and anti-radical Conservative, who wrote both as a member of and an apologist for the Victorian era, sets the date for middle-class unease with the death of Edward VII in 1910.[2] Much that happened in the following two years brought into question political and social relationships and disputed the hegemonic powers of the middle class.

A constitutional crisis occurred throughout 1911 into 1912 over a bill to curb the power of the House of Lords. The Lords had refused to accept the budget of the Liberal government and the government were forced to promise Home Rule for Ireland in exchange for the support of the Irish Nationalists in the House of Commons. This was not, in the end, given and the Irish problem began to move towards the Easter Rising and to enter an even more violent stage. Threatened with the abolition of the House of Lords, which would be replaced by an elected second house, the Conservative peers split and submitted to having their powers curtailed in a debate marked by deep acrimony as they took sides as either 'hedgers' or 'ditchers'. This could be said to mark the end to surviving rights and privileges of the aristocracy. They would never be able to exert such power again after 1912.[3]

There are other theatrical events that might lead us to 1912. Ignoring politics, Pellizzi assesses that year as the pinnacle of excellence for the middle-class drama. By no coincidence Priestley returns to that year twice; his *Eden End* (1934) is set in October 1912. The play is an autumnal piece dealing with relationship conflicts in a Yorkshire doctor's home. Here Priestley asserts the sense of a failing among the middle classes to have grasped opportunities that were there at the turn of the century, when Dr Kirby might have taken risks and been more ambitious; although his daughter, Stella, has taken risks she has become no more than a jobbing actress. In a scene between the two, in Act III, sc. ii, Dr Kirby ironically looks forward to a time, in the 1930s, when there will be a cleaner, more sane and happier world. People living then will not understand the muddle of life in 1912. However, in 1948 he turns to the year 1912 as the setting for *An Inspector Calls* (1948) – which achieved such recent success in Stephen Daldry's 1990s production. Here Priestley marks the year as the time when the behaviour of the wealthy middle class is called into question over their abuse of privilege. The year 1911 begins the period of labour troubles which is known as The Long Unrest. In 1912 there was a Miners' Strike, which the workers failed to sustain because they could not achieve a two-thirds majority to carry on, but drew from Lenin the optimistic judgement:

> The miners' strike positively represents a new epoch . . . Since the strike the British proletariat *is no longer the same*. The workers have learned to fight . . . A change has taken place in the relation of social forces in England which cannot be expressed in figures, but which everyone feels.[4]

The aristocracy fragmented and declined, the middle class trembled at close scrutiny and the working class were exultant (but still oppressed). The lower-middle class regretted the missed opportunities of times past and the social muddle and lack of direction of the present time. Esmé Wingfield-Stratton, rejoicing in the excitement of a new production of the latest Shaw play at the Royal Court, places the social criticism of the new realist drama in an aesthetic rather than political context. He records an 'extraordinary bitterness of political and social controversy . . . A time when, if ever in history, it was counsel not only of patriotism but of elementary sanity to sink all party and sectional differences and present to the world the face and spirit of a united people.'[5]

The 1914–18 War and its aftermath

The First World War signalled the end of a

> golden age of continuously expanding territories and markets,
> of a world policed by the self-assured and not too onerous
> British hegemony, of a coherent 'Western' civilisation whose
> conflicts could be harmonised by a progressive extension of the
> area of common development and exploitation, of the easy
> assumptions that what was good for one was good for all and
> that what was economically right could not be morally wrong.[6]

The war eventually produced the national unity which Wingfield-Stratton had earlier called for, but not on the recherché basis he had expected. Society was turned on its head and in no other field was this more obvious than in the theatre.

> Of all the follies committed by the English Government of
> 1914, none was worse than the neglect to check the efforts of
> the English Theatrical Trust to dominate the whole financial
> interests of the theatre. And none was of more far-reaching
> consequences as to the effect on the mind and spirit of the
> English people. It was equal to making financiers, speculators,
> and profiteers the sole guardians of theatrical expression in
> particular in London.[7]

> The financial speculators settled on the theatre like a cloud
> taking advantage of its vulnerability and the carelessness it
> displayed about its reputation in those hectic four or five years.[8]

The process whereby from the 1880s the profitability of the long run had attracted speculative investment in productions and also enabled actor-managers to use their profits to build their own custom-built theatres had taken deep root by the beginning of the First World War, with one or two significant changes. The actor-managers were dying off, often leaving their theatres to relatives with no interest whatsoever in performing or in producing plays. Theatres became a source of non-speculative income, with the search for stages becoming desperate as speculators jockeyed to have a foot in the West End. Norman Marshall sums up this process by stating that during the First

World War 'theatres became just another asset on the list of properties held by business magnates, regarded as impersonally as the factories, the hotels, the chain of shops, the block of flats which also figured on the list'.[9] A system grew up rapidly in which the original disinterested owner leased the theatre to a management. Often the lease itself became a source of speculative income as a system of sub-leases grew up. The second development in theatre ownership and management was the formation of Trusts. Trusts began in the United States where managements, such as the Shubert Brothers, bought or established vast chains of theatres across America, as better communications made it feasible to control them. As William Poel noted in 1920: 'During the last 30 or 40 years the theatrical conditions have changed so much owing to the long-run system and the opening up of the American and Colonial Markets, that a play has become (spatially) a very valuable property and a contract for its lease needs just as much care in drawing up as a lease of an estate.'[10] The battle for the control of territories in which to acquire and control theatres was both bitter and violent. The potential for return on investment through control of these circuits was awe-inspiring. Managements were gods as artists scrambled to tour their act or play in vaudeville or drama presentations.

> A small theatre now running a revue started its first rental at something like £80 per week. A theatrical firm acquired the house and put it up to £110 for the next incomer. He, on subletting, charged £150 a week and the next man who wanted it had to pay £200 . . . Can you wonder, then, that so many managers, coming third, fourth or fifth in the list of renters, lose even on plays that appear to be successes? Also can you wonder that some 'bricks and mortar' managers make such big fortunes? And to make matters worse, every new tenant of most West End theatres had to allow for a certain number of seats handed down from renter to renter in succession, for disposal by sale or otherwise, generally increasing with each deal so that sometimes as many as 70 seats have had to be granted by the last tenant . . .[11]

Numerous critics and theatre commentators of the era noted the prob-lematics of a system which allowed for an almost purely profit-making agenda. They also noted the ways in which this economic situation was shaping the content of London theatre productions.

> Under these exacting conditions it is difficult to see how any play can succeed financially unless it is a modern drama or farce, having a small but inexpensive cast and intended for a long run. It is inaccurate, therefore, in the circumstances, to infer that the public refuses to give its support to good plays. In reality it was the additional expense of the annual £4000 premium, paid to the sub-tenant, which made it impossible for London to have better plays.[12]

The legacy of Victorian finance capitalism was the abuse of power forcing standardisation upon the English theatre in order to minimise risk. One result of this was that the First World War arguably swept away the high level of realist drama which Pellizzi later extols so strongly.

What then took its place and for whom was it intended? Minor changes had already occurred in the audience. Sir Arthur Pinero confidently attributed the decline of the Edwardian musical comedy and the go-as-you-please revue to 'feminine influence'. Macqueen-Pope, also lacking any sense of gallantry, says of the pre-1914 years, 'But already there was a shudder of female unrest in the land . . . Already, in the late nineties, women were going into the City to work there.'[13] Complaining that girls were being trained as clerks and typists instead of being brought up for marriage, he lists the post office as major employer in its telephone service. 'Slowly, almost imperceptibly, but very steadily and resolutely they were sapping the defences and undermining the outworks [of the City].'[14] The advancing facility for women to move more freely began to change theatregoing habits.

> Before 1914 an evening at a West End theatre was a social event. Patrons of the pit and gallery did not put on evening dress but looked for this courtesy from the Stalls and Dress Circle.[15]

But women's influence upon theatre of the immediate pre- and post-First World War years was far more substantial than this might suggest; for example, the work of the Actresses Franchise League was instrumental in changing, amongst other things, attitudes to women as professionals in the theatre industry.[16] Equally, the struggle for the female franchise had led Edwardian playwrights like Elizabeth Baker and Cicely Hamilton to turn 'to the stage as a vehicle for feminist agitation'.[17]

Huntley Carter suggested that the 1914–18 War shattered the 'new ideology of civilised man' and that a 'swift and violent succession of passions and paroxysms took its place'. For Carter, 'ideas and ideals long since buried beyond resurrection (or so it was hoped) reappeared to riot amid shocking ruin'.[18] In the course of chronicling the Maude Allen v. Pemberton Billing libel case centred on Wilde's *Salome*, Phillip Hoare investigates into the sex life of the war period – and after. He quotes Diana Manners, later Lady Duff Cooper, on life in the early part of the war.

> With the outbreak of war in August 1914, life turned upside down. Diana Manners became a V.A.D. at Guy's Hospital. It was a schizophrenic life dealing by day with death and disease, while at night, 'I would fly out of the ward . . . Five minutes would see me painted and powered and dressed (as I hoped) to kill and into the arms of friends or a friend'. They held parties dubbed the 'Dances of Death'. War turned the make-believe decadence of the Corrupt Coterie into the real thing. The young were dancing a tarantella frenziedly to combat any pause that would let death conquer their morale . . . Wine helped and there was wine in plenty.[19]

Sex and theatre entertainments

As the war progressed, London, as the clearing house for the Western Front, with Paris, which suffered a similar fate, became inundated with young men going to the front and those lucky ones on leave from the front, always conscious that soon they must return. Many of the Americans and colonial troops were straight off the farms they had lived on all their lives, and had never seen a major city. Again, according to Huntley Carter:

> Soldiers hot from the trenches or straight from the Colonies thought they were perfectly justified by being soldiers in throwing overboard every moral, social and marital tie, in order

to have a rousing time. They set up voluntary relations resulting in ruin to many a virtuous girl; they contracted bigamous marriages, knowing they could drop them when they wanted. Women encouraged it. They married for the war allowance, some married several times and got several allowances. Married women packed their husbands off and then went looking for others. They simply flouted marriage and divorce laws, and scattered morality to the winds.[20]

At first a number of patriotic plays, largely melodramas and intended for recruiting purposes, appeared in the regular diet of musical comedies, revues and light comedy. The Trusts did not really get their acts together until late in 1916. For Huntley Carter, 'Towards the end of 1916 . . . the exploitation of an unparalleled wave of sexuality became the predominating theatrical feature'; the civilians blamed the soldiers for their own debased tastes. Notwithstanding Carter's caveat, the manager of several theatres stated that 90 per cent of theatregoers were soldiers and their friends. There circulated a rumour at one time that the government surreptitiously supported the theatres in the belief that putting on intellectually light entertainment would make the troops happy to go back to the front.[21] In default of any organised activities to cover the ten-day leave period, there were certain welfare organisations like the YMCA; otherwise it was left to the Trust theatres and prostitutes, professional and amateur, to entertain the troops. The licence to present lewd, suggestive and salacious plays was aided by the relaxing of censorship from the start of the war, to the extent that some practitioners declared there were no battles with censorship to be won.

The plays which so shocked public morality and drew the soldiers, their women and others in such great numbers would be more likely to draw derision than applause today. In the context of their time they were scandalous. William Poel, in his *What is Wrong with the Theatre?* gives many quotations from press reviews, for example, in relation to *The Bing Boys:*

> At the Alhambra there is a trio sung which, if it isn't called 'Another Drink' contains the words at the end of each refrain. The scene is a private hotel or restaurant, time midnight and champagne is being freely drunk by women as well as men . . .

And at the Garrick Theatre

> a young lady has been inveigled into drinking more champagne than is good for her, and, though a married woman, she persuades the bridegroom to drink more wine than he should, and the two are seen embracing each other as the bride enters the room . . . At the Lyceum there is a play called *Women and Wine* . . . I cannot recall at the moment any play I have recently seen in which 'drinks' are not brought on the stage . . .[22]

Huntley Carter trumps this with a retired Indian judge who is clearly an expert on the subject: 'The Ambassadors was pretty well in the lead for undress . . . There was one scene in which the leading lady disrobed herself on stage down apparently to the very last item of her clothing . . .'[23] Carter quotes from an article by the censor, Sir H. Smith-Dorien, in the *Weekly Dispatch*, 22 October 1916. Other quotes from the article list *Little Miss Mustard*, a revue, full of inanities and dealing in the main with ladies underclothing, containing a scene where a girl is measured for pyjamas. A riot of bedroom and pyjama plays include *Please Get Married*, *A Sleepless Night*, *The Parlour, Bedroom and Bath*, *Up in Mabel's Room*, *The Dancer*. In *The Naughty Wife*, the woman says she 'is damn sick of men'. Revealing dresses on-stage move off-stage into the ballrooms, where they enter high fashion. Without a doubt the two greatest successes of the war period were *A Little Bit of Fluff* and *Chu Chin Chow*. *A Little Bit of Fluff* ran for 1,241 performances and was a farce concerning an injudicious night out which ends with breakfast and a set of wild escapades to conceal the facts from the central character's wife. The play, by Walter W. Ellis – a very successful revue writer – was still being resurrected well into the 1950s and is spoken of with affection by those who played in it. In some ways it leads the way to Ben Travers and the Aldwych farces but it lacks their sophistication and field of social reference. *Chu Chin Chow*, a musical version of *Ali Baba and the Forty Thieves*, opened 31 August 1916 and ran for 2,235 performances, a record at that time. An over-elaborate spectacle, in its own time it appeared daring. There are twenty-five songs at least one of which, 'The Cobbler's Song', holds its place in the concert repertoire. The text has wit and sophistication.

(There was nothing new in using oriental settings to add spice and spectacle to productions – Gilbert and Sullivan ran *The Mikado* in 1885.) Oscar Asche, who wrote the script and produced *Chu Chin Chow*, had presented a forerunner, *Kismet*, at the same theatre in 1911. Reviews of the production stressed the sumptuousness of sets, costumes, and particularly the colour schemes. *The Times'* critic extolled its virtues:

> Mr Asche's second excursion into the region of fantastic, polyphonic, polychromatic orientalism . . . (is) everything by turns and nothing long – a kaleidoscope series of scenes, now romantic, now realistic, now Futuristic or Vorticist but always beautiful . . . There is perpetual gyrating and posturing and madcap dancing. It is such a rich beauty show . . . A gorgeous heap of coloured stuffs.[24]

The Era remarked that 'the contrast between the dark chilliness outside and the glow and gorgeousness inside the theatre is irresistible. . .'[25]

Chu Chin Chow outran the war, continuing to set new levels for female (and male) exposure. Whether the sensuality and nudity of the spectacular shows or the prurient innuendoes of the farces can be said to have raised the sexual desires of the population, or simply to have pandered to them, is debatable. Certainly, the soldiers had little need of theatrical stimulation to set them on the way to sexual indulgence. What is certain is that between 1914 and 1918 sex seemed to be the common denominator for drama in a time when previous modes of behaviour and conformation were thrown overboard in the social chaos provoked by the war. Three months after the war ended G.E. Morrison, dramatic critic of the *Morning Post* and President of the Critics' Circle, wrote a number of articles summing up the situation in the theatre:

> To millions who rarely or never visited the theatre before, the war had made it a solace almost as familiar as their newspaper or their pipe. In becoming a nation of warriors we may have become also a nation of theatre-goers. Even if this be not so it is high time that the theatre was sternly taken in hand. Nor has

the public reason to be satisfied with the entertainment set before it as an audience. The war has not brought in the theatre that quickening of spirit some foretold. Our managers have not risen to the occasion; rather may some of them be said to have stooped to the opportunity.[26]

Theatre and society after the First World War

There was a family in Birmingham which came to London once a month for nearly five years to see *Chu Chin Chow*! These demented people saw that melancholy entertainment more than fifty times. A gentleman, who had spent his vigorous years in shooting big game, spent his declining years in going to see *Chu Chin Chow* – he died of it. Hundreds of civilised and expensively educated people frequently went to see this singular piece ... we cannot deny that a people which mainly nourishes its mind on that sort of fare must be in a feeble state of health.[27]

St John Ervine's *The Organised Theatre*, from which the above originates, is a disappointment. Taking his cue from Matthew Arnold's battle cry: 'the theatre is irresistible: Organise the theatre', we might expect the sometime playwright and theatre critic for the *Morning Post* in the 1920s to find a plan or an outline of some plan on which to organise the theatre, but Ervine spends much of his book in a contemptuous and indiscriminate attack on the American academics who charted the new movement in European theatre and who paid scant respect, if any, to the British theatre in the 1920s. J. C. Trewin quotes an anonymous critic in 1925: 'A year of prodigious activity with not even the pencil sketch of a plan.'[28] While Ervine finds a basis for the future of the theatre in the ruins of the repertory theatre movement which had collapsed at the outbreak of war, he fails to see, or record, that in some areas the theatre was very busy organising itself.

Organising the theatre

In August 1919, at Stratford-upon-Avon, the British Drama League [BDL] and the Workers' Educational Association jointly called the first British Theatre Conference. The conference presented a resolution calling for the formation of a national theatre linked with faculties of theatre at British universities and colleges. The conference pledged itself 'to promote and assist collective and individual efforts in the development of Acting, Drama, and the Theatre as forces in the life of the Nation'. Other resolutions deplored the lack of a policy adequate to the cultural needs of the people and that theatre no longer related to the lives of the people: the theatre had become isolated, remote. Formed in 1919, the British Drama League arose out of a small group in the Workers' Educational Association. It should be borne in mind that underlying the fabric of inter-war British theatre lies the BDL, working as a resource centre for the unseen theatre – the amateurs, repertory theatres and other attempts to create a popular theatre throughout Britain, with both settled and touring companies. The origin of the BDL says much of the class shift; there had been amateur theatres throughout history but from the early years of the twentieth century there had been a consistent growth of amateur groups in the regions outside London, reflecting the growing popularity of theatre during the Edwardian years. After the war a consistent and organised movement of Little Theatres developed; this movement was to some extent developed by and co-ordinated through the BDL. One strong feature of the movement of 'little theatres' was a need to offer some alternative to the rundown state of West End theatre and theatre companies touring the provinces. In its repertoire it harked back, to some extent, to the pre-war theatre. There was a prolific growth of amateur Gilbert and Sullivan companies reaching many more people than the original productions had done and, in a way this was a cultural catching-up by a new emergent class on the heritage offered by the immediate past. Out of some of these 'little theatres', new repertory theatres began to emerge. During the 1920s Sheffield Rep. moved to employ professional actors – Donald Wolfit was one of the first – and directors, on the way to becoming a fully professional theatre. This development arose as a collective effort. In some cases the old-style patronage, which had marked the early repertory movement of Annie Horniman in Manchester, was carried on by wealthy backers, such as Barry Jackson, whose enthusiasm and money supported not only Birmingham Repertory Theatre, the Malvern Festival and the Shakespeare Memorial Theatre but also reached out to influence the West End. The 'Little Theatre Movement', the repertories, Sunday Play Societies and personal initiatives, such as J. T. Grein's and Nancy Price's People's National Theatre and the small London Club Theatres presented a varied repertoire, each according to its own nature, including some immediate pre-1914–18 plays, the whole range of the cultural heritage, translations of foreign plays and experimental productions. Later, some groups began to take a more political line, and throughout the inter-war period a series of politically inspired and engaged theatre groups emerged through the Worker's Theatre Movement and, later, the Unity Theatre. Many of these initiatives have been well documented and assessed elsewhere.[29]

In 1919, a further attempt was made to organise the theatre, this time from the actors through the formation of the Actors Association, which immediately began the task of unionising a profession which had notoriously considered itself to be above such things. Delegates were sent to the Trades Union Congress in 1923, and negotiations were attempted with managements for a minimum wage of £3 a week and for progress towards a closed shop with binding contracts in all areas of work. In all, negotiation was attempted on fifteen points. These were, of course, totally rejected by the managements, although some of the largest, and most successful, managements could see the advantages and injustices. C. B. Cochran objected to unionisation *per se* but claimed that a salary of £3 a week was ludicrously low and that personally he had never employed anyone for so low a figure. As well as Cochran, André Charlot and Arthur Bouchier were in support of the actors, even though many actors found themselves in support of management politics. In 1924 the managers formed an organisation of their own, the Stage Guild; the bizarre situation arose where managers supported the Actors Association and prominent actors joined the Stage Guild.[30] The managements attempted to negotiate on a basis of the £3 minimum with certain exceptions. Members with fewer than forty weeks of working experience could be employed below the minimum and managers could take on between 20 and 25 per cent of unpaid 'learners', and so began what was known as the 'war of the theatres', with discrimination on both sides. A long struggle culminated in the formation of the British Actors Equity Association in 1929, the name taken in acknowledgement of the encouragement given by the example of the American Actors Equity. Recognition granted by the managements was later achieved in the face of a threat of strike action by a significant number of leading actors and actresses. But it was never possible to organise the theatre through unionisation in any watertight way. As the theatre began to appeal to a lower-middle-class audience it drifted from the patronage of the Edwardian upper-middle classes. Such popularisation also meant a steady increase of actors coming into the theatre throughout the inter-war period, around one-fifth every year.[31] There were also managements in the provinces who were trying to jump on the bandwagon of the Trusts' success and make easy money for themselves. Among the submerged problems of the theatre was the standing of the new 'actors'. C. B. Cochran, who was a trustee of the Actors' Benevolent Fund, complained that people came into the profession and few weeks later made a claim on the Fund, which he had to pay because they had joined the Actors Association.

One of the significant features of the post-First World War theatre world was the diminishment of the numbers of actor-managers, a group that had so dominated the pre-war period. Their eventual, literal, demise enabled the Trusts easily to take over the West End.[32] Only Gerald du Maurier who died in 1932, enormously respected, survived into the 1920s.[33] The work of the Actors Association was a brave attempt to protect less fortunate actors, an unselfish action on the part of many star names. An example is Dame Sybil Thorndike, who was very active in the agitation, and who seems hardly to have paused between engagements in the whole period.[34]

During this period, many actors who were in high demand did very well financially out of desperate managements. Before the war it was working practice to base the recovery of production costs on a 50 per cent house, which would give a profit after a hundred performances. Post-war, this figure rose to 80 per cent business. This pressure created a demand for star actors who could be counted on to bring in the customers, creating a wide differential between the stars and the rest.

In order to guarantee their rent and share of the profits, theatre managers demanded a say as to who would star in a production before admitting it into their theatre. It would, perhaps, be fair to say that problems over managements in the 1920s, by and large, lay not with monolithic grasping tyrants but with too many managements trying to get their snouts into the trough. The split between theatre managements, who owned the buildings, and production managements, who financed and put together the productions, was a particularly destructive feature of the theatre in the 1920s – and beyond the inter-war period – but in the 1930s there was a settling down, as well as a growth of managements who combined both functions. A situation of the 'survival of the fittest' began to shake out the West End theatre and the weak fell by the wayside. This placed power in fewer hands, but did allow much less interference in the process of getting the planned show on to the stage. Most of the best theatre of the 1930s came either from these management companies or from the smaller, suburban theatres such as the Lyric, Hammersmith, and the Embassy, Swiss Cottage, which were free of the West End chaos and therefore carried very much lower costs.

Decades apart: differentiating between the 1920s and 1930s

It is difficult in many areas of social and theatrical life to give a coherent picture that will cover a whole period. It is relatively much easier to differentiate between the 1920s and the 1930s, at which latter point significant and startling changes come over both society and the theatre. We can with near certainty put a date of 1930 for the change-over but, of course, not everything changed overnight. Allardyce Nicoll states that what was done after the Armistice was largely a rounding-off or an elaboration of what was present in 1914: 'evidence is varied and scattered and complex, but cumulatively it suggests that the theatrical change which occurred round about the year 1930 was, in fact, as great as any to be discovered in the stage's annals'.[35] Macqueen-Pope, a leading theatre publicist for West End theatres of the 1920s, viewed the situation as follows.

> It was a strange world that emerged from the holocaust of
> 1914–1918. Much that had belonged to the previous era had
> been distorted or destroyed. It was a hurried and precarious

world in which the habits of leisurely elegance no longer found
scope or encouragement. For more than four years the young
people had been servants of the war machine . . . Reacting from
the squalor of battle, they had devoted their short and precious
leaves to obtaining what pleasure they could. They wanted
bright lights . . . warmth . . . and acceptable moral values often
went by the board. It was no use the purists complaining, for life
seen through the eyes of impending dissolution conjures up a
transcending ethic of its own.[36]

The search for pleasure continued well into the 1920s, regardless of the
social conditions surrounding the 'bright young things'. In some ways
it is reasonable to see that life after the war simply continued the
horror. Internationally, the influenza epidemic of 1919 killed more
people than died in the 1914–1918 War and killed with no regard for
class or wealth. The post-war boom which had followed the Armistice
had petered out by May 1921, putting an end for many to relief that the
war was over.

When industries were beginning to work normally again and
the first peace-time reaction of extravagant spending had died
down, a trade depression was revealed in the growing
unemployment-rate and in the frequent strikes [culminating in
the Miners' lock-out and the General Strike of 1926]. The Ex-
Serviceman who lost his temporary employment was no longer
a hero but a good-for-nothing living on public charity.[37]

The government cut housing plans and, in the aftermath of the war,
spending on conquered territory and 'protectorates' was draining
wealth. Britain began to feel like a fragmented society; a society with a
distribution of wealth and privilege based neither on any rationale nor
on any principles of social or moral justice; a society from which the
structure had been removed as successfully as the filleting of a fish in
one of the new fashionable restaurants which were springing up all
over London. The alternative to this lay in attempts to organise the
unemployed and to strengthen working-class unity. Outside this, a
style of life developed from importations from the United States.

Cocktails became fashionable, overturning an ancient prejudice against gin which, owing to the nineteenth century, had always been seen as a working-class drink. Ragtime and dance sensations had been imported from the United States around 1915, with the advance guard around 1912. The jazz craze followed the war. Dance halls, dance clubs and tea dances began to spring up everywhere and hotels offered music, dancing and cabaret, as well as the traditional dining. Bottle parties extended to drinking clubs.

Women's new-found independence, propelled by their contribution to the war effort, by the partial franchise in 1918 and the full franchise in 1928, meant that they had new freedoms within the public domain. The encouragement of contraception, led by Dr Marie Stopes (who incidentally had also written a number of plays for West End theatres), combined with programmes established for sex education, made possible a sexual freedom that may have begun during the war, but now could be practised in better circumstances. These new freedoms included, of course, those of homosexuality.[38]

The young post-war generation did not so much rebel against the Edwardian values of their elders, for those had already been shaky when the war finally put paid to them, as wander off in search of values with little to guide them. The death of the war generation had consequences of the most catastrophic kinds – not least in politics, where constant reference was made to governments of second-class brains. The brightest and best perished in the trenches, where the average life expectancy of a Junior Officer was three months. In 1939, at the end of the period covered in the present volume, J. C. Trewin wrote of Terence Rattigan's *After the Dance*:

> it could have been taken as a *Vortex* of 1939. And here, on the very rim of a second world war, the first world war was being blamed for it. 'You see', said a girl to a whisky-soaked writer of 38, 'you see, when you were eighteen, you didn't have anybody of twenty-two or twenty-five or thirty or thirty-five to help you because they'd all been wiped out. Anyone over forty you wouldn't listen to, anyway. The spotlight was on you and you alone, and you weren't even young men; you were children . . .'

DAVID: . . . What did we do with this spotlight?

HELEN: You did what any child would do. You danced in it.[39]

J. C. Trewin called his review of the decade *The Gay Twenties*, but why? The year 1920 is named the year of chaos; 1921 the year of failure – not the time for experimentation. Excellent though his book is as a source of reference, Trewin never manages to make the case for gaiety in the drama. The major dramatic advances over the decade were in revue (see James Ross Moore's chapter in this volume) and in farce. Grand Guignol made a return (see John Stokes' chapter here). Otherwise, the past continued into the present. *Chu Chin Chow* was joined in 1919 by *Afagr*, a musical set in a harem, and followed by *Cairo* in 1921, which added scantily clothed men and staged a frenzied bacchanalia, climaxing in semi-naked bodies collapsing in heaps on the stage. The craze for orientalism carried on unabated as managers sought to grab their share of the profits from the payload that *Chu Chin Chow* had opened up. A lot more money was spent and lost chasing *Chu Chin Chow* than profits were made from it. Serious dramatic producers looked for a way of getting at the profits through a similar formula but with more pretensions to art. One answer lay in James Elroy Flecker's *Hassan* (1923), directed by Basil Dean. The Baghdad settings were as sumptuous as anything in the musical world. The incidental music was by Frederick Delius. Flecker – who died in 1915 – had written a dramatic poem with scenes of rare poetic beauty. But the play has little of *Chu Chin Chow*'s glib and easy plotting. *Hassan* needs an audience to respond to the poetry, not to the sets, and it contains scenes and actions whose cruelty borders on the gratuitous and the vicious.[40]

When audiences had finally seen enough of plays oriental, the European musical comedies which replaced them had settings which were just as fanciful.

> Life as seen through the rose-and-amber-tinted spectacles of the musical comedy convention becomes a sentimentally erotic dream. Its romantic appeal is an escape from here and now into an artificial world of somewhere else or some time past . . . some imaginary Balkan state . . . removed as far as possible from the waking realities of the spectator.[41]

Phillip Godfrey makes the point that whatever the setting the musical followed certain formalistic conventions. There must be two senti-mental lovers and two comic ones to counter the sentimentality, a convention that well outlived the inter-war period, with certain imagi-native inversions and changes of balance. He also takes a moral stand-point at what he sees as prurient insertions in the action, objecting to the fact, for example, that in *Wild Violets* (1932), set in a girls' board-ing-school, the girls' dormitory is set placed down stage on a high rostrum.

Deprived by the censor of putting living figures on stage, play-wrights in the 1920s made plays out of cultural icons, beginning with John Drinkwater's *Abraham Lincoln* in 1919, followed variously by *Clive of India*, *Mary Stuart*, *Robert E. Lee*, *Robert Burns*, *Oliver Cromwell*, *Charles and Mary* (Lamb), *The Lady with the Lamp*, *Rose without a Thorn*, (Catherine Howard), *She Passed through Lorraine* (Joan of Arc), *Richard of Bordeaux*, *Gallows Glorious* (John Brown), *The Barretts of Wimpole Street*, *And so to Bed* (Pepys), *Mrs Fitzherbert*, *Will Shakespeare*, and, in one single year (1933), *The Brontës*, *Wild Decembers*, *The Brontës of Haworth Parsonage*, come one, come all. Allardyce Nicoll saw the origins of these plays in Louis Napoleon Parker's pageant plays from the turn of the century (see Mick Wallis's chapter). Nicoll also sees the influence of the novel as a source for drama, and quotes B. W. Findon from 1919:

> We have cast aside the old models, our old ideas of what constituted a good play, and appear to have formed a drama more or less based on the lines and conventions of a film production with its inconsequent procedure and incidental trivialities.[42]

Pellizzi takes into account the fact that there have been history plays before or plays on historical personages, but none of the new plays looks for an internal drama: 'Once Drinkwater [and by implication others] had grasped the *leit-motif* of his hero, he sings variations on it through the three or four acts, as if reciting a prayer or chanting and repeating a war song.'[43]

Audiences and social class

In 1935 Pellizzi questioned whether the public had become tired of drama that was incapable of dramatic emotion and no longer had any real, widely felt, problem which audiences expected dramatists to treat. However, Pellizzi here missed the point. The anecdotal historical biography plays are indicative of a large shift in the socio-economic make-up of the audience. This process was not simply a shift from upper to lower class, although that is what was happening, but, rather, a new class was forming and the plays, in which Drinkwater, for example, perceives this as happening, rehearse the cultural icons on which the new class intends to build its identity. As the 1920s move into the 1930s the plays, and the choice of icons, display a growing self-confidence.

Heavy rises in the levels of income tax and super tax during the war and after it, effectively reduced the numbers of the very rich, a process which slowed down after 1925.[44] Death duties had a decimating effect on the landed aristocracy, and many large estates were sold piecemeal to tenant farmers. The processes by which finance capitalism works led to a redistribution of social roles and the creation of many new jobs through the attendant growth of institutions such as those of stockbrokers, accountants and solicitors. Two groups of people lost out in the economic decline which existed between the two world wars: investors and capitalists – who relied on the market rising – and the poor. For many others there was a steadily growing prosperity, particularly for those in sheltered employment. During the 1920s there was a conspicuous decline in the older heavy industries on which the prosperity of Britain had depended in the past. These, on which so much of the empire markets depended, tended to be grouped in the north and west of Britain near the seacoasts, and the major impact of the slump was manifested here:

> Meanwhile wholly new science-based industries were growing . . . Building (with related industries like furniture and wallpaper, as well as building materials) was also rapidly expanding. But by far the greatest increase in employment was in distribution, hotels and catering and various service trades

(laundries, cleaners, hairdressers, entertainment) and these, like the newer manufacturing industries, were already concentrated in the South East and the Midlands, and continued to grow there. This was the main cause of growing economic prosperity and increasing population of these districts.[45]

There was massive development in house building in the south-east in the early 1920s and, in spite of a drop after this due to government restrictions, the boom continued in selective areas. The middle classes moved to the suburbs; the working class on to council housing estates.[46]

Other features affecting the class structure of British life in the 1920s and 1930s were, first, the sporadic growth of small family businesses and factories, many of which were later taken over and swallowed up by large conglomerates, in the process adding to the number of white-collar workers (often the original owners) needed by the increase of administration. Small but significant industries were growing, of which radio broadcasting was one, all of which needed technicians, writers, announcers; a mass of what could be called the socially unclassified or unclassifiable workers.

In the theatre, indicators of the changing social structure, for example, were the downgrading of settings from Somerset Maugham's London flats and stockbroker country houses to J.B. Priestley's Acacia Avenue and middle-class villas under economic strain, as well as a new genre of theatre, which we might call 'professional plays'. For Pellizzi these plays seem to have been both written and seen out of curiosity about the working lives of sections of the population; such plays include the immensely popular *Nine till Six* (Aimée and Philip Stuart, 1930), set in a West End dressmakers; *Her Shop* (1930) and *Supply and Demand* (1931); *London Wall* (John Van Druten, 1931) showing life in a London solicitor's office; and *Service* (Dodie Smith, 1932), set in a London department store. In some ways the development of the genre resembles that of the pre-war plays of Granville Barker, Elizabeth Baker and others, but in the professional plays moral enquiry, according to Pellizzi, has to some extent descended to the level of mere curiosity.

These are the last sparks of realism, which, having sprung from a lofty and moral and social passion, lost, after the war, its real content and source of inspiration, both epical and ethical, and now feebly survives in the form of a curiosity, something very banal, about all human things; it is the curiosity of wanting to peep into closed places, of wanting to penetrate into the habits and feelings of people with whom we have no intimate contact in ordinary life.[47]

Pellizzi is, of course, speaking from an affinity with the recently departed Edwardian middle classes. An alternative reading of the significance in popularity of such plays would posit the natural wish of any emerging group or class to take over the cultural forms of the departing class and to see themselves portrayed on the stage.

Two further subsections of the new society audience can be identified, the educated working class and women. It is not easy to establish either of these groups absolutely, as most of what was written at that time is written from a class-conscious and critical point of view. St John Ervine, he of the jaundiced view of the cultural demolitions effected by the presence of women, gives as evidence:

There were Gallery Boys before the War. After the signing of the Armistice, they had almost disappeared, and in their place came the Gallery Girl, whose capacity for emotional excitement was almost inexhaustible.[48]

It is easy to treat St John Ervine as a figure of fun, but he was representative of widely held views at that time. Pinero, for one, expressed similar charges against women. James Agate, one of the most influential critics of the period and provider of the most panoramic views of the theatre written at that time, or just after, deals with the many women playwrights who addressed this section of the new audience at small length and relegates them, erroneously, to a minor category (see Maggie B. Gale's chapter). The new playwrights were in many cases dealing with the romantic dreams and disappointments of their audience. Others examined the experiences of women thrown into a time when gender and social roles were being renegotiated. Perversely, St

John Ervine wrote one of the best of the few problem plays written in the 1930s: *Robert's Wife* deals with the dilemma faced by a clergyman and his wife when the former's chances of promotion are jeopardised by his doctor wife adding a birth-control clinic to her surgery. The argument – not an uncommon one in plays of the period – revolves around whether a wife should put her own ambitions and interests before those of her husband.

By the late 1920s there was a general movement away from the new freedoms which had developed in the aftermath of the war. Women's fashions became less androgynous:

> Some people suggested that the turn towards femininity in fashion was the result of a subconscious desire for security, for a retreat from the hazards of the new freedom. But in fact the new fashions were in tune with the spirit of the romantic, escapist make-believe world which dominated the films and popular songs of the day.[49]

It seems that from the end of the 1920s marriage came back into favour against all the various alternatives that had been loosely followed before. Social manners changed and in the 1930s it was no longer considered proper to discuss sexual matters in mixed polite company. As the Gay Twenties crumbled into the Anxious Thirties, Noël Coward, ever a barometer or weather-vane for fashions, dropped his scandalous and risqué themes and, well before the end of the 1920s, went from the nostalgic romance of *Bitter Sweet* (1929), to the patriotic guyed melodrama of *Cavalcade* and stayed in comedy, this side of propriety, thoughout the 1930s.

With so much unemployment reaching across classes, and the newly introduced possibility of house-ownership for all, security became a priority. Hence the rapid increase of employees in the insurance business, wandering the streets, knocking on doors for the premiums. Arthur Calder-Marshall describes the people of the new classes, and new audiences, as 'perfect "tweenies", whose terror is to fall into the class below and ambition to rise to the higher class . . .'.[50]

Educational opportunities had been increasing since the turn of the century, from which time we can place the redbrick universities.

Gradually the number of free-place children in secondary schools was increasing through a scholarship examination at age 10 or 11 years. Added to these were the children of the increasing lower-middle class as fee-paying pupils. During the 1920s and increasingly in the 1930s (in spite of savage government cuts) the number of students admitted into the redesignated grammar schools increased, with some going on to university, where they were hopelessly outnumbered. Expenditure on education trebled between 1913 and 1931 and, in particular, free places in secondary schools doubled between 1919 and 1931. Arthur Calder-Marshall, from his lofty public school position, was not impressed by the education given:

> This consists chiefly in supplying old boys with a distinctive tie and a veneer of the 'public-school manner'. The educational training is on a very low level, matriculation being the ideal of most parents in this class: the social training creates a pathetic shadow of refinement.[51]

A great many minds were opened in the 1920s, and were later fed by the publisher Penguin's paperback books – from 1935 – and lending libraries. Along with those emerging from the established intellectuals' cliques were many who were radicalised by their experiences; however, although they appeared to be conscious of what was happening they had little idea how to change things. Of the Auden Isherwood circle:

> A personal love–hate relationship with the values of their public schools . . . remained an important preoccupation in much of their work. Nevertheless they shared a belief – half-regretful, half-exultant – that the old order was doomed, that some kind of revolution ('death of the old gang') must come, and that the only hope lay with the oppressed workers (who as people remained more or less unknown).[52]

There were other groups of intellectuals who identified with the workers' political cause, fighting in Spain, writing, documentary film-making and organising political and cultural work. Between these groups, the Group Theatre, Unity Theatre, the Left Book Club and the

Left Book Club Theatre groups were brought into existence with solid working-class involvement. Such groups have been recently covered and in great detail.[53]

That a new audience began to enter the theatre during the 1920s is clear, as are the broad outlines of its social composition. To a certain extent we can accept a shift in class values and we can see that the nature of the circumstances surrounding the rise of this audience inclined it towards prioritising a sense of security.

Theatre and political change

The process of radicalisation moved theatre intellectuals towards a very 'milk-and-water' identification with the cause of the working class, but the direction was not clear-cut. The 'adopted' Russian director Theodore Komisarjevsky showed a lack of commitment in the opposite direction. In the introduction to his *Theatre in a Changing Civilisation*, he stated:

> The author of this work professes neither the Bolshevik, Fascist, Nazi or any other political faith. But he welcomes Fascism, Communism and Nazism as powerful forces which will help to open up the road towards a new life of cultured, disciplined *individuals*, united in corporations under the leadership of enlightened men for social, scientific and artistic work.[54]

Small wonder that Pellizzi insisted that in their crisis the English needed strong government, but their traditions were against it.

Richard Findlater is prepared to extend this lack of commitment on either side for strong government and, perhaps, for the wish to appease the dictatorships when he sums up the post-war period in theatre:

> Apart from the inadequacy of theatrical organisation, there was, and still is, a time-lag between Britain and the rest of Europe. In the theatre, as in other areas, it seemed as if the country were caught in some air-pocket of history, sealed off for a couple of decades from the social, intellectual and political changes which were gathering momentum across the Channel. We

apparently did not want to *know* about many facts of twentieth century life: and the theatre helped us to ignore them.[55]

However, British theatre did meet and reflect what was happening in the world, if only indirectly or by default. The first remarkable event in the wake of the General Strike of 1926 was the total eclipse of Ruritania, not to appear until well into the 1930s through the work of Ivor Novello. In J.C. Trewin's opinion:

> There, surely, was an anachronism at the core of the Gay Twenties . . . Ruritania had become a blank on the map . . . the stage had seemed oddly bleak since a curtain had slid down upon the Balkan states.[56]

It seemed as though the cynical escapism of the post-war years was moving towards more serious considerations, although critics were still bewildered by a seeming lack of any pattern in plays. Trewin commented that 'everything seems to be in a state of flux, or dependent on the whims, caprices, and the capacity of individual magnates or syndicates for making profitable deals'.[57] In retrospect it is possible to see emergent patterns of genres in the drama, such as the traditionally male form of Grand Guignol, and farce; in many ways both reflected the social unease precipitated by the political climate, even though plays rarely confronted such unease directly.

Grand Guignol and farce

In 1926 one of the new and popular women playwrights, Clemence Dane, produced in *Granite* a female version of the traditionally male form, Grand Guignol. Sybil Thorndike took the role of Judith, a lonely island woman who swears to sell her soul to the devil in exchange for the love of her brother-in-law. An escaped convict is the instrument by which both the husband and his brother are murdered and Judith becomes imprisoned for life with a man whom she accepts as the devil. Thereafter Grand Guignol became part of the theatre until the outbreak of the Second World War. Principal among the early writers of the genre was Edgar Wallace and after him Emlyn Williams (see John Stokes' chapter), but there were many others; Bridie's *The Anatomist* and Patrick Hamilton's *Rope* and *Gaslight* are among the more accomplished of these plays. Of Edgar Wallace, Pellizzi says:

> These plays were derived on one hand from Grand Guignol, on the other hand from the American 'dramas of action' . . . Including detective plays, secret service plays and so on. Wallace was a clever purveyor of thrills. The Anglo-Saxon thrill is a slight shiver in the bones, which is desired, waited for, and received with relief; it is a slight intoxication of which we rid ourselves with a little internal electric discharge – something like a sneeze . . . [a] reacting with the nerves against the heaviness and boredom of the environment.[58]

Pellizzi points out that these plays are simply a manipulation of theatrical devices which have existed throughout the centuries. What makes them remarkable here is their popularity in the 1930s. For Pellizzi the horror plays exist because there is no longer any real, widespread and widely felt problem which the public expects their playwrights to treat – the avoidance is all. It should be noted that the horror play is a version of fantasy dressed up as reality. It is a game played with the audience, for whatever reason to provoke the reaction which Pellizzi proposes.

One play which is exemplary of Grand Guignol is one which makes a joke of it – the widely loved *Ghost Train* by Arnold Ridley (1925). Here, a group of passengers are trapped overnight in a haunted railway waiting room outside of which a ghostly train runs through the station. The audience knows there is no train but cannot tell how the effect is made. The empathetic sense of horror still works and backstage visits after the show were frequent. *The Ghost Train* bridges the gap between two theatre forms popular in the late 1920s and the 1930s, horror and farce. The Aldwych farces, which began as early as 1922 did not start with Ben Travers, traditionally associated with Aldwych farces, but with *Tons of Money* by Will Evans and 'Valentine'. The farces were based upon a continuing company of typecast actors, and were superbly crafted with parts for actors which actors love to play and can shine in.

The farcical effect here lies in the action of the plot, and in the
situations, and relies chiefly on the popularity of certain special
actors, whom Travers has in mind when he writes . . . the heroes
of these farces are more typical in their action than in their
character. Being undifferentiated characters from the middle-
classes, they can for the most part, represent Tom, Dick and
Harry; anyone in the audience can imagine himself in the
situations in which they find themselves; the comic-dramatic
stimulus springs from this generic similarity, from this possible
confusion between the spectator and the character – also the
language used, taken from ordinary slang, makes easier this
cordial, humorous collaboration between the actors and the
pit.[59]

Pellizzi compares the Aldwych plays to the Latin farces and the interludes of the Mystery Plays with one major exception. Although the
Aldwych plays do include some working-class characters they are not
intended for the working classes. The clowns are middle class and
designed to amuse a middle-class audience. Another interesting point
about the Aldwych plays, which supports the general thesis of this
chapter, is the way in which the dominance of the characters changes
as the period moves on. The three central male characters are the aristocratic blithering idiot, played by Ralph Lynn; the bullying and
corrupt bourgeois, played by Tom Walls and the much put-upon lower-
middle-class worm, played by Robertson Hare. In the early plays, the
pecking order runs Walls, Lynn and Hare, but as the period develops,
Robertson Hare moves more into the centre of the plotting until
towards the end of the 1930s he plays the major character around
whom the plot revolves.

    J. C. Trewin introduces the last chapter in his survey of theatre
in the 1920s by finding little apart from Sean O'Casey's *The Silver
Tassie* and R. C. Sherriff's *Journey's End* – other than Coward's *Bitter
Sweet* – to recommend. Other war plays of a very high standard preceded *Journey's End* in time without such success. For *Journey's End*,
excellent play as it is, the times had changed and the past had to be
examined to determine the way to the future. The wonder is that no

one ever seemed to be influenced by Sean O'Casey the one playwright of the period in tune with continental theatre techniques and experiments. Many British plays differed not only from O'Casey's work but also from anything written abroad, and it was left to the small independent theatres and to a few pioneering provincial repertory lessees and directors to bring foreign plays into Britain. There was an easing of censorship between the wars but the victims of the censor's blue pencil, in the main, were progressive and political plays from the Continent: Strindberg, Pirandello, Schnitzler, O'Neill, Toller, Bruckner and Wedekind are included in this list of honour.

O'Casey keeps company in the 1930s with several playwrights in either retiring from the stage or writing very little for production. O'Casey offered only one full length play during the 1930s, *Within the Gates* (1935), a full Expressionist play set in Hyde Park, surrounded by a distant chorus of the unemployed. It failed in London but was a huge success in New York. Set against Auden, Isherwood and Doone it shows an understanding of style and a sympathy with content equal to that of these more celebrated playwrights.

For various and usually undisclosed reasons, other playwrights well-established in the 1920s disappeared in the 1930s or were driven from the stage by poor response, to be replaced by another generation. Only three major playwrights crossed the dividing line, Shaw, Coward and Clemence Dane. Edgar Wallace died, as did Pinero after submitting three small and insignificant plays. Galsworthy wrote nothing after 1929, Drinkwater produced *A Man's House* in 1934 after a long absence. Frederick Lonsdale, author of many very successful, stylish social comedies, wrote only one play in 1932 which had a run of only fifty-eight performances. Somerset Maugham who vied with Lonsdale for skill and success gave up very early in the 1930s in the belief that he had lost his audience. Both these playwrights had epitomised those who had found a formula and stuck with it. The fact that Maugham thought he had lost his audience after he had tried one play, *Sheppey*, with a central character socially lower than his usual range, is a great pity. His last play, *For Services Rendered*, is arguably the best play written in the 1930s (see the last chapter of this book).

Others continued writing plays and comedies of situation

throughout the period. One last major playwright who disappeared was J. M. Barrie, who made a comeback with *The Boy David* in 1936. The production opened in Edinburgh, starring Elizabeth Bergner – a very popular star of the day. A great deal of pre-publicity heralded the success to come: in the event, it failed to excite or even interest and Barrie retired from the stage. The 1930s were replete with biblical plays, which, as a genre, seemed a way of saying something about a moral situation in terms which made it easy to ignore any possible contemporary relevance by clouding the issues. James Bridie kept one foot in the horror camp and one on the Bible. Bridie's view of the function of the theatre was to give the British theatregoer what s/he wanted and this could be defined as giving, for a short time, people living in a safe world the illusion that they were living in a dangerous one. This clearly will stand a great deal of pondering. Who could have thought of the 1930s as a safe time? Surely the point was to remove danger to a realm of fantasy so that people living in a dangerous world could be given the illusion that they were living in a safe one. Violent death only happens in plays. Which is not, of course, what Bridie said but something which he turned into many of his successful plays.

Notes

1. Camillo Pellizzi, *The English Drama: the Last Great Phase* (London: Macmillan, 1935).

2. Esmé Wingfield-Stratton, *Before the Lights Went Out* (London: Hodder & Stoughton, 1945), pp. 240–1.

3. A good account of the life and politics of the aristocracy at this time is: Lord Willoughby de Broke, *The Passing Years* (London: Constable, 1924). Lord Willoughby was one of the main organisers of the opposition to the bill. Outside of politics and the life of the landed gentry he had a passion for the theatre, in which he invested. Unfortunately, as his wife records in the preface of the autobiography, he became so involved in writing up the political events of 1910–12 during an illness in 1923 that he died without writing the final chapters of his book. 'his intention was that Chapter XIV (the penultimate), should be devoted to the Drama – always to him a most interesting subject . . .' (p. xv).

4. Quoted in Allen Hutt, *British Trade Unionism* (London and New York: Lawrence and Wishart, 1941). Notwithstanding Lenin's discounting of numbers, the membership of unions rose rapidly and substantially.

5. Esmé Wingfield-Stratton, *Before the Lights Went Out*, p. 14.

6. E. H. Carr, *The Twenty Years Crisis: 1919–1939* (London: Macmillan, 1981 [revised edition]), p. 207.

7. William Poel, *What is Wrong with the Theatre?* (London: Allen and Unwin 1920), p. 17.

8. *Morning Post*, 13 June 1924, quoted in Huntley Carter, *The New Spirit in the European Theatre* (London: Ernest Benn Ltd., 1925).

9. Norman Marshall, *The Other Theatre* (London: John Lehmann Ltd, 1947), p. 15.

10. William Poel, *What is Wrong with the Theatre?* p. 10.

11. *Referee*, 5 December 1915, quoted in William Poel, *What is Wrong with the Theatre?* p. 24.

12. The *Monthly Letter*, September 1917, quoted in William Poel, *What is Wrong with the Theatre?* pp. 24–5.

13. W. MacQueen-Pope, *Twenty Shillings in the Pound* (London: Hutchinson & Co., 1948), pp. 140–1.

14. *Ibid.*, p. 141.

15. Ernest Short, *Theatrical Cavalcade* (London: Eyre and Spottiswoode, 1942), p. 62.

16. See Julie Holledge, *Innocent Flowers* (London: Virago, 1981), and Viv Gardner, *Sketches from the Actresses Franchise League* (Nottingham: Nottingham Drama Texts, 1985).

17. Sheila Stowell, *A Stage of Their Own: Feminist Playwrights of the Suffrage Era* (Manchester University Press, 1992), p. 7.

18. Huntley Carter, *The New Spirit in the European Theatre* (London: Ernest Benn, 1924), p. 15.

19. Phillip Hoare, *Wilde's Last Stand* (London: Duckworth, 1997), p. 9. Hoare is quoting from *The Lady Diana Cooper Scrapbooks* (London: Hamish Hamilton 1987).

20. Huntley Carter, *The New Spirit in the European Theatre*, pp. 33–6.

21. *Ibid.* For a recent monograph on the role of theatre in the First World War see L. C. Collins, *Theatres at War, 1914–18* (London: Macmillan, 1998).

22. *Era*, 6 September 1916, quoted in William Poel, *What is Wrong with the Theatre?*, p. 20.

23. Huntley Carter, *The New Spirit in the European Theatre*, pp. 142–6.

24. *The Times*, undated, quoted in Kurt Ganzl, *The British Musical Theatre: Volume II* (London: Macmillan, 1986), pp. 32–5.

25. *Ibid.*

26. G. E. Morrison, 'Reconstruction of the Theatre', *Morning Post*, 13–17 February 1919.

27. St John Ervine, *The Organised Theatre* (London: Allen and Unwin, 1924), p. 53.

28. J. C. Trewin, *The Gay Twenties* (London: Macdonald, 1958), p. 69.

29. See P. P. Howe, *The Repertory Theatre* (London: Martin Secker, 1910); Cecil Chisholm, *Repertory* (London: Peter Davies,1934); G. Rowell and A. Jackson, *The Repertory Movement* (Cambridge University Press, 1984); Richard Jerrams, *Weekly Rep* (Droitwich: Peter Andrew Publishing Company, 1991); Norman Marshall, *The Other Theatre* (London: John Lehmann, 1947); Andrew Davies, *Other Theatres* (London: Macmillan, 1987); Colin Chambers, *The Story of Unity Theatre* (London and New York: Lawrence and Wishart, 1989); Samuels, Cosgrove and MacColl *Theatres of the Left* (London: Routledge and Kegan Paul, 1984), and R. Stourac and K. McCreery, *Theatre as a Weapon* (London: Routledge and Kegan Paul, 1986). Ann Lindsay, *The Theatre* (London: Bodley Head, New Development no. 5, 1948) is the source of the material on the 1919 British Theatre Conference. This is a pamphlet of sixty-four pages and is general in its coverage but, because of Ms Lindsay's own involvement in community and education theatre, is full of insights which others do not have. Would she had written more.

30. Sir John Martin Harvey, who had spoken in favour of a Labour Party Theatre at the 1919 Conference, found himself later the subject of an Actors Association (AA) boycott.

31. A good account of the life of the struggling professional is to be found in Stanley Heather, *That Struts and Frets* (Ilfracombe: Arthur H. Stockwell, 1972). This is a poignant social document and records engagements in the 1930s offered at half of the paltry £3 demanded by AA. An excellent volume on the Edwardian theatre is Michael R. Booth and Joel H. Kaplan, eds., *The Edwardian Theatre: Essays on Performance and the Stage* (Cambridge University Press, 1996).

32. Beerbohm Tree died in 1917, Alexander in 1918 and Wyndham in 1919.

33. His biography, *Gerald*, written by Daphne du Maurier (London: Gollancz, 1934) ran to four impressions in its first year. Laurence Olivier is known to have said that his generation of actors had no models to copy. They had to make up their own way of working, except that they had du Maurier. Du Maurier was President of the Stage Guild for a period.

34. See H. R. Barbour, *The Theatre: An Art and an Industry* (London: The Labour Publishing Company [undated]), and J. McLeod, *The Actors Right to Act* (London: undated).

35. Allardyce Nicoll, *English Drama 1900–1930* (Cambridge University Press, 1973), p. 4.

36. W. Macqueen-Pope, *St James: Theatre of Distinction* (London: W. H. Allen, 1958), p. 190.

37. Robert Graves and Allan Hodge, *The Lost Weekend* (London: Faber and Faber, 1941), p. 69.

38. See Martin Taylor, *Lads: Love Poetry of the Trenches* (London: Duckworth, 1989), and Nicholas de Jongh, *Not in Front of the Audience* (London: Routledge, 1992). One of the more interesting (and best-written) plays of the 1930s arises out of this frenzied scene after it had passed its peak and was in decline. Mordaunt Shairp's *The Green Bay Tree* deals with the homosexual relationship between a rich collector and a young man corrupted by luxury – a very moral tale. The censor initially missed the nature of the relationship and his later understanding set back homosexual themes for many years (see John Deeney's chapter).

39. J. C. Trewin, *The Turbulent Thirties* (London: Macdonald, 1960), p. 129.

40. Flecker spent much of his life in the Middle East.

41. Philip Godfrey, *Back Stage* (London: Harrap and Co., 1933), p. 55.

42. Allardyce Nicoll, *English Drama 1900–1930*, p. 133. The *Play Pictorial*, xxxv, no. 213: 93 and xlii, no. 250: 1. It is possible that some ideas on epic structures from the Continent might just have slipped through.

43. Camillo Pellizzi, *English Drama*, pp. 199–200.

44. Ross McKibbin, *Classes and Cultures: England 1918–1951* (Oxford University Press, 1998), p. 38. See also Charles Loch Mowat, *Britain Between the Wars 1918–1940* (London: Methuen, 1955).

45. Noreen Branson and Margot Heinemann, *Britain in the Nineteen Thirties* (London: Weidenfeld and Nicolson, 1971), pp. 44–5.

46. For a valuable monograph on housing and poverty between the wars see G. C. M. McGonigle and J. Kirby, *Poverty and Public Health* (London: Gollancz, 1936).

47. Camillo Pellizzi, *English Drama: the Last Great Phase*, p. 284.

48. St John Ervine, *The Theatre in My Time*, pp. 138–40.

49. Noreen Branson and Margot Heinemann, *Britain in the Nineteen Thirties*, p. 234.

50. Arthur Calder-Marshall, *The Changing Scene* (London: Gollancz, 1938), p. 160.

51. *Ibid.*, p. 159.

52. Noreen Branson and Margot Heinemann, *Britain in the Nineteen Thirties*, pp. 269–70.

53. In addition see Michael J. Sidnell, *Dances of Death – the Group Theatre of London in the Thirties* (London: Faber and Faber, 1984), and Robert Medley, *Drawn from the Life: a Memoir* (London: Faber and Faber, 1983). For an inter-

esting source of visionary speculation of the inter-war period see John Palmer, *The Future of the Theatre* (London: George Bell and Sons, 1913).

54. Theodore Komisarjevsky, *The Theatre in a Changing Civilisation* (London: The Bodley Head, 1935), p. ix.

55. Richard Findlater, *Banned!* (London: MacGibbon and Kee, 1967), pp. 145–6.

56. J. C. Trewin, *The Gay Twenties*, p. 84.

57. *Ibid.*, pp. 90–1.

58. Camillo Pellizzi, *English Drama: the Last Great Phase*, pp. 278–9.

59. *Ibid.*, p. 290.

2 Body parts: the success of the thriller in the inter-war years

JOHN STOKES

> There are no trunks or cupboards or wall paper or floorboards. There are no hands taped together and there is none of that awful business that you have read about of having to cut quickly and efficiently at the neck in order to stop the screaming. But the body is still there, and there are all the usual criminal precautions to be taken; the locked doors, the muffling of sounds so that the neighbours won't hear . . . But in the end (and this is the real similarity between the secret and the crime) in the end, just like in all the worst cases that you've ever read about, what it all comes down to in the end, and what will finally lead you to being caught, is the fact that there is a body. Not a slip of the tongue or a sum of money or a slip of paper. A body.
>
> Neil Bartlett, *Mr Clive and Mr Page*[1]

In any murder story there will always be two kinds of body, the living and the dead; but if the story is enacted on stage, if it is performed, then that distinction becomes far more palpable. The dead bodies may not be visible (though they must surely be somewhere) while the living bodies are not just seen and heard, they may, if they belong to well-known actors, actually be familiar. In the 1920s and 1930s a number of performers realised that their physical presence was enhanced, made more complex, when it was it countered by the silent fact of an inanimate corpse.[2]

There is a celebrated moment in an otherwise forgotten thriller of 1927 called *Interference*[3] in which the actor-manager Sir Gerald du

Maurier remained alone on stage in the company of a dead body for ten whole minutes, not speaking a single word. Du Maurier played Sir John Marlay, a distinguished specialist, second husband of Faith, who is being blackmailed by Deborah Kane. Deborah has discovered that, long ago, Faith lived as the mistress of the man who eventually became her first husband. In a richly improbable coincidence the first husband, previously believed to have been killed in the war, arrives at Sir John's surgery for a consultation in the course of which he manages to steal some prussic acid. A confrontational scene at Deborah's flat culminates with this first husband (they too have had an affair) lacing her brandy with the acid, an act the audience witnesses. But this is what happens in the immediately following scene when Sir John, already suspicious, arrives at the flat, discovers the body, and assumes that Faith has committed the murder:

> SIR JOHN (*gently*). Anyone here? Miss Kane! (*Goes to writing-table R., puts latch-key on it, then lights a match. Finds the switch and lights go up. He stands looking round the room. Sees* DEBORAH.) MISS KANE! (*Moves to her side and kneels, takes her hand and turns her over on her back.*) GOD! (*He goes down to bedroom L. returns to table, picks up tumbler, smells it. Is just about to telephone when he sees* FAITH's *bag lying on the floor R. At the sight, for a moment his mind becomes blank with horror. He picks up the open bag, examines its contents: the cheque he wrote for her and puts it in his coat pocket. Glances at his wrist-watch. His eye settles on the poison bottle, which he recognises as one of his own. He covers his eyes with his hand and sits thinking. Suddenly he straightens up with a new and intense expression. From this point onward his actions are extraordinary. He takes gloves and black silk handkerchief out of pocket; puts on the gloves; takes off his coat, places it on chair at back of table; picks up poison bottle from table; tries to remove its label with a knife from the tray. He then empties poison tumbler into bowl of flowers on writing-table; places poison bottle in a glass of water which he takes from jug at back. Takes brandy bottle, thoroughly cleans it with handkerchief. This done he replaces brandy bottle on the table*

c. He then removes poison bottle from glass and scrapes off the red label, which he puts on table c., and places the poison bottle in DEBORAH'S R. *hand. At this moment the voices of two men are heard approaching: their shadows appear on the glass window – they stop – one rings the bell – they are evidently calling on* DEBORAH *to try and get a drink – the other persuades his friend that it is too late and they go away talking. At the sound of voices and appearance of the shadows* SIR JOHN *is arrested in what he is doing. He backs to the wall, moves down to the bedroom door L., hesitates – the two men go away, he registers relief and hurriedly carries on. Rinses glass, pouring contents into bowl, wipes it with handkerchief; pours brandy into glass, wipes knife; wraps his gloves in handkerchief and puts the lot in trousers pocket. He takes coat and goes to table, picks it up and puts it in his pocket. Returns to door, opens latch with his coat, switches off lights and passes gently out of the front door, latching it.*

(p. 52)

The spectators were taken through this silent sequence, as one critic put it, 'cinema fashion'; watching 'with such breathless interest that one can assume that every individual member of the audience has a personal interest in learning how to conceal the crime'.[4] But the lessons went beyond the merely criminal. No matter that in the effort to protect his wife Sir John has made a potentially fatal mistake, reconstituting the scene as if the dead woman were right- rather than left-handed; no matter that the poisoner will eventually confess to the offence, the audience have seen a public man reveal a steely, almost instinctive, capacity for deception in a thorough demonstration of the uses to which his professional dexterity can be put. And all this has been reproduced, theatrically, by an actor in total command of the stage. As Sir John Marlay Sir Gerald du Maurier has, once again, shown his audience how to create an almost flawless falsehood. James Agate made the point, characteristically, by invoking Hamlet: 'There are other roles besides the philosopher's in which one can be bounded in a nutshell, and count oneself a king of infinite space.'[5] These other roles include that of the actor who creates and re-creates with exquisite bodily skill: 'One might say that Sir Gerald du Maurier's performance gives infinite pleasure,' wrote Agate, 'But that would be to speak loosely. His acting last night gave one pleasure of a finite, definite, almost concrete sort. You could pin down, and nail to the counter, each and every one of its many admirable qualities – vigour, ease, precision, attack, balance.'[6]

In the history of the British stage thriller the influence and example of Gerald du Maurier is crucial, as actor, director, entrepreneur and collaborator. His suavity, his celebrated naturalness, was so seemingly absolute that it even provoked suspicions that it must conceal some elusive duplicity. After an early career working for John Hare, establishing himself by doubling Captain Hook with Mr Darling in *Peter Pan* (1904), he had scored tremendous success with the 'amateur cracksman' 'Raffles' in the 1906 stage version of E. W. Hornung's popular, Conan Doyle-inspired, crime stories. Like his nineteenth-century precedents, Raffles is considerably smarter than the detectives who try to track him down, but he is no class impostor, rather an aberrant symptom of rigid social mores and pretension. He is a moral outsider who has no need to pose as an social insider, because he actually is one: an Old Harrovian and a first-class cricketer, entirely at home in the country houses he subsequently loots. Raffles is a resourceful Englishman who has no need to make an effort, who breaks all the rules without, at some fundamental level, compromising his own integrity, which is why du Maurier replaced the brooding melodramatic intensity of, say, Irving's Mathias in *The Bells* with an apparently throwaway style that responded to changing ideas of criminality, of class, of sexuality.[7] Although 'not at all conventionally handsome', du Maurier, as the late Sir John Gielgud recalled, 'could slouch and lounge and flick his leading lady behind one ear as he played a love-scene, never seeming to raise his voice or force an emotion'.[8] His speech was both slow and staccato, but he moved quickly, smoothly. Social malevolence was replaced by stylish self-interest and a witty deceit that had little to do with Lombrosian criminal abnormality. This attractiveness ensured that it was the Raffles type, rather than Galsworthy's pathetic victim in *Justice* (1910) or Shaw's sophistical burglar in *Heartbreak House* (1919), who survived as the classic criminal-hero.

Raffles was sufficiently popular for the play to be revived during the First World War, but in 1921, at a time when heroism urgently needed redefining, the character re-emerged, admittedly with some significant changes, when du Maurier, having helped to re-draft 'Sapper's original script, staged *Bull-Dog Drummond* at Wyndhams, his own theatre.[9] It is not just that the upper-class hero now solved crimes rather than committing them, but that the dramatic interest was unashamedly spurred by violence.

The play opens with Drummond placing a newspaper advertisement, a paragraph that was actually reproduced in the theatre programme:

> Demobilised officer, finding peace incredibly tedious, would welcome diversion. Legitimate, if possible, but crime, if of a humorous description, no objection. Excitement essential. Reply at once Box X 10.

Drummond has a flat in Half Moon Street, is keen on golf and racing, and goes around with a posse of side-kicks, friends also left over from the war. In the first act he is called upon to help Phyllis Benton, sister of another old comrade whose life he had saved in the trenches. Phyllis is worried that a gang of international criminals, the sinister Carl Peterson, his daughter, and Henry Lakington, an evil doctor, are blackmailing her rich but fallible uncle. First, Phyllis has to be reassured by one of Drummond's chums that he really is the man for the job:

> We soldiered with the old bird in France and all that sort of thing . . . As a matter of fact, Peter and I were both at school with him, and he's the sort of fellah who never says very much – but always seems to get away with the goods . . . I mean, he's got a face like a motor mascot, and all that – but the old grey matter rotates all right.[10]

'I think he's got a very nice face', interrupts Phyllis, already won over. Together she and Drummond set out to investigate her uncle's plight but are eventually taken prisoner by the gang. At the climax of the

Body parts: the success of the thriller

Bulldog Drummond Baited by the Villainous Doctor.

DR. HENRY LAKINGTON TORTURES PHYLLIS BEFORE DRUMMOND: SIR GERALD DU MAURIER, MR. GILBERT HARE, AND MISS OLWEN ROOSE.

One of the most thrilling scenes in "Bulldog Drummond," the melodrama at Wyndham's, takes place in what purports to be Dr. Henry Lakington's nursing home. The villainous "doctor" tortures Phyllis Benton, and then lets the impotent Bulldog Drummond see her in a fainting condition. Drummond is, however, equal to every situation, and though he is tightly bound with chains and leather, he manages to get free through the aid of Phyllis, who "comes to" at the right minute, and he is able to turn the tables on the Doctor very prettily. *(Photograph by Stage Photo. Co.)*

1. Dr Henry Lakington tortures Phyllis before Drummond: Sir Gerald du Maurier, Mr Gilbert Hare and Miss Olwen Roose. From *Bull-Dog Drummond*. Reproduced in *The Sketch*, 22 February 1922

Bulldog Drummond's Bite, Grip, and Strangle·Hold.

DOWNING THE VILLAINS: SIR GERALD DU MAURIER AS THE HERO
OF "SAPPER'S" MELODRAMA.

Sir Gerald du Maurier has a busy time as the hero of the "thick ear" play "Bulldog Drummond," which has been running successfully at Wyndham's for nearly a year. He has to deal with two cunning and unscrupulous villains—Dr. Henry Lakington (Mr. Gilbert Hare) and Carl Peterson (Mr. Alfred Drayton), and is shown on our page at grips with them both in thrilling moments in the play.

Photographs by Mage Photo Co.

2. Downing the villains: Sir Gerald du Maurier as the hero of 'Sapper's' melodrama. Reproduced in *The Sketch*, 22 February 1922

third act, they find themselves bound to chairs, threatened with torture by the coldly scientific doctor. With a cunning feint Phyllis succeeds in loosening Drummond's bonds. The du Maurier touch is unmistakable in the extended sequence that follows: first, a gun-shot that breaks the deadlock, and then a couple of pieces of stage trickery whose obvious absurdity is masked by the sheer speed and surprise of the acting:

> (DRUMMOND *rises, motions* PHYLLIS *to* R. *up, wheels invalid chair to up* R.C., *glides cautiously down to switch by door* L., *turns off light. Only green from sofa and red from fire, which lights* PHYLLIS' *face left on.* DRUMMOND *then crouches behind sofa, marks his eye with carmine whilst on floor.* LAKINGTON *comes through doors, sees semi-darkness, dashes down to* R.C. *shouting.*)
>
> LAKINGTON: My God, where is he?
>
> (*Pulls out his revolver, sees* DRUMMOND'S *head which just appears over top of sofa. Fires at him.* DRUMMOND *falls behind sofa, bullet goes through picture up on* L. *wall with a crash. Picture falls with another crash. This is worked by a piece of lead on string hanging through hole in centre of glass of picture: when shot goes, it is pulled, and the picture is allowed to fall from back. When* DRUMMOND *rises,* LAKINGTON *fires again. Hits* DRUMMOND *in the hand.* DRUMMOND *binds his hand up with a blood-stained handkerchief. Apparently now there are more shots in revolver.* LAKINGTON *throws the revolver on desk, seizes knife from mantelshelf, and with a* 'Take that, damn you,' *he hurls it at* DRUMMOND. *By a trick the knife appears to have stuck in the back wall* L.C., *and vibrates vindictively. This worked by having a trick knife in a steel tube fastened on back of scene, and at the word cue* 'Take that, damn you', *man at back pushes it through.* LAKINGTON *at the same time smuggles his knife inside his coat, and dashes off into the laboratory* R. DRUMMOND *puts foot on chair under where knife is stuck, makes a grab at it. It naturally doesn't come out. He then seizes champagne bottle and hurls it at him through*

folding doors. There is a crash off. Bottle is caught in a net off R.)
DRUMMOND: GOT him!

(pp. 68–9)

Not that this is the end of the play; in the final act Peterson offers
Drummond a chance to come in on the blackmail racket. Drummond
refuses but the criminal mastermind escapes: a social menace has been
scotched not killed, and there will be opportunities for future confron-
tations.

Drummond is Raffles as he might have become had he been to
the Front, an example of the figure of the returning soldier who features
so strongly in works of the post-war years, often to provide some sort of
heavily weighted moral understanding. In Robins Millar's remarkable
Thunder in the Air,[11] for example, a combination of melodramatic
thriller and ghost play, a dead soldier returns as an apparition to confront his family and friends and to reconcile them with their knowledge that in real life he fell far short of the heroic masculinity that
sanctimonious posterity has conferred upon him. In the case of *Bull-
Dog Drummond*, however, violence is still expressed within an atmosphere of camaraderie where male values are held to have been betrayed
rather than undermined by the war. At the same time, sex begins to
make a surreptitious entrance with Phyllis, the kind of girl who appre-
ciates a brawl. As du Maurier announced from the stage after a 'tremendous' curtain on opening night:

> We've given you the sex play and we given you the 'highbrow'
> play. Now we want to give you a change – and here's what
> 'Sapper' and I think is perhaps best described as a 'thick-ear'
> play![12]

Privately du Maurier had his own explanation for the play's success:
'*Bull-Dog Drummond* appeals to the youth of the country because they
can recognise the sort of leadership they badly need and aren't getting
any more.'[13] In other words (though du Maurier would hardly have seen
it this way), violence would now hold centre-stage as a release for the
frustrations of a wounded officer class fighting hard to claim its place
in the modern world, a claim bolstered by imperialist racism (in the

form of Asian servants as well as foreign villains) and comic Cockney by-play from what remained of the other ranks.

Naturally there were, even in the 1920s, more sophisticated explanations than du Maurier's for what seemed to be a universal fascination with brutality. William Bolitho's *Murder for Profit* (1926)[14], a collection of studies of serial killers of the past, claimed that the contemporary taste for verbatim reports of murder trials in the papers had come about because of the need for the kind of ritual event that the modern world failed to provide:

> A murder trial is the celebration of a human sacrifice by
> suffocation, to which modern men are excited in a crowd by the
> recital of some bloody deed, whose details awaken hate and fear
> to which the coming execution is the foreshadowed, fore-tasted
> complementary. Everything there, prayers, codes, robes and
> bars, is devised to create that hoarse atmosphere in which alone
> modern men, in a state of peace, can work themselves up to a
> corporate killing, and to whose terrible reality the witnesses
> respond so that they speak truthfully and unlock themselves.
>
> (p. 9)

Bolitho thought that the modern theatre was unlikely to match the compulsive appeal of an actual event since 'it is its reality, not its drama, wherein lies the core of the interest of murder' (p. 9). While the subsequent history of British theatre in the inter-war years would tend to disprove Bolitho's argument – for one thing, plays continually drew upon real-life cases – his sense that the re-enactment of murder fulfils deep needs relating to the social world at large was certainly borne out. Bolitho's chapter on the serial killer G. J. Smith, of 'Brides in the Bath' fame, stresses that when he was tried in 1915 Smith's 'affairs competed for public interest with the first defeats of the Russians in Galicia and the first victories of the Italians in the Dolomites. Under the weight of contrast, Smith's deeds seemed more terrible than the crash of armies, his tin baths more evil things than bridge-destroying artillery, this minor devil more sinister than all the hell outside' (p. 195).

Contrasts and comparisons among individual acts of aggression and the enormity of war crimes, as well as between the self-interest of the thug and the high-minded patriotism of the soldier, are made continually in the drama of the 1920s. They even permeate the work of Edgar Wallace.

A uniquely successful and prolific novelist since *The Four Just Men* in 1905, it took time for Wallace to make any impact in the theatre. The change came through collaboration with du Maurier. To the business of the stage thriller the two men brought complementary talents: Wallace had a hard-boiled American style and his own brash and reactionary sense of morality, du Maurier was the great creator of theatrical excitement. In Wallace's *The Ringer*, which du Maurier produced in 1926, a mysterious criminal (given his nickname because he continually 'rings the changes' on his appearance), returns to London intent on revenge. Real name 'Ernest Milton', he is a war hero who refused the DSO; his first act after the war is to kill the officer who had his best and only friend executed on a false charge of cowardice. Since then, 'The Ringer' has married a woman who is herself guilty of shooting a man who insulted her in a dance-hall. He is now thought to be back in London intent on tracking down a notorious criminal who once abused his sister, Gwenda. This is Meister, certainly the most interesting character in the play, a 50-year-old dandy who affects perfectly fitting clothes, snowy-white spats, top hat, yellow gloves, and a large buttonhole. Meister also carries a cane topped with an ivory ball which is both a sword-stick and his secret hiding place for the cocaine to which he is heavily addicted. He is, we are told, a brilliant musician and an art connoisseur, as well as a fence for stolen goods.

The action of the play moves between Scotland Yard, a Dockland police station and Meister's house in Deptford, which features a secret panel that flashes with a red light when it is operated. In general attendance are a bevy of police officers (one of whom, Bliss, just back from America, we are encouraged to think could possibly be 'The Ringer' in disguise) and Lomond, a Scots criminologist whose name is almost an anagram, since he comments in a 'Lombrosian' way ('prognathic process of the jaw suggest a rabid homicide')[15] on the nature of criminality.

In many respects *The Ringer* follows conventions established in the late nineteenth century: London still has the same cultural topography based on East and West Ends, Meister is a hangover from *fin-de-siècle* decadence, and 'The Ringer' is a witty rebel distantly related to Raffles. It goes without saying that both men are much cleverer than the police, though even the Met. is struggling to catch up with the modern world. At the time the play seemed advanced because the action, when it takes off, is so rapid, because it makes allusions to America, because the female characters, though still subsidiary to the male, have a greater degree of independent life, and finally, vitally, because, by all accounts, the audience found plenty of opportunities for laughter along with the excitement.

The characteristic movement is from fairly static passages of speculation to incidents of melodramatic intensity and hectic business. Sword-stick and red light both come into play at the climactic end when 'The Ringer' finally appears and unmasks himself.

(*The lights go out. There is complete darkness except for red light glowing over door. We hear a strange voice, rather weird tone. It is really* LOMOND, *The Ringer.*)

THE RINGER: Where are you, Meister?

(*The piano ends on a discord and* MEISTER *gurgles.*)

The Ringer's come for you.

(*There is a stifled groan from* MEISTER.)

(*Loudly*) That's for Gwenda!

(*A woman's scream is heard. Then there is much confusion in the darkness. The red light goes out.*)

WEMBURY: Stand by that door.

LOMOND: Put up those lights! Who was it screamed? Put up the lights, you damned fool!

(*The policeman puts up the lights. Positions are the same except for* WEMBURY, *who is front of panel,* L. *of door* C., *and* MEISTER, *who is leaning with his back to door with the sword part of his own sword-stick through his breast, with a green spot on him.*)

(BLISS *has come down to back of* LOMOND *with an automatic in his hand.*)

LOMOND: You can tell me, eh! Then who is The Ringer?

BLISS: (*pointing pistol at* LOMOND's *back*). You're The Ringer!

(BLISS *moves in front of* LOMOND *and whips off his hat and throws it up stage. This is a trick affair, a distinctive hat, the replica of the one* LOMOND *has worn and carried all through the play, but with a false fringe of grey hair fixed inside, so that the whole lot comes off together. At the same time* LOMOND *whips off his moustache, leaps up with a ?!)*

LOMOND: What the hell – ?

WEMBURY: Stand still.

LOMOND: Bliss!

(*Bliss leaps back to* L., *still covering* LOMOND, *and* THE RINGER *stands revealed, a young man.*)

BLISS: *Not so much of the Bliss! I want you, Henry Arthur Milton. Search him!*

(pp. 67–8)

As with *Bull-Dog Drummond* this is not, of course, the end of the play. Always with an eye on the possibility of a sequel, Wallace has 'The Ringer' manage to disguise himself as a policeman and make a successful break for it. Nor is it merely a convenience that it should have been Lomond, the cod criminologist, who has concealed the identity of the slippery criminal. The joke underlines Wallace's habitual point that it has long been time to move on from late nineteenth-century 'criminal anthropology' to a more modern sense of the offender as an extreme product of a new world where disguised vigilantes are more to the point than easily identifiable biological aberrations. The Ringer set the pattern for a string of Wallace hits including *The Squeaker*,[16] *The Flying Squad*[17] and *On the Spot*,[18] all of them fast-moving and international in their frame of reference.

It followed that the most appropriate form of discovery for these modern masters of disguise should often have been a kind of contrived theatre, as in the penultimate scene of *The Ringer*. But there are plenty of examples of a more extreme self-referentiality, of thrillers where the theatre provides the location as well as the analogy for crime. *The Big Drum*,[19] by Harold Holland, opens with a view of what purports to be the stage of a provincial theatre but immediately involves the whole auditorium: shots ring out from the real audience, the leading actress falls to the ground, a policeman climbs on-stage where he is eventually joined by the supposedly guilty man, also from the audience. After many twists and turns it turns out that the entire 'play within a play' has been an elaborate stunt designed to drum up business for an unsuccessful melodrama. *Murder on the Second Floor*,[20] written by Frank Vosper,[21] with himself in the leading role, has a playwright compose a thriller based on the fellow inmates of a Bloomsbury boarding-house; as the imagined plot proceeds so the commonplace lodgers all turn into potential criminals and what has begun as a *jeu d'esprit* becomes for a while what appears to be a real-life murder mystery. Emlyn Williams' *A Murder has been Arranged*,[22] written with du Maurier in mind during the run of Wallace's *On the Spot* (in which Williams appeared) is set in the St. James's Theatre where it was later performed. A millionaire is about to celebrate his birthday with a fancy-dress party which the guests are required to attend as famous ghosts from history. Although he is murdered in the course of the evening by Maurice Mullins, a vengeful cousin, the host mysteriously reappears as a ghost before finally becoming a corpse:

> *The dead body lies in the armchair.*
> MULLINS *stares, quite uncomprehending. Then, suddenly, he leaps to the curtains and tears them together.*
> MULLINS (*hysterical*): You didn't see that! You didn't see that! You didn't see that! You didn't see that – there's nothing there! Look! There's nothing there! There's nothing there – look!
> *He tears back the curtains again. The dead body . . .*
> *He stares, quite motionless for a moment, then gives a long scream of terror.*
> *He totters and collapses.*
> *A loud clanging noise, high above. He looks up.* (*Dully*): What's that coming down? *The safety curtain begins to fall, slowly and implacably.* It's a wall . . . A prison wall! . . . (*Falling to his knees, in a crescendo of madness*): Shutting me in! Shutting me in . . . Shutting me in . . .

The safety curtain will not rise again. But it need not. A murder has been arranged; a murder has taken place; and the murderer has been brought to book. The evening's adventure in the St. James's Theatre, London, is over.[23]

Williams' final coup, a comment on theatre itself, locks the character in with his deed and obliges the audience to go home still puzzling over what they have seen: a conscious variation on the traditional satisfying ending.

By the early 1930s, if not earlier, it becomes possible to distinguish between the increasingly theatricalised mode of the thriller and the more domestically contained world of the detective story. While both came to prominence at much the same time, and while there were certainly overlaps among performers and directors, there are identifiable differences in terms of narrative structure. A thriller in the Wallace mould is usually constructed so that in order for everything to make sense in the end, after many complicating adventures, much of the essential information must be present, though often hidden, at the outset. Live theatre, not being suited to 'flashback', obeys this rule quite strictly – more so than fiction, and certainly more so than film. Detective stories, in contrast, tend to start with a central event or crime and work backwards to the cause – though again, in the theatre, this must normally be achieved without retrospective incidents; the past must be recalled in other ways. Yet quite often the two narrative patterns came together – or ran alongside one another – so that detecting the guilty involves risks and dangers characteristic of the thriller. A good example would be *The Fourth Wall*[24] by A. A. Milne, in which an efficient murder, a faked suicide, is witnessed by the audience in the first act, but not solved by characters on stage until the end of the third. Milne's title, of course, plays on a familiar phrase used to describe the passive, voyeuristic role of the audience in conventionally realistic theatre.

It nevertheless remains true that while thrillers are driven by a sequence of ever-more threatening events culminating with a headlong revelation, detective stories tend to pursue a slow backwards unravelling that explores the psychology of the investigator along with that of the culprit.[25] The modern detective story arrives on the British stage, again with du Maurier as midwife, in 1928 with an adaptation of Agatha Christie's *The Murder of Roger Ackroyd* under the title *Alibi*[26] starring Charles Laughton as Hercule Poirot. 'Clearly, he has been produced by du Maurier', wrote Sydney W. Carroll of *The Times*, 'No one else could have taught him how to roll that cigarette so admirably, whilst he watches sideways his victim or plays with a situation as a kitten with a ball.'[27] Whereas du Maurier had discovered the charismatic power of languor, Laughton's went even further, making Poirot, the detective who possesses access to other people's minds, the most private figure on stage. Laughton was always physically awkward and mentally poetic. Reviewers praise the way in which he built up the part from a quiet beginning, spreading the emphases, 'so that fairly commonplace dialogue is made to appear startlingly good',[28] and in his extended tribute Carroll devoted paragraph upon paragraph to Laughton's 'thick, sensitive lips, the fat cheeks, the dimple, the weird, sly smile', to his hands, 'quickly indicative of every passion, every thought, and every mood', to his feet, 'one foot turns over whilst the other tip-toes on the carpet'. Yet, for all that, Carroll concludes: 'he is something lacking in the lovable. There is very little charm in the fellow. He amuses you. He excites. But there is always some strange undercurrent of unwholesomeness that you cannot explain or understand.'

At the end of the play, just as Poirot the detective is left with his secrets – the fact that he has persuaded the murderer to kill himself, his unrealisable passion for the murderer's sister – so the actor remained half hidden behind the technical brilliance of his art. Indeed, when Poirot returned to the stage in Agatha Christie's *Black Coffee*,[29] this time with Francis Sullivan in the part, one or two critics preferred his interpretation to Laughton's on the grounds that he 'does not tie "character" labels all over the part, but plays it quietly and firmly, trusting that the story will do its own work of entertainment',[30] and because whereas 'Mr Laughton's Poirot was a diabolically clever oddity; Mr Sullivan's is a lovable human being.'[31]

Some younger actors of whom Laughton was one, Emlyn Williams another (both, not insignificantly, homosexual) knew how to

mine a vein of inner mystery that, while undoubtedly present in the
Wallace thrillers, had remained relatively unexploited apart from melodramatic effect.[32] Laughton and Williams acted in Wallace plays
sometimes together; already Williams specialised in a kind of psycho-
pathic creepiness, in the kind of men who are heroes only to themselves. As Lord Lebanon in *Frightened Lady*[33] he played an aristocrat
suffering from hereditary madness who has discovered during his time
in India how to strangle people 'Thuggee-style' with silk scarves. Until
it is guessed by Tanner, a notably calm police detective, only Lebanon's
mother and a couple of bodyguards know his secret.

> LORD LEBANON: You know that room my mother wouldn't
> show you? Well, that's all padded, you know. Rubber cushions
> all round the walls. I have to go there when I realise things.
> TANNER (*smiling*): When you get a little tiresome?
> LORD LEBANON (*shouts at him*). When I realise things I know
> what I'm saying! (*Calm again.*) You know, when I'm quite well
> I'm mad – I don't realise anything! It is only when I get excited
> that my brain gets clear.[34]

Such roles depended not only on psychotic shifts of mood but on an
unmistakable physical presence that an audience would soon come to
recognise. There was an inevitable risk – sometimes a temptation –
that actors well known for their representation of unusual states of
mind might also become associated with other shady areas, including
forbidden sexuality. One result was a fascination with crimes in which
the need to maintain a façade of respectability concealed violent incli-
nations and might even be said to have caused them in the first place. If
Raffles, the fictional gentleman crook, was one lingering inheritance
from Edwardian England, then the real-life criminal, Hawley Harvey
Crippen, the little man with a big secret, was another. In 1910 Crippen,
an American resident in London, had been hanged for the murder of his
second wife, having been apprehended on board a transatlantic liner as
he tried to make a getaway with his secretary mistress – the suspicious
captain contacted Scotland Yard by radio. The remains of Crippen's
wife were found under some floorboards at his home. His story contained all the essential elements of a modern murder: dismemberment,

concealment, and a conviction based on forensic evidence that made the pathologist almost as famous as the criminal. No wonder it haunted the cultural memory. T. S. Eliot incorporated elements into his aborted avant-garde thriller, *Sweeney Agonistes*[35] in 1923, and, as late as 1939, the eminent poet turned up at a fancy-dress party dressed as the murderer.[36] Thoughts of what respectability might both conceal and engender continued to inspire powerful plays. Frank Vosper's *People Like Us*[37] is based on the notorious Bywaters and Thompson case of 1923 (also of interest to Eliot)[38] in which a young woman was found guilty of being an accomplice to the murder of her husband by her lover after a string of her passionate letters had been read out in court, while *Love from a Stranger*,[39] which Vosper adapted from a short story by Agatha Christie, features an American serial killer who manages for a time to set up a domestic ménage in Oxford.

As Tanner, the sanguine detective, observes in Wallace's *Frightened Lady*: 'Homicide is not one of the peculiar habits of the criminal classes, but as a rule the recreation or amusement of amateurs who want to get on in the world, such as labourers, lawyers, insurance agents and stockbrokers.'[40] In contrast, Wallace's own central characters had tended to be high-flying international figures who were not murderers by inclination, who destroyed mainly to advance their financial, political or retributive ends. Nevertheless Crippen, typically, took pride of place among more than a dozen domestic killers invoked by Wallace in an article entitled 'Truth about Sex Murders' which appeared in the sensationalist weekly, *John Bull*, in 1924. Protesting that 'publicists and preachers are telling us that the cause of these sex murders is traceable to the Great War and to the deadening of the moral sense', Wallace offered his own explanation for the apparent increase in murder:

> They can trace such crimes to the growth of paganism, to the breaking down of family ties, to a thousand and one fantastic causes; but the truth is that the sex murder is immediately connected with the wave of Puritanism, the blatant hypocrisy and the stupid gentility of the mid-Victorian period . . . Until seventy years ago, the crimes which are constantly appearing

nowadays in the newspapers were practically unknown. The motive of 70 per cent of murders was robbery or revenge.[41]

Respectability and prudery, fear of looking absurd in the eyes of women, the English vices, are the root cause of modern violence, practised to an overwhelming extent by males.[42]

Wallace is said by those who knew him well to have been unusually hostile to any hint of unorthodox sexuality and it is noticeable that his rationale for the domestic murder mixes frankness with reticence; in the name of sex it actually diminishes sexual motivation. He left it to others to reap the rewards of sex crime, pre-eminently Emlyn Williams. At this stage in his life a bi-sexual man living in a largely homosexual milieu, Williams was all too familiar with the importance of façade, the way that the forces of society would turn a calculatedly blind eye to what was clearly under its nose, almost encouraging self-display, only suddenly to pounce. Bolitho's *Murder for Profit* had no keener a reader; for Williams the book was an inspiration, a bible which he discovered very early on and continued using for the rest of his life, right up until his book on the Moors murders in 1967. One chapter in particular held him in thrall. This dealt with Fritz Haarmann, the Hanover homosexual and informer, who in the early twenties systematically murdered boys and, or so it was said, sold their flesh.[43] In 1924 Williams actually travelled to Germany to re-trace Haarmann's steps.

Bolitho precedes his analysis with an exemplary warning:

No one can nowadays dare to reproach such men, after a collective killing of such magnitude as we have all committed, of an exclusive mark of blood-stain. All our foreheads are smeared. Those who innocently persist in imagining that mass-murderers are different from themselves simply in that they had the awful courage to kill and repeat their act, a faculty to which they are to some a gloomy monopoly among the sons of men, I refer to the printed achievements of the heroes of the war; or if they are unwilling to read them again, I call the witness of all the ex-combatants that at the Front it was never found difficult to induce even the mildest recruit to kill.

(pp. 275–6)

Williams' fascination with the figure of Haarmann does not, of course, mean that he necessarily endorsed this view. Nevertheless, the postwar idea of the murderer as Everyman, of the mark of Cain, does feed into the complex process whereby he was to learn how to manipulate three kinds of deception, drawing parallels, suggesting distinctions: the homosexual or bisexual man masquerading as exclusively heterosexual; the criminal, at worst a murderer, not too convincingly disguised as a respectable member of society; the professional actor, such as himself, who is paid to dissemble. Although homosexuality is never directly represented, its contemporary codes and conventions are frequently alluded to. In Williams' *Night Must Fall*[44] Dan, a young Welshman, punishes the women who find him sexually interesting, murdering two of them, keeping the head of one in a hat-box. As vain as most murderers were usually held to be, Dan exploits a selfish, stupid mother-figure whose susceptibility is just possibly Williams' harshly self-critical representation of his own real-life passion for a Welsh boy named Fess – though it should be noted that Williams himself claimed to have been prompted to write the play by a number of well-reported murders as well as by the Haarmann affair.

As Williams read and re-read Bolitho on Haarmann so he must have absorbed the reference to Friedrich Nietzsche's ideas concerning the addictive 'pleasure of the knife' (p. 279). Williams' one real rival among thriller-writers, the novelist and playwright Patrick Hamilton, was even more taken with Nietzschean philosophy, fascinated not only by the mutuality of love and hate (his own sexual interests inclined strongly to the sado-masochistic), but by the political potential of those supposedly superior men who can execute the most monstrous crimes without trembling. In the thirties Hamilton eventually sought ideological security in classical Marxism, though this failed to curtail his interest in the *acte gratuit* that lies 'beyond good and evil', and that might in some circumstances have intellectual links with the evil attractions of fascism.[45] In *Rope*,[46] which is based on the Leopold and Loeb case in Chicago in the 1920s, when two young college men were found guilty of killing a third for the existential thrill of it, Hamilton has his two cultural stereotypes, Brandon, the blond athlete, a model of Saxon *sang-froid*, and Granillo, an impulsive panicky Spaniard, encourage the family and friends of the man they have murdered to eat a buffet supper off the chest in which his fresh remains have been placed. Brandon's philosophical justification for this grotesque scenario is thoroughly Nietzschean, and only at the very end of the play is it satisfactorily countered. Rejection of his moral nihilism falls to Rupert Cadell, a wounded poet and dandy hero, another jaundiced war veteran indirectly in the line of Bull-Dog Drummond and 'The Ringer'. Initially Cadell voices the post-war mood all too knowingly:

> One gentleman murders another in a back alleyway in London for, let us say . . . the gold fillings in his teeth, and all society shrieks out for revenge upon the miscreant. They call that murder. But when the entire youth and manhood of a whole nation rises up to slaughter the entire youth and manhood of another, not even for the gold fillings in each other's teeth, then society condones and applauds the outrage, and calls it war.[47]

In the end, with a great cry of 'You are going to hang, you swine! Hang – both of you – hang!' (p. 86), Cadell, an amateur detective figure who has long suspected the truth but who has now seen the contents of the chest, summons the police in the name of a society whose hypocritical values he had previously scorned.

Patrick Hamilton was a great renovator. His preface to *Rope* claims the play as an attempt to make good contemporary use of the decadent form that he believed the thriller had become. The true thriller, as he argued elsewhere, has 'no interest in the physical whatever and thrives purely and simply on suggestion and the nightmare things of the mind'.[48] With *Gaslight*[49] he was to create a brilliant pastiche of the Victorian melodrama that by its use of fluctuating light and sound effects conveyed raw terror within an historical environment, and yet culminated by having the victim turn on her male persecutor with a modern, if still disturbing, relish.

Melodrama has often survived because of its adaptability and because, given its origins in the Gothic, it remains the ideal medium for fantasy. The plays of Williams and Hamilton, in particular, match, almost too exactly, the most influential accounts of Gothic horror to have appeared in recent years; Julia Kristeva's post-Freudian concept of the abject: 'The corpse, seen without god and outside of science, is the utmost of abjection. It is death infecting life, from which one does not protect oneself as from an object. Imaginary uncanniness and real threat, it beckons to us and ends up engulfing us.' For Kristeva, though, and this is precisely where the British thriller diverges from her paradigm, true abjection follows 'what disturbs identity, system, order. What does not respect borders, positions, rules. The in-between, the ambiguous, the composite. The traitor, the liar, the criminal with a good conscience, the shameless rapist, the killer who claims he is saviour.'[50] In a British stage thriller, 'borders, positions, rules' invariably reassert themselves, not just because morality intervenes, and the ambiguity of criminal behaviour is usually ironed out, but because the smooth outline of the accomplished actor in total control, pioneered by du Maurier in the 1900s, but by the 1930s embracing even Ivor Novello,[51] was invariably re-established. And in the same way that the British thriller touches, and then retreats from, areas of profound psychological disquiet, so it flirts with formal or continental experiment, never quite committing itself: it adopts a theatrical self-consciousness of almost Pirandellian complexity, but stops short of any philosophical conclusion; it draws on melodrama's fondness for grating sounds and silent shadows, but never quite makes the transition to full-blown expressionism; it hints at grotesque objects, mutilated bodies and severed heads, but they remain hidden in chests and hat-boxes, preventing any Artaudian visual frisson. This is largely because, as forms of commercial entertainment, the thrillers were ultimately tied to West End methods, to the Lord Chamberlain, and the moral conventions of the time. For some people though, the explanation for their success must surely have lain in the secrets they were obliged to keep.

Notes

1. Neil Bartlett, *Mr Clive and Mr Page* (London: Serpent's Tail, 1996), pp.140–1.
2. For thriller novels, some of which were dramatised, see Michael Denning, *Cover Stories: Narrative and Ideology in the British Spy Thriller* (London: Routledge and Kegan Paul, 1987); Jerry Palmer, *Thrillers: Genesis and Structure of a Popular Genre* (London: Edward Arnold, 1978); Richard Usborne, *Clubland Heroes* (London: Constable, 1953, repr. 1974).
3. Roland Pertwee and Harold Dearden, St. James' Theatre, 29 January.

4. Hubert Griffith, unidentified cutting, Theatre Museum, London.

5. Unidentified cutting, Theatre Museum, London.

6. See Daphne du Maurier, *Gerald: a Portrait* (London: Gollancz, 1934) and James Harding, *Gerald du Maurier* (London: Hodder and Stoughton, 1989).

7. In 1927 the veteran critic H. Chance Newton published *Crime and the Drama* (London: Stanley Paul, 1927), a ramshackle survey running from Marlowe to *The Bells*. He concluded with a challenge; 'Are these dramas any worse, indeed are they not better, and certainly cleaner and more wholesome, than many plays and so-called "comedies" of the eternally triangular and wretchedly "Sexual" types which now disfigure and degrade the British Drama?'(p. 273). To ask the question betrays Newton as a member of a generation for whom crime and sex supposedly occupy entirely separate realms. The twentieth century had already been more forthright. For an informative account of late nineteenth-century ideas see Cary M. Mazer, 'The Criminal as Actor: H. B. Irving as Criminologist and Shakespearean' in *Shakespeare and the Victorian Stage*, ed. Richard Foulkes (Cambridge University Press, 1986).

8. John Gielgud, *Backward Glances* (London: Sceptre, 1993), p. 148.

9. 'Sapper' (H. C. McNeile) and George du Maurier, *Bull-Dog Drummond*, Wyndham's Theatre, 29 March 1921.

10. 'Sapper' and Gerald du Maurier, *Bull-Dog Drummond* (London: Samuel French), 1925, p. 38.

11. Duke of York's Theatre, 5 April 1928.

12. *Era*, 30 March 1921, p. 5.

13. Interview with Gerald Fairlie, model for Sapper's original character, *The Times*, 14 December 1974, p. 6.

14. William Bolitho, *Murder for Profit* (London: Jonathan Cape, 1926)

15. Edgar Wallace, *The Ringer* (London: Samuel French, 1926), p. 17.

16. Apollo Theatre, 29 May 1928.

17. Lyceum Theatre, 7 June 1928.

18. Wyndham's Theatre, 2 April 1930.

19. Adelphi Theatre, 14 November 1927.

20. Lyric Theatre, 21 June 1929.

21. Frank Vosper (1893–1937), an actor and author who specialised in writing thrillers, in some of which he played the leading role.

22. Strand Theatre, 9 November 1930, transferred to the St. James' on 26 November. For Williams in general see his remarkable volumes of autobiography, in particular *Emlyn* (London: The Bodley Head, 1973), and Richard Findlater, *Emlyn Williams* (London: Rockcliff, 1956).

23. Emlyn Williams, *A Murder has been Arranged: A Ghost Story in Three Acts* (London: William Collins 1930), pp. 121–2.

24. Haymarket Theatre, 29 February 1928.

25. J. B. Priestley's parody, *Mystery at Greenfingers* (London: Samuel French, 1937), written for the *News Chronicle* Amateur Dramatic Contest, boasted no murder and no police though it was still, according to its author, 'a detective play'. Priestley's interest in the genre was to result in *An Inspector Calls* (1946), in which the nature of crime and authority remain ambiguous to the very end.

26. Adapted by Michael Morton, Adelphi Theatre, 14 November 1927. For a careful analysis of Christie's popularity, see Alison Light, *Forever England: Femininity, Literature and Conservatism between the Wars* (London: Routledge, 1991).

27. *The Times*, 14 June 1927. For Laughton's acting in general see Simon Callow, *Charles Laughton: a Difficult Actor* (London: Methuen, 1987).

28. G. W. B., unidentified cutting, Theatre Museum, London.

29. Transferred to St. Martin's Theatre on 9 April 1931 after a try-out at the Embassy Theatre, Swiss Cottage.

30. Ivor Brown, unidentified review, Theatre Museum, London.

31. W. A. Darlington, unidentified review, Theatre Museum, London.

32. It is said that the friendship between du Maurier and Wallace that led to *The Ringer* began when du Maurier complained to Wallace about his having written a muck-raking article claiming that the London theatre was being permeated by sexual perversion. See Margaret Lane, *Edgar Wallace: The Biography of a Phenomenon* (London: William Heinemann, 1938), p. 313, D. du Maurier, *Gerald*, p. 149, and *Edgar Wallace by His Wife* (London: Hutchinson, 1932). The topic was certainly in the air. According to Emlyn Williams, du Maurier asked Laughton at the outset of *Alibi*, 'Are you a bugger?' To which Laughton stammeringly replied: 'N- -no, Sir Gerald. Are you?', *Emlyn*, p. 157. Noël Coward's biographer, Philip Hoare, quotes Robert Flemyng's comment that du Maurier 'probably should have been gay – he was a very effeminate man – but of course he wasn't, and was consequently violently anti-gay'. Philip Hoare, *Noël Coward* (London: Sinclair-Stevenson, 1995), p. 136.

33. Wyndham's Theatre, 18 August 1931.

34. Edgar Wallace, *The Case of the Frightened Lady* (London: Samuel French, 1932), p. 67.

35. Performed by the Group Theatre in 1934.

36. Peter Ackroyd, *T. S. Eliot* (London: Abacus, 1985), p. 246.

37. Strand Theatre, 3 November 1930.

38. Peter Ackroyd, *T. S. Eliot*, p.143.

39. Wyndham's Theatre, 2 February 1936.

40. Edgar Wallace, *The Case of the Frightened Lady*, p. 24.

41. *John Bull*, 24 May 1924, p.13. Also see Edgar Wallace, 'The Passionate Murderer', *John Bull*, 7 June 1924, p. 13.

42. This was a very common view at the time: 'Most criminals are great egotists and inordinately vain, but these two qualities are found in excess in murderers', Fryn Tennyson Jesse, *Murder and its Motives* (London: William Heinemann, 1928), p. 10.

43. In 1973 Werner Fassbinder produced, and Uli Lommel directed, a film based on Haarmann, *The Tenderness of Wolves*, as a tribute to Fritz Lang's *M*.

44. Duchess Theatre, 31 May 1935, transferred to the Cambridge Theatre on 9 July 1936.

45. See Nigel Jones, *Through a Glass Darkly: The Life of Patrick Hamilton* (London: Scribners, 1991) and Sean French, *Patrick Hamilton: a Life* (London: Faber, 1993).

46. Sunday night try-out at the Strand Theatre 3 March 1929, opened at the Ambassador's Theatre 25 April. *Rope* was performed on radio 31 January 1931 and on television 8 March 1939. For mention of thrillers and detective stories on radio see Jean Chothia, *English Drama of the Early Modern Period: 1890–1940* (London: Longman, 1996).

47. Patrick Hamilton, *Rope* (London: Constable, 1985), pp. 60–1.

48. *Sunday Referee*, 24 January 1932, p. 3.

49. Richmond Theatre, 5 December 1938, later transferred to the Apollo Theatre (January 1939) and then the Savoy (May 1939).

50. Julia Kristeva, *Powers of Horror: An Essay on Abjection* (New York: Columbia University Press, 1982), p. 4.

51. Novello starred in his own *Murder in Mayfair*, Globe Theatre, 5 September 1934.

3   When men were men and women were women

JOHN DEENEY

> The abyss of unpleasantness to which the telling of such a story
> might descend is all too apparent. Yet – and this is the aptest
> tribute to the production – at the play one's mind was occupied
> only with a dream of beauty . . . It was a production compounded
> of fine reticence and secret business.[1]

> Mr. Shairp handles a theme commonly labelled 'unpleasant'
> with a cool detachment that will do as much as is possible to
> commend his play to all who do not find his theme irreparably
> distasteful.[2]

Between October 1932 and January 1933 two premières in London's
West End acceded to the possibility, as contemporary reviews lay
claim, of material 'unpleasant'. Christa Winsloe's *Children in Uniform*
and Mordaunt Shairp's *The Green Bay Tree* share little beyond a syn-
chronistic presence in time and space. Winsloe's play, originally
produced in Germany as *Yesterday and Today* and catapulted to international fame by Leontine Sagan's 1931 film version, *Mädchen in
Uniform*, is set in a girls' boarding school in Prussia. Manuela, a newly
arrived pupil, forms an emotional attachment to a young schoolmis-
tress. The result is a scandal and Manuela, punished for her proclama-
tions of love, commits suicide. *The Green Bay Tree* concerns one
Dulcimer, a resident of London's Mayfair, and his 'adopted' son Julian.
Dulcimer has rescued Julian from a drunken and neglectful father, providing him with education, cultivation and 'luxury'. When Julian falls
in love with Leonora and desires marriage Dulcimer terminates
Julian's allowance. Unable to support himself, Julian once again

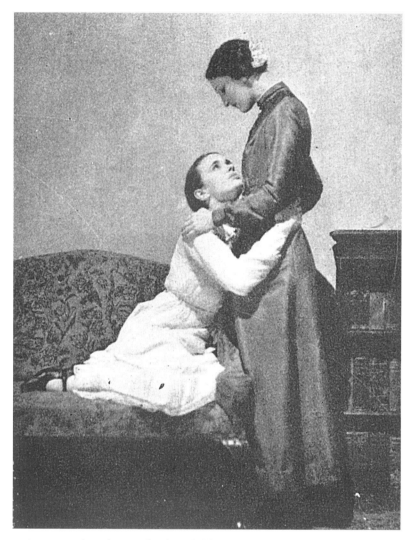

3. Jessica Tandy and Joyce Bland in *Children in Uniform*, the Duchess Theatre (1932).

becomes the property of Dulcimer. But the contract is short lived; Julian's father, now reformed and a preacher, kills Dulcimer. The final image – Julian arranging flowers – mirrors one of Dulcimer's activities in the opening scene.

For critics and readers today, *Children in Uniform* and *The Green Bay Tree* testify to the possibility of same-sex passion between women and between men, that which the critics Burnup and Brown name as 'unpleasant'. *Children in Uniform* has been described in more recent times as 'lesbian-themed',[3] as fitting 'quite tidily into the model of the "lesbian fairy tale"'.[4] *The Green Bay Tree* has been termed a 'play about homosexuality'[5] and 'possibly the first contemporary drama about homosexuality'.[6] Such labelling assists in the construction of a lesbian and homosexual dramatic, theatrical and cultural history, a process which opens the closeted door of history. As this important and belated project continues, methods of analysis are characterised by the employment of dramatic and theatrical subjects to describe the emergence and representation of lesbian and homosexual identities, and the legal and moral oppression of such identities within and beyond the theatre as both art form and industry. The inter-war period in British theatre offers numerous opportunities in this respect.

A number of popular dramatists working in the period – most eminently Noël Coward, Terence Rattigan and Somerset Maugham – have been identified as gay, dramatists who, as Sean O'Connor suggests: 'share a particular way of looking at the world, a strategy of discussing relationships and a similar agenda . . . They are certainly all traditionalists.' O'Connor goes on to suggest:

> it seems appropriate to consider these avowedly commercial playwrights and how far their personal dilemmas as gay men affected their agendas as revealed in their work intended for a popular audience.[7]

One can therefore group playwrights in relation to their often post-career declarations of sexual orientation, but this can lead to simplistic and generalised analysis. An alternative to what might be called the 'grouping method' is a consideration of 'plays that are more explicitly "about" homosexuality', into which category *The Green Bay Tree* would fall.[8] Nicholas de Jongh has observed:

> any closer viewer of the plays about homosexuality placed upon the stages of New York and London in the inter-war period will be struck by a certain diversity, by a sense that there were slight but significant attempts to qualify the predominating sense of the evil, sinister homosexual.[9]

The important distinction between these two approaches is the different emphases given to the subjects of 'dramatist' and 'text', while both simultaneously proceed to a discussion of the significance of perceived homosexual representations – textually and theatrically. Significantly, neither approach is able to accommodate a discussion of representations of lesbianism within the theatre. I would like to suggest that this framing of the homosexual and homosexuality in actual reality (the playwright and his social world) and virtual reality (the play and its stage performance), while in current vogue – pushing open that closed door of theatre history – de-contextualises the theatre practice in question. Such studies seem discerning in that they account for the legal, social, medical, positions and oppression of the homosexual and homosexuality within a given period. Commentators such as O'Connor and de Jongh also pay some attention to the attempted subjugation of provocative texts through the censoring powers of the Lord Chamberlain's office. These powers of censorship, as Steve Nicholson argues, appear to have been particularly relevant to theatre production in the 1920s, 'when social traditions and the economic order were perceived to be splitting apart, the theatre was subject to a particularly tight system of censorship'.[10] The policing of sexuality therefore gained a new impetus. However, the problem with the approaches described is that in foregrounding a homosexual, even homosocial, discourse other dramatic concerns and, most importantly, marginalised yet inter-related theatrical developments are made peripheral. Further, in pursuing this discourse, the stage picture of homosexuality is relegated to exploration 'through the subterfuge of heterosexual relationships'[11] or the establishment of 'a clandestine stage iconography'.[12] It is important that the generality of such assumptions is challenged. Homosexuality found a presence in inter-war British theatre and one not always requiring a 'decoding system'.[13]

Contexts within contexts

In 1912, 'The White Slave Act' amended criminal legislation by tightening up 'the law regarding "bullies", procurers and brothel keepers, and reaffirmed flogging, which chiefly affected homosexuals'.[14] Jeffrey Weeks argues that the Act reflected 'a deflection . . . of real, and urgent, anxieties, the product of major social disruptions, on to the sphere of sexuality'.[15] The Act, nineteenth century in spirit and character, is symptomatic evidence of the 'belief that roots of social stability lay in individual and public morality'.[16] The combined forces of social puritanism and the law triumphed, notoriously, in the third 1895 trial of Oscar Wilde, thereby dissolving the distinction between 'private' and 'public'. Wilde was accused of gross indecency with another male person (private), yet the case was brought to prosecution due to a relative of a member of the government being named (public). The intervention of the state into private adult heterosexual relations did not apply. Weeks concludes, 'there is a strong case to be made that the moralistic campaigns around sexuality encouraged, as a response, a more radical position'.[17]

In the late nineteenth century such a position was to gain ground through propagation within the social sciences of new methods of theorising about sexuality. The writings of such figures as the sexologist Havelock Ellis and Sigmund Freud were significant in that they not only located sexuality in a new arena – outside the agencies of the church and the law (sin and crime) – but both took advantage to different degrees of so called objectivism. Ellis set out to describe a range of sexual behaviours (inversion, sadism, transvestism, necrophilia, etc.) as variations within the biological make-up. By way of identifying that there was an aim to sexuality – the continuation of the species – Ellis reinforced the paradigm of dominant male/responsive female. Like Ellis, Freud believed that heterosexuality was the preferred standard, although he did lay emphasis on the ingenuous practice of non-procreational sex. Edward Carpenter – who labelled the homosexual the 'intermediate sex' – along with sexologists like Ellis and psychoanalysts like Freud offered description and analysis in a field where it had hitherto been absent.[18]

In social and cultural terms the impact of sexology and psychoanalytically derived discourses on sexuality cannot be underestimated, particularly as they gained currency from the 1920s onwards. However, whilst their appropriation – particularly that of Freudianism – into cultural discourse contributes to persuasive readings of individual texts, the focus on single-identity readings eclipses other developments impacting on the inter-war period. Maggie B. Gale has drawn attention to the conflict between Freudian psychoanalysis and the women's movement: 'Women who wanted to follow what were traditionally seen as "male" pursuits, encompassing independence and a professional life, were problematised and seen as having an unresolved relation to the castration complex as proposed by Freud – the perception was often that, effectively, independent women wanted to be men.'[19] It was a woman psychoanalyst, Karen Horney, who challenged Freud by pointing to the fact that 'the developmental context of psychoanalysis ... [was] ... a world dominated by the needs of the male, as was the law, morality and religion'.[20] The social and political significance of the 'woman question' is paramount here. Sexology both strengthened the maternal function of womanhood and gave credence to the sexually liberated woman. Christine Bolt points out that before the Second World War this rekindled 'fears of free love which had so long embarrassed Socialists and feminists', resulting in 'the sexualisation of spinsterhood and the stigmatisation of lesbianism'.[21] The attempt in 1921 to make lesbian practices illegal failed, because the authorities did not wish to advertise the very existence of such practices:

> 'Deviant' sexual behaviour by women, of whatever kind,
> remained unacceptable ... one can understand why, in the
> 1920s, older feminists, who had already witnessed the
> denigration of the spinster before the war, and now saw the
> invention of the frigid woman and attacks on the sexual
> abnormality of the independent 'new woman', preferred to
> address themselves to the rights and problems of married
> women and children, because here they might expect some
> sympathy from conventional men and women.[22]

Bolt's analysis points to a state of flux in the women's movement as part and parcel of a changing sexual ideology. During the inter-war period, conceptions of 'womanhood' and 'femininity' were to take on new dimensions, and this coincided with what Lesley Hall has called 'a crisis of masculinity characterised by intense misogyny'.[23] The image of the dominant and aggressive male, whose appetites are spontaneously (and therefore unproblematically) resolved has remained unchallenged until relatively recently. S. M. Gilbert and S. Gubar posit that modernist literature was haunted by 'male fears of a debilitating no man's land', while wartime poets expressed not only 'generalized sexual anxiety' but also 'anger directed specifically at the female, as if the Great War were primarily a climactic episode in a battle of the sexes that had already been raging for years'.[24] However, Hall suggests that the emergence of both the 'crypto-patriarch' and the 'sexually wounded denizen of no man's land' may represent an 'optical illusion'.[25] Drawing on the immense correspondence generated by Marie Stopes' marriage manual *Married Love* (1918), Hall proposes that requests for advice to the author by men paint a more complicated picture. Men's revealed ignorances about matters sexual point to the way in which a whole 'generation of young men had been exposed to a revelation of how much they had been deceived by their elders about the romance and chivalry of war'. The momentum in social change, particularly around the institution of marriage, provides a context for the emergence of the 'new man', which must be differentiated from an alternative reading of the very same material – 'man in a new world'.[26]

If new, emerging identities and relations between the sexes point to a crisis both in femininity and masculinity after the war, was such a crisis contingent on heterosexual identity and experience? This is a dangerous question, for it reinvents the legal and social oppression of 'alternative' sexualities through historical discourse, perpetuating a pattern of marginalisation. Further, the histories of homosexuality and lesbianism form distinguishable narratives. Weeks reveals how this distinction might inform the answer.

> Male homosexuality and lesbianism have different social
> implications. For men, homosexuality is seen as a rejection of
> maleness, with all its socially approved connotations. For
> women, it can be an assertion of femaleness, of separateness
> from men, and of identity.[27]

Alan Sinfield presents a persuasive argument for the emergence of the 'dominant twentieth century queer identity' as a construction 'out of elements that came together at the [Oscar] Wilde trials: effeminacy, leisure, idleness, immorality, luxury, insouciance, decadence and aestheticism'.[28] Furthermore, the Wilde trials did constitute a 'labelling process' which cast a shadow over male fraternity. If Oscar Wilde does represent the birth of a modern 'queer' identity, this is complicated by the fact that Wilde was also married, a father and an Oxford-educated Irish Protestant with Republican sympathies. None of this suggests a direct link between the emergence of a homosexual identity and a ostensible crisis in male heterosexual identity, but rather positions both in a 'complex elaboration of socio-sexual discourses'.[29]

Significantly, Sinfield has also drawn attention to the link between homosexuality and the theatre, where 'homosexuals are simply supposed to be histrionic, flamboyant . . . which may indeed be one way of coping with stigma'. However, the 'notion of homosexuality as theatrical is susceptible to hostile infection: consider the word histrionic, and how ominously its scope runs from "pertaining to actors and acting" through to "pretended, artificial, affected".' Sinfield moves on to propose a cultural materialist reading; that theatre and deviant sexual activity frequently occupy the same inner-city terrain, that they are both 'contingent, cultural phenomena – subject to the pressures and limits of a specific historical moment and figuring differently in different parts of the social order'. He locates such a pattern in the first half of the twentieth century (notably the 1920s and 1930s), alongside the 'uneven development of a modern homosexual identity and the dominance of the urban middle-classes in West End theater audiences'. In noting that an association between theatre and homosexuality had already been established in the nineteenth century, Sinfield deduces a pattern of 'discretion', such as that in wider society, sustained by the law, namely the Lord Chamberlain.[30] Sinfield's argument seems incisive because of the strong contextualising emphasis, and the observation that '[the] closet did not obscure homosexuality . . . it created it'.[31] However, such a thesis is based, somewhat ironically, on generalised assumptions regarding the theatre's position as both a cultural institution and a leisure activity. The perception that the urban middle classes dominated West End audiences, while not in itself incorrect, is characteristic of the approach – Nicholas de Jongh goes somewhat further.

It seems another world now . . . Flappers and chorus girls,
gangsters and silly asses in monocles, femmes fatales and heart-
throbs fill its stages. The audience, well-heeled and high-heeled,
sumptuous in their starched and careful formalities, regarded
the playhouses as after-dinner relaxations. The stars were
remote icons to be reverenced.[32]

Another typical (and generally accepted) understanding of London
theatre during the 1920s was that post-war meant party time, and the
West End, with its collection of bars, clubs and theatres provided
meeting-places for a leisured and middle-class youth. If the theatre had
any responsibility here, it was to entertain; this was the Jazz Age;
hedonism rather than hermeneutics ruled the night. However, this is a
view which needs qualifying. The impact of the war meant that new
types of audience were also in circulation. Alongside the sons and
daughters of the wealthy Victorian middle classes were servicemen
and officers on leave, and 'women moving into the public field of work
might seek an evening's entertainment in the West End'.[33] A change in
the make-up of the audience partly explains the popularity of the revue
and the thriller after the war. It is also important to note that this dem-
ographic shift is both class- and gender-orientated.

In 1930 H. M. Tyrer, of the London Public Morality Council,
notified his concern to the Lord Chamberlain's Assistant Comptroller
that 'the crowded dress circle (in which I counted about 20 men) did not
express any sense of offence' at a performance of Noël Coward's *Private
Lives*.[34] Writing just three years later, the critic St John Ervine points to
the dangers of a theatre that has become 'womanised', a disparity
'apparent in every part of the theatre, from the stalls up to the gallery'.[35]
Ervine observes that tragedy has been all but banished from the modern
stage, a form that had 'prevailed among the great races of mankind at
the period of their greatest power, and that a decline towards comedy,
and eventually to spectacle and sheer buffoonery, coincides with the
appearance of degeneracy'. St John Ervine not only equates 'degeneracy'
with 'womanisation' but also the 'lack of able men of vision . . . as a
result of the Youth Movement'.[36] This combination of meta-narrative

and social observation to critique the corrupted state of the modern West End theatre is further and most revealingly directed at theatre production, reception and the behaviour of audiences.

> The most daring English dramatist would not have dreamt of introducing a homosexualist into the cast of a play before 1914. After the War, it became common to see perverts of both sexes on the stage. Young girls in the gallery giggled very knowingly when an effeminate youth wriggled his way across the stage in a musical comedy and were quick to point out to each other notorious youths in the stalls, especially at the Russian Ballet, who were, so gossip said, addicted to unnatural vice.[37]

And 'unnatural vice' was restricted neither to the stalls nor to the ballet:

> I took my aunt . . . to see *The Ghost Train*. We were in the gallery and I realised then, my instinct. Nobody told me. I kept on looking at the back and it was jet-black and crowded, crowded full of people standing, although there were a lot of empty seats. And that was, I think, my first realisation that this was a scene I wanted to join in, I went back two or three days afterwards to see *The Ghost Train* and stood at the back and what was going on there was nobody's business! They were big meeting places . . . I went round those theatres quite a lot.[38]

This last quote might support a theory that the darkened auditoria of West End theatres during the 1920s and 1930s were but another locus for homosexual subcultural activity. More importantly, the evidence taken together problematises the notion of the 'stable respectable playgoer'. This is important, for it is upon such a construct and that of 'a knowing subculture of privileged insiders' (homosexual, but by necessity leisured, bohemian) together with the exploitation of the 'split between the two audiences' that the reading of homosexual representations pivots.[39] Once such a model is established, 'discretion' is practicable and coding systems can be activated. Sinfield suggests that in the work of Noël Coward and others, the theatrical form of revue was particularly appropriate: 'the whole manner invites a knowing wink across the footlights. Revue may be more hospitable to innuendo because it does not pretend to naturalistic illusion, and it therefore can play more freely and ambiguously with the audience and with levels of fictiveness and knowledge.'[40] However, revue also fell outside the Lord Chamberlain's remit, as no submission for a licence was necessary. In 1920, a 'revusical vaudeville' called *Splinters* played at the London Coliseum. *Splinters* consisted entirely of ex-servicemen impersonating women: the group continued to perform until the late 1930s. While *Splinters* and other concert-party groups clearly built upon the dame tradition of Victorian pantomime, they and other such groups represent a split from that tradition. *Splinters* brought forth a 'new breed of drag queen . . . a "woman" confiding about her experiences with men now becomes an almost transparent cover for homosexual flirtation'.[41] Such a reading is demonstrably inter-textual, and there is little to suggest that audiences at *Splinters*, made up of large numbers of ex-servicemen, would read any innuendo into the grotesquely comic effect of putting a man – not only a performer, but one of their own kind – into a dress. The popularity of such shows in the 1920s and 1930s might be better explained by 'nostalgia', a reminder of life and entertainment in the forces. Nevertheless, the example is useful because it further demonstrates the dangers inherent, particularly in contemporary discourses, of appropriating theatre practice – both its production and reception – and conveniently generalising its characteristics in any given period for the motive of pursuing itemised representational agendas, particularly within the domains of gender and sexuality. It may indeed be argued that such a 'scholarly' strategy differs little from the more subjective, journalistic, quotidian – call it what you will – approach, which runs along the lines: 'Gay writers earlier this century . . . evolved a particular style which heightened the importance of subtext, for the subtext is the queens' realm'.[42]

The loves that must not speak their name

Christa Winsloe's *Children in Uniform* is a formidably difficult play to place, which might be dismissed as a theatrical oddity. However, its production in 1932 was an enormous critical and commercial success, running for 263 performances.[43] Critics at the time were so enthusiastic, many claiming it to be the best play in town, with one going so far as to say that 'the London stage has been redeemed of tawdriness and once more made glorious'.[44] The 'lesbian theme' of *Children in Uniform* (the word 'lesbian' is, of course, not mentioned in the play) appears rendered through Manuela's public declaration of love for Fräulein von Bernburg. Her subsequent suicide performs the 'necessary' task of casting Manuela not simply into the role of 'tragic heroine' but 'lesbian as tragic figure', thus lending some explanation to the play's production in 1932 being permitted. However, the play's very status – its licensing, its German origins, the all-woman cast – combined with aspects of Winsloe's dramaturgical strategies, exposes this oddity as a remarkable 'outing'.

The Lord Chamberlain referred *Children in Uniform* to his advisory committee.[45] Lord Cromer initially thought the play should be denied a license, not due entirely to its 'unnecessarily doubtful themes' but principally because of the parallels which might be drawn between a 'Prussian girls' school and the usual run of girls' schools in this country'. There is little to suggest that Cromer actually read the play, but rather was working from the Reader's Report, which states, 'Such an ordinary thing as the "passion" of a schoolgirl for a mistress is not to be confused with adult Lesbianism.' From the committee came the sole dissenting voice of Allardyce Nicoll: 'While there is certainly a distinction to be made between Manuela's feelings for F. von Bernburg and adult Lesbianism, it still remains true that the former are clearly leading towards the latter and that Manuela, innocent though she may be, is in the grip of potentially unnatural passion.' Nicoll was also concerned that a 'bad production' would introduce an 'atmosphere'. The play was licensed on the proviso that the 'setting . . . remain German'.[46] The Lord Chamberlain's file on *Children in Uniform* is revealing in a number of ways. The conflicting views on the nature of Manuela's 'passion' are indicative of the 'invisible' and confused status surrounding lesbianism and how Winsloe and her translator Barbara Burnham exploited this in its representation. It is important to note that the play's production in England came one year after the film's release.

Their differing titles, *Mädchen in Uniform* (also the play's international title) and *Children in Uniform*, in themselves occasion two different readings, the term *Mädchen* invoking 'female adolescence'. A reviewer at the time was quick to note that 'To call them children alters the whole meaning and tendency.'[47] Yet at Manuela's arrival her status as 'child' is immediately qualified:

> FRÄULEIN VON KESTERN: So you are our new pupil? You are a
> tall girl for fourteen.
> MANUELA: (*correcting her – quite simply*): Fourteen and a half.
> FR. VON K.: Nearly a grown-up lady! We have many girls
> younger than you here.[48]
>
> (p. 19)

The ambiguity around Manuela was further worked through in performance, with the casting of the 23-year-old Jessica Tandy in the part. The reviews not only celebrate her portrayal for its 'virginal innocence' but also for its 'beauty', 'intensity' and 'nervous sensitiveness'. Tandy's performance effectively eroticises innocent but 'misplaced' girlhood feelings. Manuela's declaration of love for Bernburg occurs after the performance of the school play, Voltaire's *Zaire*, in which Manuela plays the lead male role of a 'knight'. A party ensues in which Manuela grows intoxicated from the 'punch'. At the moment of revelation Manuela is 'beyond herself' and 'boastful' (p. 76). The declaration itself is driven by Bernburg's gift, earlier on, of a chemise:

> MANUELA: ... I was to wear it and think of her. (*Softly*) She
> didn't say that ... (*Aloud*) But she doesn't need to tell me
> anything. Her hand on my head tells me everything – sweet,
> good, dear white hand, that can hold so tenderly ... (*Smiling
> blissfully on all*) Nothing can happen to me now – nothing can
> touch me – nothing in the whole world ... She loves me!
>
> (p. 77)

The declaration is framed in the perpetuation of a 'performance' by a performance and such framing allows Winsloe to forge a disruptive spectacle. Manuela's appearance 'in her "silver armour" and "unbound hair"' (p. 67) seems to combine both masculine and feminine, maybe even 'invert' and 'feminine invert', but Tandy's heterosexual eroticisation of the role negated any such possibility. Winsloe, of course, proceeds to provide the necessary 'closure'; the retribution of the school's headmistress, and a final avowal from Bernburg immediately prior to Manuela's suicide:

> This house is a rat-trap. It is a house of death. You kill the soul, the spirit! This galvanised oppression is spiritual death. Only women can do such terrible things to women.
>
> (p. 103)

Bernburg is of course speaking of Germanic 'galvanised oppression' and German 'women'. *Children in Uniform* certainly critiques an authoritarian educational system, and it might be argued that lesbianism is merely muted within this. Is it lesbianism which is made tragic or female innocence and beauty, physical beauty at that? The final lines come from the headmistress: 'What shall I tell the Grand Duchess? We shall tell her there has been an accident. An accident' (p. 104). In the realist tradition, this ultimate silencing establishes 'order' through 'closure', albeit an uncomfortable order. However, to read Manuela's death as a 'silencing' is based on misplaced but deep-rooted assumptions regarding realist narrative. As Sheila Stowell has noted, such a definition of 'closure', 'negates the possibility of cumulative experience, arguing that because a so-called "order" is restored at the end of the play, the work's overall cerebral and visceral meaning is erased . . . [denying] the significance of a play's process . . .'[49] *Children in Uniform* stages the possibility of same-sex passion through its process, through a textual–theatrical strategy which, in a momentary spectacle, circumvents a linguistically driven model of censorship (the Lord Chamberlain's men were reading plays, not seeing theatre). Thus the ambiguity of Manuela's 'passion' serves its purpose. Yes, it is muted, even made tragic through realism, but it is not 'coded' for any group of 'insiders'. Almost every review of the production points to the possibility of 'wrongful passion', demonstrating collusion in a pervasive censorship. Through negating such passion, *Children in Uniform* permits its presence.

Lillian Hellman's *The Children's Hour* (1934) seems to fail where *Children in Uniform* succeeds. Banned until 1960, it did however receive a critically and commercially successful 'private' production in 1936 at the Gate Theatre, Dublin, under the direction of Norman Marshall. Karen Wright and Martha Dobie run a small private girls' school in small-town America. Martha's aunt, Lily Mortar, is an unemployed actress working at the school whose general ineptitude spurs Martha to send her on a round-the-world trip, thus using up the last of her savings. An argument erupts in which Lily imputes that Martha is jealous of Joe, Karen's fiancée, and that her relationship with Karen is 'unnatural'. The argument is overheard by a badly behaved pupil, Mary Tilford, who uses the eavesdropping to extract herself from punishment. Parents withdraw their children from the school as news of the accusation is disseminated by Mary's grandmother. Lily departs and Karen and Martha are left to pursue a libel case, in order to free themselves from the allegation of lesbianism (again, the word itself is never used). The libel action fails and the two schoolteachers are left destitute. After Joe has told Karen that their relationship cannot be reconstituted, Martha tells Karen her true feelings:

> MARTHA: ... I lie in bed night after night praying that it isn't true. But I know about it now. It's there. I don't know how. I don't know why. But I did love you. I do love you. I resented your marriage; maybe because I wanted you; maybe I wanted you all these years; I couldn't call it by a name but maybe it's been there ever since I first knew you –.[50]
>
> (p. 66)

Martha then commits suicide, which act is followed by her aunt's return and the arrival of Mary's grandmother, bearing the revelation of Mary's lies.

The Children's Hour was not banned simply because it contained a lesbian character, adult and self-declared, even though Martha could not 'call it by a name', but also because of the way in which the lesbian theme is provoked through a child's distorted imagination.[51] While lesbianism might seem the defining layer in Hellman's thematic nomenclature, Martha and Karen are first of all independent women, and it is particularly Martha's independence – she has no fiancé –

which strengthens the accusation against them. As Gale has observed of the play, 'the issue of lesbianism is used as a device to indicate a social attitude to women who make the choice to remain independent'.[52] *The Children's Hour* exposes the fragility of social structures, and how puritanical manoeuvrings are coalesced against women who seek both a role and function outside marriage and motherhood.

Neither *Children in Uniform* nor *The Children's Hour* fits easily into a lesbian canon. It has been argued that the latter's canonisation in modern drama is indeed dependent on baseline homophobia, through the literal extinction of Martha and therefore the extinction of the possibility of a lesbian identity, of a 'referent' (the same might be said of *Children in Uniform*). Anne Fleche cogently argues that there is an alternative response to the play's 'negativity': Hellman: 'abstracts the lesbian – cuts her out, abbreviates her, conceives her as a problem of representation', and it is this 'problem' which might be pursued.[53] However, no one should ignore the play's historical positioning, its radicalising potential in 1935 as demonstrated by its banning, and the broader questions around womanhood and the societal matrix which it clearly engenders. If *Children in Uniform* and *The Children's Hour* abstain from providing a 'lesbian referent', it is, indeed, upon such abstention that the construction of a referent must submit to.

The Lord Chamberlain's policing of sexuality extended far and wide. John van Druten's originally banned *Young Woodley* (1925) dramatises the love of a school prefect for his housemaster's wife, Laura. Characters such as Laura have been positioned in a long line, from Mrs Erlynne to Blanche Dubois, as women who 'represent' the 'tensions and ambiguities of homosexual desire'.[54] When Simmons, Laura's husband, discovers her and Woodley kissing, he waits for a less scandalous excuse to have Woodley removed from the school. Laura's parting words to Woodley might be offered as evidence of a homosexual subtext, casting her into the role of 'outsider', articulating the predicament and complex surrounding homosexuality:

LAURA: You're young . . . you have the whole world before you. I want you to be happy. Don't let me be a bitterness and a reproach to you always . . . don't let me spoil love for you. It's the most precious thing in the world . . . but it is so often wasted and can be so cruel. It can turn so easily to hate and bitterness. Don't let me feel that I've done that for you.[55]

(pp. 236–7)

However, Woodley's 'abnormal' love and its reciprocation from Laura cannot be hermetically sealed in this manner, for the context of the English public school is all-important here. Laura is indeed an 'outsider', for she has transgressed the boundaries of middle-class respectability and opened herself up to the possibility of public vilification.

The gender–class matrix is also significant in *The Green Bay Tree*. We identify Dulcimer as 'homosexual', not simply through the play's action, but because he is a man of leisure, effete and opulent. Julian is in his snare because Dulcimer is the ultimate 'sugar daddy'. However, readings of the play tend to centre all too conveniently on the homosexual stereotype wrapped in Shairp's melodramatic form. Peter Burton suggests that Shairp 'distorts established gender values'; Dulcimer becomes 'Dulcie' – 'decidedly feminine' – and Leonora, Julian's fiancée, becomes 'Leo' – 'decidedly masculine'.[56] John Clum proposes therefore that 'the woman is the strong positive adversary of the evil, homosexual influence', exposing 'the "problem" in this melodrama [as] the sexual corruption of a working-class boy by an older upper-middle-class man'.[57] However, Leonora is not simply 'masculine', she is an economically independent woman, a trained veterinarian; Shairp describes her as 'a beautiful girl . . . modern in the best sense of the word' (p. 63). For Julian, Dulcimer's battle with Leonora is not simply a battle with 'good' but a battle with a 'new woman'. In the final scene, six months after Julian's father has murdered Dulcimer and Julian has inherited his property and wealth, Julian sees marriage as the logical next step, for he now has the money to look after his wife-to-be. But this is not acceptable to Leonora, the association with Dulcimer being too great. Leonora's exit line, 'I don't wonder he's smiling' (p. 97) refers to Dulcimer's death mask, ordered in his will. The line is preceded by Julian stepping symbolically into Dulcimer's role. Leonora's exit is not simply a triumph for the dead Dulcimer; the point is that she is able to make this exit, knowing that she has a role to play that lies beyond this world. Julian's 'crisis' does not so much relate to his sex role (homosexual/heterosexual) as his gender role (bachelor of inherited wealth/working husband). Whatever he chooses he is 'dependent', either on the dead or the living, and the roots of this dependency rest in his class origins.

That *The Green Bay Tree* was 'the most dishonest and morally disreputable play about homosexuality' to reach the London stage between the wars is not easily challenged.[58] However, the 'Wildean' Dulcimer fitted the mould perfectly, and the critics of the day took note; Ivor Brown wrote of Dulcimer's 'nimminy-pimminy aestheticism'.[59] That the play was permitted a license begs analysis. Sinfield suggests that the Lord Chamberlain, by licensing such work, 'was helping to make theater a place where sexuality lurked in forbidden forms', knowing full well that it could not be 'eliminated'.[60] Such a reading lends a degree of sophistication and strategy to the process of censorship which is not evidenced in the Chamberlain's correspondence. Rather, not unlike *Children in Uniform*, the licensing of *The Green Bay Tree* is more readily explained by a degree of confusion surrounding such matters, and the censor's questionable ability in ascribing significance to the languages of theatre and performance, not merely to the unmediated dramatic text. Dulcimer's significance is inscribed through the 'theatrical', through the performance of a 'role'.

The 1920s had arguably seen some moves to challenge the dominant homosexual stereotype. J. R. Ackerley's *The Prisoner's of War* (1925) and R. C. Sherriff's *Journey's End* (1928) employ the background of the First World War to shield a latent eroticism underlying intense homosociality.[61] Ackerley's play is particularly revealing in its dramatisation of a captain's attachment to a lieutenant. A less sympathetic challenge to the dominant stereotype might be found in Patrick Hamilton's *Rope* (1929). When two students murder a fellow undergraduate, their action seems motiveless. The symbiosis of Brandon and Granillo's relationship produces what Brandon describes as an 'artistic' murder, a perfect performance. When Rupert, a poet, whose 'affectation verges on effeminacy' (p. 27) discovers their guilt, he describes it as 'a very queer, dark and incomprehensible universe, and I understand it little' (p. 84).[62] However, the suggestion that Hamilton uses the thriller form to demonise and criminalise homosexuality needs to be counterbalanced with the more obviously homosexual figure, Rupert, the discoverer of the crime. *Rope* ingeniously complicates the question of male sexuality through its absence of psychological motivation, moving any apparent discourse on sexuality into the thriller's very 'action', where its circulation means it is less easily verified or labelled.

The Coward complex

In 1939, on the eve of the Second World War, Noël Coward's *Design for Living*, written in 1932, was produced in London, after having finally been granted a licence. The story of Gilda the interior decorator, Otto the painter and Leo the playwright and their various couplings, decouplings and final regrouping for a *ménage à trois* originally proved too much for the Lord Chamberlain. By 1939 it was, 'despite the immorality of its themes . . . only an artificial comedy of manners'. Indeed, the Assistant Comptroller felt able to riposte to a complaint from a member of the public that 'the principals are objects for compassion rather than for disgust'.[63] Bohemians had already graced the West End stage in plays like Rodney Ackland's *Strange Orchestra* (1932) and Terence Rattigan's *French Without Tears* (1936), so it seemed only a matter of time before the ban on *Design for Living* would be lifted. The play's symmetrical plotting eventually brings Otto and Leo together. In Act II, Sc. iii they comfort each other and agree they can live together without Gilda. Yet this realisation is immediately defined by their very desire for Gilda:

> OTTO: We shall both miss her.
> LEO: She's the only really intelligent woman I've ever known.
> OTTO: Brilliant!
> LEO: She's done a tremendous lot for us, Otto. I wonder how much we should have achieved without her?[64]
>
> (p. 91)

The final image of the act – 'they sob hopelessly on each other's shoulders' (p. 92) – might still imply homosexual love. However, as Christopher Innes notes, 'the symmetrical patterning of the plot covers a void that it does not attempt to disguise, while being too artificial in its exact duplications and parallels to serve as a substitute for reality'.[65]

Coward's own reflections on *Design for Living* were that it was 'a project rather than a play', conceived for Lynn Fontanne, Alfred Lunt and himself.[66] The playwright's projection into in his own work, as an actor, is crucial in this respect, indicative of what Innes describes as the substitution of 'action' for 'acting'.[67] This does not simply refer to the characteristic Coward 'style', lean yet shrewd, 'camp' yet complex. In the London production of *Design for Living*, six years after the Broadway première, different actors took the leads, and there were clear ramifications, as James Agate's review demonstrates:

> Miss Fontanne and Messrs. Lunt and Coward had the easy task of exploiting their own genius for the tart, cynical and impish, for presenting human beings as gargoyles. The task for Miss Diana Wynyard and Messrs. Anton Walbrook and Rex Harrison was quite other, and one reflected that honey can never suggest vinegar . . . His English cast let him [Coward] down by its very niceness . . . They pretend that the day is sunny, and ask us to join in their basking.[68]

This reveals the dangers inherent in devolving Coward's work from its stage history and performance context. *The Vortex* (1924) not only established Coward as a playwright, it also marked his entry into theatrical stardom. Meanwhile, the play lends itself remarkably to an Oedipal reading derived from Freudian psychoanalysis. The cocaine-addicted Nicky Lancaster, obsessed with his nymphomaniac mother, Florence, is engaged to Bunty. But she prefers Florence's latest acquisition, Tom, who describes Nicky as 'up in the air – effeminate' (p. 198).[69] Act III sees an encounter between Nicky and Florence, now both jilted, where he admits his drug dependency and compels his mother to admit her fickleness:

> NICKY: It doesn't matter about death, but it matters terribly about life.
> FLORENCE: I know –
> NICKY (*desperately*): Promise me you'll be different – promise me you'll be different.

FLORENCE: Yes, yes – I'll try.
NICKY: We'll both try.
FLORENCE: Yes, dear. – Oh, my dear – !
*She sits quite still, staring in front of her – the tears rolling
down her cheeks, and she is stroking NICKY'S hair
mechanically in an effort to calm him.*
CURTAIN

(pp. 244–5)

While the Freudian reading may extract Nicky as homosexual, supported by the character's emotional and physical demeanour, the play's
shocking effect in the 1920s cannot be disconnected from a personality
constructed around Coward through his performance of Nicky. The
Daily Mail was overwhelmed by 'a skill that frankly astonished'.[70] In
every respect, Coward 'caught the moment', popularising the neuroses
of the 1920s which so characterised the leisured classes, and providing
it with a referent in Nicky/Noël. For 'gay readings', Nicky represents
considerable refinement of the Wildean 'stereotype', for here we have
anguished youth alongside unconventional sexuality.

Private Lives (1930) is both a scathing and humorous attack on
the institution of marriage. Amanda and Elyot have been divorced for
some years. Both are now honeymooning in France with their new
spouses, Victor and Sibyl, when they accidentally meet. Both reveal
that they are already bored by their partners and respective social
circles and decide to elope to Paris. However, their attempts to quell
the bickering that was the cause for the divorce cannot be stopped, and
full-fledged wrestling ensues. Act III sees the tables turned with Victor
and Sibyl scrabbling, 'as AMANDA and ELYOT go smilingly out of the
door, with their suitcases' (p. 90).[71] The plotting and structure of
Private Lives clearly anticipate *Design for Living* in its use of symme-
try. The Lord Chamberlain penned on the Reader's Report, 'An
immoral play written in this writer's amusing style',[72] but of course
'immorality' is centred here on the familiarity of the marriage institution, not the less familiar perpetuity of bohemia in *Design for Living*.
Terry Castle makes the interesting suggestion that the famous publicity shot for *Private Lives*, Noël Coward and Gertrude Lawrence facing

one another across a table, with tilted cigarette-holders held high and placed firmly in their mouths, is an indication of the period's sexual style, of an 'implicitly "homosexual" confounding of traditional sex roles'.[73] However, if masculinity and femininity lose their definitions here, it is also because marriage is less able to contain preconceived fixed gender roles.

The texts highlighted here represent only a sample of those plays discoursing alternative sexualities and patterns of living which were produced on the London stage during the inter-war years. It is important to stress the impact of censorship and criticism on such texts. Such a strategy lends explanation to their emergence in a theatrical and wider social climate and possible attempts to harness and negotiate a changing sexual ideology. Such a strategy also complicates the straightforward categorisation of, for example, a 'gay drama' or a 'lesbian drama', terms in themselves which privilege the notion of 'lineage' and deny the challenge of context, particularly theatrical context. No individual 'dominant patterns' are deducible through this process, for this must rely on discarding key elements in the production and reception of theatre – for example, the make-up of theatre audience. Rather, the plays discussed here, when re-contextualised, reveal how readings of gay texts as coded texts often disallow for the arbitrary nature of systems and working processes of censorship, and equally undermine the social variety and cognisance of audiences of the time. That men were men and women were women thus becomes an ironic proposal, for the inter-war years did not create such stable possibilities for sexuality.

Notes

1. Peter Burnup, *Sunday Reference*, 9 October 1932.
2. Ivor Brown, *The Observer*, 29 January 1933.
3. Terry Castle, *Noël Coward and Radclyffe Hall: Kindred Spirits* (New York: Columbia University Press, 1996), p. 24.
4. B. Ruby Rich, 'From Repressive Tolerance to Erotic Liberation: Mädchen in Uniform', Corey K. Creekmur and Alexander Doty, eds. *Out in Culture: Gay, Lesbian and Queer Essays on Popular Culture* (London: Cassell, 1995), pp. 137–66, p. 151.

5. Nicholas de Jongh, *Not in Front of the Audience: Homosexuality on Stage* (London: Routledge, 1992), p. 35.

6. Peter Burton, introduction to Mordaunt Shairp, 'The Green Bay Tree', in Michael Wilcox, ed., *Gay Plays* (London: Methuen, 1984), p. 53.

7. Sean O'Connor, *Straight Acting: Popular Gay Drama from Wilde to Rattigan* (London: Cassell, 1998), p. 10.

8. *Ibid.*, p. 9.

9. Nicholas de Jongh, *Not in Front of the Audience*, p. 22.

10. Steve Nicholson, 'Unnecessary Play: European Drama and the British Censor', *Theatre Research International* 20:1, pp. 30–6, p. 30.

11. Sean O'Connor, *Straight Acting*, p. 21.

12. Nicholas de Jongh, *Not in Front of the Audience*, p. 16.

13. See Alan Sinfield, 'Private Lives/Public Theater: Noël Coward and the Politics of Homosexual Representation', *Representations* 36 (1991), pp. 43–63.

14. Jeffrey Weeks, *Sex, Politics and Society* (London: Longman, 1981), p. 92.

15. *Ibid.*

16. *Ibid.*

17. *Ibid.*, p. 91.

18. *Ibid.*, p. 141–59.

19. Maggie B. Gale, *West End Women: Women and the London Stage 1918–1962* (London: Routledge, 1996), p. 33.

20. Quoted in *ibid.*, p. 34.

21. Christine Bolt, *The Women's Movements in the United States and Britain from the 1790s to the 1920s* (London: Harvester Wheatsheaf, 1993), pp. 230–1.

22. *Ibid.*, pp. 270–1.

23. Lesley A. Hall, 'Impotent Ghosts From No Man's Land, Flappers' Boyfriends, or Crypto-Patriarchs? Men, Sex and Social Change in 1920s Britain', *Social History* 21/1 (January 1996), pp. 54–70, p. 54.

24. S. M. Gilbert and S. Gubar, *No Man's Land: The Place of the Woman Writer in the Twentieth Century: Volume 2: Sexchanges* (New Haven, 1989), quoted in Lesley A. Hall, 'Impotent Ghosts', pp. 54–5.

25. Hall, 'Impotent Ghosts', p. 55.

26. *Ibid.*, pp. 67–70. Also see Lesley A. Hall, *Hidden Anxieties: Male Sexuality, 1900–1950* (Cambridge: Polity, 1991).

27. Jeffrey Weeks, *Coming Out: Homosexual Politics in Britain From the Nineteenth Century to the Present* (London: Quartet, 1990), p. 101.

28. Alan Sinfield, *The Wilde Century: Effeminacy, Oscar Wilde and the Queer Moment* (London: Cassell, 1994), pp. 11–12.

29. *Ibid.*, p. 14.

30. Alan Sinfield, 'Private Lives/Public Theater', pp. 43–4.

31. *Ibid.*, p. 48.

32. Nicholas de Jongh, *Not in Front of the Audience*, pp. 18–19.

33. Maggie B. Gale, *West End Women*, p. 39.

34. Lord Chamberlain's Correspondence Files [LCCF] of Licensed and Unlicensed Plays, file on *Private Lives*. Housed in the Manuscript Section of the British Library, the files contain applications, readers' reports, letters, memoranda, etc.

35. St John Ervine, *The Theatre in My Time* (London: Rich and Cowan, 1933), p. 27.

36. *Ibid.*, pp. 128–9.

37. *Ibid.*, pp. 116–17.

38. Quoted in Hugh David, *On Queer Street: A Social History of British Homosexuality 1895–1995* (London: HarperCollins, 1997), p. 66.

39. Alan Sinfield, 'Private Lives/Public Theater', p. 53.

40. *Ibid.*, p. 54.

41. Roger Baker, *Drag: A History of Female Impersonation in the Performing Arts* (London: Cassell, 1994), p. 188.

42. Sean O'Connor, *Straight Acting*, p. 9.

43. See Maggie B. Gale, *West End Women*, pp. 198–237, for a list of plays by women on the London stage (1918–1962), including dates and number of performances.

44. Peter Burnup, *Sunday Reference*, 9 October 1932.

45. This was not a requirement when there was a question over a play's suitability for a licence. Referrals seem to have been made on an *ad hoc* basis.

46. LCCF, file on *Children in Uniform*.

47. J. T. Green, *The Illustrated London News*, 29 October 1932.

48. Christa Winsloe, *Children in Uniform*, in *Famous Plays of 1932–1933* (London: Golancz, 1933).

49. Sheila Stowell, 'Rehabilitating Realism', *Journal of Dramatic Theory and Criticism* 6/2 (Spring 1992), pp. 81–8, p. 86.

50. Lillian Hellman, *The Children's Hour* (New York: Dramatists Play Service, 1981).

51. LCCF, file on *The Children's Hour*.

52. Maggie B. Gale, *West End Women*, p. 185.

53. Anne Fleche, 'The Lesbian Rule: Lillian Hellman and the Measures of Realism', *Modern Drama* 39/1 (Spring 1996), pp. 16–30, p. 26.

54. Sean O'Connor, *Straight Acting*, p. 22.

55. John van Druten, *Young Woodley*, in *Famous Plays of To-day* (Gollancz, London: Gollancz, 1929).

56. Peter Burton, in *Gay Plays*, p. 53.

57. John M. Clum, *Acting Gay: Male Homosexuality in Modern Drama* (New York: Columbia University Press, 1994), pp. 93–4.

58. Nicholas de Jongh, *Not in Front of the Audience*, p. 35.

59. Ivor Brown, *The Observer*, 29 January 1933.

60. Alan Sinfield, 'Private Lives/Public Theater', p. 45.

61. J. R. Ackerley, *The Prisoners of War*, ran for 25 performances, and R. C. Sherriff, *Journey's End*, ran for 593.

62. Patrick Hamilton, *Rope* (London: Constable, 1961).

63. LCCF, file on *Design for Living*.

64. Noël Coward, *Design for Living*, in *Coward Plays: Three* (London: Methuen, 1979).

65. Christopher Innes, *Modern British Drama: 1890–1990* (Cambridge University Press, 1995), p. 249.

66. Noël Coward, introduction to *The Collected Plays of Noël Coward: Play Parade Vol. I* (London: Heinemann, 1934), p. xvi.

67. Christopher Innes, *Modern British Drama*, p. 250.

68. James Agate, *The Sunday Times*, 29 January 1939.

69. Noël Coward, *The Vortex*, in *The Collected Plays*.

70. William Pollock, *Daily Mail*, 28 November 1924.

71. Noël Coward, *Private Lives*, in *Coward Plays: Two* (London: Methuen, 1982).

72. LCCF, file on *Private Lives*.

73. Terry Castle, *Noël Coward and Radclyffe Hall*, p. 27.

4　Girl crazy: musicals and revue between the wars

JAMES ROSS MOORE

Writing in 1926, James Agate recalled an incident during the First World War when he overheard a group of 'lively young men' trying to decide what to do after dinner. Offering himself as a reliable guide, *The Times* critic asked whether they would like to 'see a play of spiritual purpose and noble intent' and was immediately rebuffed: 'Good God, no! We don't wish to see anything of the sort. We're on leave!'[1]

Agate went on to assert gloomily that the English theatre-going public always considered itself on leave. Yet, to judge from his reviews, Agate seemed perfectly at ease with the musical theatre of his time, a multi-headed genre which has always assumed its audiences were 'on leave' in one way or another. It was only when Agate caught a whiff of musicals aspiring to art or the delivery of messages that he unloaded his richest scorn: it was not their place.

Agate and his peers had little to complain about during those inter-war years when the book musical provided endless hours of escapism. As in the previous half-century, silly plots, punning humour, untaxing tunes and stock characters were enhanced by regular parades of decorative 'ladies' – often distinguishable from their 1870s ancestors only by thinner clothing and more rapid movements. The West End was girl crazy in a properly British way and British in its unwillingness to seem serious about what it was doing. Not for Britain the often surreal, biting political and social satire which characterised the American musical stage during the 1930s; not for the book musical. But widen the focus to include variety and its partial offshoot revue and everything changes. Variety grew large; revue became the era's most vital, innovative and influential form of musical theatre. Through its increasingly deft sketches – actually 5- or 10-minute playlets at first derived from variety turns and short burlesques – revue honed the skills of librettists and playwrights and stretched the versatility of its stars, people like Gertrude Lawrence, Jack Buchanan, Jack Hulbert, Cicely Courtneidge and Beatrice Lillie, subsequently leading performers in all the era's media. Composers who began in revue wrote the era's most significant book musicals. Sometimes, these playwrights, actors and composers were the same person: Noël Coward, Ivor Novello. Beginning in 1912, revue most quickly promoted the various dance crazes and especially during the 1930s it offered shelter to a newborn native ballet. Revue also readily incorporated the serious experiments of repertory groups and other manifestations of what Norman Marshall later called 'the other theatre'. Gradually abandoning brainless spectacle – Hippodrome chorus girls on a 'joy plank' extending over the audience's heads, tossing balloons to the bald-heads ogling below – British revue chose stylish, sophisticated intimacy and gradually changed the musical stage's world.

Revue is the binding ribbon for this journey through an era when all genres struggled with an economy that never perked up, years when the musical stage survived fierce competition from radio (and later on from television), whose stay-at-home devotees vastly preferred musical entertainment to improving their minds. During these inter-war years, the musical stage gradually recovered from the latest of its periodic Americanisations, and especially during the dreary days of the 1930s slump, it rediscovered essentially British subject-matter and found fresh ways of bottling more familiar wine.

Our journey begins in 1918, when 'on leave' was not a figurative term and the book musical offered familiar solace. *Chu Chin Chow*, Oscar Asche's reworking of *Ali Baba and the Forty Thieves*, was a must-see for servicemen, possibly because its home, His Majesty's Theatre in the Haymarket, was apparently a marvellous place for picking up women. But it would be churlish to assign the show's 2,238-performance run solely to such urgent opportunism; *Chu Chin Chow* managed to combine the joys of pantomime with perhaps the most enduring form of British musical escapism – a free-ranging orientalism which dates at least from the exotic importations and derivative creations popularised by Arthur Liberty's department store beginning in 1875 – a precursor to Gilbert and Sullivan's 1885 *The Mikado*.[2] A quick trawl through musical comedy titles of the preceding two decades confirms the sturdiness of the genre: *The Geisha, San Toy, A Chinese Honeymoon, The White Chrysanthemum* and *My Mimosa Maid*. In these years one could also escape to fanciful versions of the Balkans (*The Balkan Princess*) or Asia Minor (*The Persian Princess*); and there were always complete fantasy-lands – *Floradora, The Arcadians* and the ever-popular Ruritania.

Imitation always being the sincerest form of show business, during the reign of *Chu Chin Chow* another escapist saga of robbers (fewer than forty), *The Maid of the Mountains*, held the boards for 1,352 performances. The First World War extended the length of show runs to exaggerated proportions. There were fewer West End shows than before the war – during the 1918 season only one-half of the 1914 number – and a clear distinction developed between winners and losers with attendant pressure upon finding a winning formula. This quest for a formula undoubtedly fitted snugly with a somewhat Americanised movement towards consolidation: variety 'chains' grew large indeed. Wartime psychology tended to make its mainly 'on leave' audience wary of experimentation – if this is the last show I may ever see, well, then . . . But to suggest, as Huntley Carter does in *The New Spirit in European Theatre: 1914–1924*,[3] that wartime created a deadly standardisation in musical theatre is far-fetched.

The legend goes that wartime profits led *nouveaux-riche* philistines into buying into the theatre, which they saw as yet another cashcow. Not only that: the hirelings (often American) of these philistines drove out the actor-managers, who were of course interested only in the aesthetic betterment of society. Thus, alas, musicals became increasingly unoriginal consumer items, not 'artful' as in the good old days. Yet entrepreneurs have always wanted pre-sold hits, and if possible in profitable series. A chain of Savoy operettas began in 1875, and the bright young things of the young century had been entertained by those virtually interchangeable escapist shows at Daly's as well as trendy and repetitious 'Gaiety' musical comedies. The history of

British musical theatre shows a consistent tendency to construct sequels to successes, often running to extended series.

Even the trend towards the creation of informal chains of theatres under one ownership or management was not quite new: George Edwardes, the 'Guv' who 'invented' musical comedy, had been regularly operating at Daly's, the Gaiety and the Empire and sometimes had five shows running simultaneously. The American Charles Frohman had established himself before the turn of the century in partnership with (Sir) Seymour Hicks; they built three theatres and vastly increased the transatlantic flow of business, underwriting the early success of composer Jerome Kern.[4] But not all American invasions were successful; the brothers Shubert never expanded beyond the Strand (formerly Waldorf). What is unarguable is the growth of large urban Variety palaces which began with the new century. This eclipse of neighbourhood music halls with their amateur sing-alongs gained irreversible momentum in 1912, when the first Royal Variety Command Performance conferred 'respectability' upon the genre. Soon the suburbs and their provinces had their own Variety palaces, courtesy of Messrs. Stoll and Moss and others, like Alfred Butt, and these chains indeed resembled American 'circuits' and 'wheels'.[5]

However, it was causes unconnected to theatre economics that changed the environment in which immediate post-war musical theatre operated. Consider the year 1912: ragtime came to England in a revue, Albert deCourville's *Hullo, Ragtime!* While indecorous American dancing had enchanted the West End before – see *In Dahomey* (1903) – the youth of late Edwardian England had not taken to its cakewalk as they now swooped on this strutting delight. 'Hitchy-koo!' they shouted – and languid British chorus lines simply had to adapt. It was 1911 when the Diaghilev ballet – the Ballets Russes – made its first visit to Britain; it is accurate to say that by 1912 the visits of the Ballets Russes were foreshadowing the transformation of dance in the musical theatre. And in 1912 George Edwardes suffered a stroke; in his remaining three years, he never regained authority. Edwardes' decline coincided with that of his light-hearted, 'up-to-date' concoction of the language and fashion of trendy late Victorian and Edwardian urbanites and suburbanites grafted on to Cinderella plots, earning the title 'Gaiety'. These included *In Town, The Shop Girl, Our Miss Gibbs, A Gaiety Girl, The Casino Girl, The Country Girl, The Quaker Girl* and a bevy of subsequent 'Girls'.

Even without Edwardes it is possible that the Gaiety–Daly's *œuvres* might have survived a while longer, but most of the factory workers had also departed. Ivan Caryll, the flamboyant composer who bridged the gap between European operetta and the dancing craze, left in 1910 for greater fame in the United States – F. Scott Fitzgerald in his 1931 essay 'Echoes of the Jazz Age' commented: 'We greybeards remember the uproar when in 1912 grandmothers of forty tossed away their crutches and took lessons in the Tango and the Castle Walk.'[6] Paul Rubens, whose sweet melodic lines influenced Kern and a subsequent generation of British tunesmiths, died in 1917. Frohman died in the sinking of the Lusitania. In 1919 the last great Gaiety–Daly composer, Lionel Monckton, professed himself disgusted by the newer dance rhythms and stopped writing altogether. And that was not all. What happened to the book musical in general but to Gaiety musical comedy in particular was revue.

Exactly when British revue began is arguable: an 1893 venture of Hicks's is often cited as the first, yet from 1903 onwards the most diligent campaigner for and practitioner of this French form was George Grossmith, Jr., whose offerings gradually expanded from 20 minutes to an hour apiece, set within Variety bills. From 1907 Harry Pelissier brought the insouciance of seaside concert parties to London with his Follies. In 1921 The Co-optimists, another but somewhat less anarchic Pierrot troupe, would begin a seven-year West End triumph. After changes in licensing laws made it possible for revues to go on their own circa 1912, the most flamboyant of producers was deCourville, who mistakenly thought in neo-Florenz Ziegfeldian terms that bigger was better; one of his chorus lines, in *Razzle Dazzle,* was 300 strong. But as Robert Nesbitt, a revue producer of later vintage, noted in conversation, '"intimate" revue happened almost by accident'. Owing to its producer's parlous finances, Cochran's 1914 *Odds and Ends* – at the Ambassadors, a tiny house completed in 1913 – was virtually devoid of scenery and boasted few personnel. But it had insouciance, topicality and a jokey book written by Harry Grattan, a variety veteran whose direct-to-the-audience approach was something new for revue. The show's success convinced Cochran's rival André Charlot – a French expatriate who had arrived in 1912 – that 'intimacy' was the future. He made the form his own.

Aside from bringing an indefinable 'style' to revue, Charlot had – amidst moving from the vast Alhambra variety house in Leicester Square to cosy venues such as the Comedy, Playhouse and Vaudeville – learned that wartime success meant ignoring the serious side of war in favour of genial, slightly saucy, sometimes pointed songs, dances and especially 'sketches.' Sometimes arbitrarily grouped around a governing theme, these pieces were performed by a small cast – rarely more than fourteen, all of them versatile, including a chorus of eight – against minimal backdrops enhanced by ingenious lighting. Light and blithe, the contents of a revue could be shuffled and changed regularly. (By his peak in the mid-1920s, Charlot was updating his revue every month.) Musical comedy was, by comparison, exhausted.

Although Charlot subsequently produced better revues than *Buzz Buzz*, which opened in December 1918 just after the Armistice and ran to 1920, setting a long-run record for revue, examining it may suggest the form's appeal. The era's essential need for delight and surprise can be found even in the title: until weeks before opening, it was *Coupons*, and many songs and sketches referred to rationing coupons. But a provincial producer had nabbed the title and anyway, rationing might soon be last year's news. Charlot kept the unifying element and changed the name. Knowing that restless audiences often decided their evening by a walkabout, Charlot had the hoardings out front of the Vaudeville painted '. . . . .'. Shortly before the opening night, he adopted the new title – it did, after all, have a Shakespearean pedigree. Charlot told no one – not even the cast – the new name, but at the interval, when audiences tumbled into the street, the hoardings read *Buzz Buzz*, the first act's closing number ('You buzz off to the city/You buzz into your office/Say "buzz off", if you're rude . . . Everything is buzz buzz now') which the cast had learned just before the opening curtain.

Buzz Buzz began with a number mainly by the chorus, which enlisted the audience's sympathy ('Here we are, waiting for the Star');

when the curtains parted, playgoers beheld a railway station at which Nelson (Bunch) Keys, as Sir Thayer Aubakkagen, was arriving.[7] Lively and saucy banter among Keys and three other principals included a passage blue-pencilled by the Lord Chamberlain's censor:

> An explorer is a man who is ever seeking to rend the veil and penetrate to the unknown.
> A CHAUFFEUSE [Gertrude Lawrence]: Yes, I've known some like that! He's not coming – in MY cab.

Within the sketch is embedded a song, 'Who killed Missis Grundy?' which suggests that wartime had undermined sexual morality, particularly when women were called upon to perform male jobs: the lyrics – by Ronald Jeans, the premier sketch-writer of his era – include, 'I, said the WAAC, I led the attack/When I drive an officer out in his car/I'm only a private, as most of us are/So I can't protest if he's going too far/I've done my bit.' That was more suggestive than anything on the musical-comedy stage, and very much in tune with the audience's mood. Next came the first of Jeans' sketches 'The Merchant of Venison': his collaborator was Arthur Wimperis, already well known for such felicitous phraseology as 'The critic left no turn unstoned.' 'The Merchant of Venison' spoofed food-rationing and black-marketeering, while keeping the tenuous Shakespearean connection going.

'Running order' was crucial in revue; not only did the sequence of song and sketch, of alternating satire and sentiment, need careful attention, costume-changing had to be figured in and a fully staged segment had to be followed by a front-cloth act (in front of the curtain) – such as the duet 'I've Been Waiting for Someone Like You,' performed by Lawrence and Walter Williams. Such songs typified revue, setting audience expectation in one direction, then causing outrage with a twist. This apparently innocent boy–girl number concludes when Williams condescends to tell Lawrence she should wake up from her daydream of him, only to be trumped: she has been waiting for someone 'richer than you'. Later in the first half came the sketch and song 'Coupons for Kisses', in which the proprietess of a kissing booth dispenses kisses of Grades 1, 2 and 3 (complete with puns: '*Couponi soit qui mal y pense'*) according to the number of coupons proffered. When Grade 1 was finally reached, a shower of pink and blue coupons preceded a quick blackout.

Revue's putative parent, Variety, was evoked with a song which might have been a separate 'turn' – 'Percy Plantagenet Ponsonby Pitt . . . was perfectly priceless', which alluded to currently fashionable night clubs such as Ciro's and Murray's as well as tut-tutting at 'Flappers of forty.' Another Lawrence song argued that for voyeurism, nothing matched the life of a woman window cleaner. Another sketch outlined the problems of newlyweds forced to choose the use of their coupons – surely not on heating? After that, 'I've Lost My Heart in Maori-Land', a spoof 'exotic' song, irreverently parodied the escapism of faraway places. The quaint-and-cute 'Miss Sunshine and Mr Rain' allowed the boy–girl lovers to enact the figurines on a barometer. The first version of *Buzz Buzz* closed with 'How It's Done', a sketch in which producers Sir Prysing Choyce and Boanerges G. Whizz (an American characterised by the size of his cigars) rewrite a patriotic melodrama into a revue sketch and the entire ensemble dance the anarchic – and topical – 'Corpse-Reviver Rag', alluding to the craze for cocktails as well as, after years of hitchy-kooing, confessing that ragtime was now tiresome. The second version closed with 'The Maid of the Mountebanks', a burlesque portraying Jose Collins (star of *The Maid of the Mountains*) as unable to accept a new engagement because she is held prisoner at The Palace (an allusion to her imprisoner Butt's house). The sketch has already reassured us that 'One Daly's play, we're glad to say/is very like the last/with robber-chief and waltz-motif/and Jose in the cast.' The spoof also burlesques the mannerisms of *The Maid of the Mountains*, including the emphatic repetitions of whatever the fierce robbers say: ('I think it's going to be fine today.' [*Fiercely whipping out knives, etc.*] TODAY!) By the end of the show all mentions of 'Coupons' and indeed of 'Buzz Buzz' had vanished – revue just happened.

Of variety, playfulness and insider-joking (including blithe self-criticism) *Buzz Buzz* had plenty, of memorable song little, of dance less than some of Charlot's shows, of inspired madness less than when comedienne Beatrice Lillie was involved; of continuity more than one might expect, of versatility and ingenuity much, of lighting effects (an excellent way of saving money on scenery) and rather pointed good humour a full measure. Audiences quickly realised that such lively fare as *Buzz Buzz* offered much more than the book musical, and entre-preneurs responded in kind. Cochran returned to revue on a rather larger scale. In April 1919 another of deCourville's American importa-tions shook the entertainment world.

Amid the general incoherence of *Joy Bells*, the latest mammoth Hippodrome offering, a brief set by five 'hot' musicians caused tumult – enough, in fact, for deCourville's star, George Robey, to insist that this 'disruptive' act be axed after one performance. So the Original Dixieland Jazz Band moved on to create further sensations at the London Palladium, and the history of inter-war musical entertainment was altered. However dubious the ODJB's claim as the first real jazz band – or even the creators of the first jazz recordings (1917) – their influence helped to revitalise a weary post-war generation. Universities quickly took up the new music and the accompanying new ballroom dances; at Cambridge the Quinquaginta Dance Club was in full swing by 1920. (By 1927 one of its graduates, Federico Elizalde, was leading the decade's most advanced jazz band.) By 1921 dance orchestras and Palais de Danse were proliferating across the land; in that year a former talent agent called Jack Hylton formed his first recording band and by the middle of the decade was presiding over a huge 'show orchestra', which patterned itself with great success upon the American Paul Whiteman's often rather sweet 'jazz' offerings.

The 'new music' gained access to the West End in many ways, none more important than the 1922 advent of both cabaret and the first broadcasts of the British Broadcasting Company. The licensing author-ities – and some entrepreneurs who were not in at the start – were so alarmed by the mixture of song, dance, food, drink and sketch repre-sented by The Midnight Follies, London's first cabaret venture at the Hotel Metropole (undertaken by Charlot, Grossmith and J. A. E. Malone) that its contents were quickly circumscribed. Subsequently bereft of sketch, it remained highly attractive, presenting the big-name stars (usually of revue) in an after-hours setting. Late-night competi-tion quickly materialised in the ballrooms of hotels old and new. The Savoy Orpheans, a dance orchestra, was quickly notable, and for good reason: the sound was no longer bounded by the Strand and the Embankment. The new BBC was soon sending the orchestra around the nation.

The hotels' approach to the new medium was considerably more enlightened than the theatres'. Charlot, who favoured buying up the BBC to put it out of business, led a faction of the Society of West End Managers opposed to any radio broadcast. Eventually a compromise was reached – portions of London shows (perhaps one act or three 'turns') could be broadcast. During the 1920s radio became known as more a partner-in-publicity than a threat and, in 1928, during a lull in his theatrical activities, Charlot created the first Radio Revue – followed quickly by deCourville.

Soon the Orpheans gained a new American leader, Carroll Gibbons, who stayed on for the rest of his life, moving smoothly into writing and directing for musical comedies. By 1926 the rage of tea-dancing was in full swing; more than thirty such venues were weekly rampant in London alone. Late-night radio became synonymous with late-night 'outside broadcasts' from the major hotels, and the inter-war years became truly the 'golden age of dance bands'. The dance band–hotel–radio–West End links grew more solid as the years passed, and by the mid-1930s the popular leader Lew Stone was simultaneously directing musical comedies and arranging some of his own compositions so the loose-limbed American expatriate Walter Crisham could dance them in a ballet for Charlot.

As we shall see, it was this new dance music, engendering a host of 'dancing musicals', which eventually helped haul the book musical out of its doldrums.[8] It did not hurt that beginning in 1923 with *Stop Flirting* the favoured theatrical home for Fred and Adele Astaire was London. But before the book musical could recover, it had to cope with further creative defections to the United States: the brightest new American musical comedies were already created by such authors and lyricists as P. G. Wodehouse and Guy Bolton. Now off went Fred Thompson and Clifford Grey, the latter – since the *Bing Boys* trilogy (1917–19) and 1919's *Kissing Time* and *Who's Hooper?* – the West End's most in-demand lyricist/librettist.[9]

There were other problems to overcome: between 1918 and 1920 the book musical depended largely upon adaptations from French farce and even German originals, with occasional original echoes of glories past, such as *A Southern Maid*, one more sentimental tour of Daly's for Jose Collins. In these years the tide of American infiltration also ran full. This was enhanced by Grossmith. Now in league with Malone, Grossmith presented a significant series at the Winter Garden (a theatre whose romantic history would extend from the Old Mogul Tavern, through closings, to a reincarnation as the New London, the long-run record-setting house of *Cats*). The first three Winter Garden musicals were built upon the music of Jerome Kern. First came *Sally* (1921) the Broadway improvement by Grey upon an original by Bolton and P. G. Wodehouse. *Sally* made a West End star of the feather-footed American dancer Dorothy Dickson, imported for a 1919 Cochran revue. Dickson – who for the next thirty years was called London's best-dressed star – repeated her Cinderella role in *The Cabaret Girl* (1922) and *The Beauty Prize* (1923), both Kern originals with weaker books nominally by Wodehouse. Dickson headed what became a virtual repertory group which included Heather Thatcher, Grossmith himself and the pop-eyed comic Leslie Henson. In a way, the 'Winter Garden shows' were doing what the Gaiety–Daly's shows had done, capitalising upon their sibling similarity and a nod to trendiness. (Why not co-opt cabaret for a plot? Wodehouse understood his remit and strength.)

Kern's three musicals were closely followed by *Primrose* (1924), an original by George Gershwin. There was every reason to hope that *Primrose* would transfer successfully to Broadway. However, it never got the chance, presumably because the gifted Gershwin had written such an 'English' score. But its plot, allowing for a few regional references, was pure American – written by Bolton with Grossmith's help. Unfortunately such plots went on to become standard for the inter-war British musical comedy: an inexperienced ingenue lives with her older, knighted guardian in a riverside mansion. Beyond its walls is moored the houseboat of a novelist writing a serial called *Primrose*. The ingénue, an avid reader, believes she is the model for the serial's heroine and sets her cap at the novelist. A secondary love interest exists between a 'sprightly maiden' and the guardian's intensely 'modern' son, supposedly promised to the ingénue. A third set of lovers are a knockabout noble and a beautician who have become engaged by flirtation. They arrive at the mansion as guests of the novelist, and soon the beautician is smitten by the latter. Somehow the scene shifts to the Hotel Splendide in 'Le Bouquet', where all the characters are celebrating Bastille Day. Slighted by the novelist's inattention, the ingénue flirts with all the boys; the novelist now becomes interested in her, but then she agrees to marry her guardian's son. Back in England the novelist, determined to break them up, engages a spiritualist, who cancels at the last moment, making it necessary for the knockabout noble to impersonate him. It works and the son's reputation is blackened. The knockabout noble continues to run amok until unmasked by the beautician. His mother turns her town house into a dancing club and the knockabout noble impersonates a raiding policeman. His mother faints into the guardian's arms. Everyone ends up with the right partner.

Aside from its absurdly arbitrary events and workings-out of intricate love interests, it is clear that for all its attempts at up-to-dateness, *Primrose* gradually becomes a showcase for the multifarious laugh-producing talents of the knockabout noble – that is, Leslie Henson. Writing material specific to performers was nothing new, and Bolton's American success was derived from his structural ability and accommodating the styles of great American comics. But Henson, a prodigious gurner once called 'our greatest droll', continued to play such roles because the public kept paying to see him, and in the later 1930s Henson found himself the focus of a series of four (the last four) musical comedies at the Gaiety – as a bankrupt hotel-owner disguised as an oriental fortune-teller, as a gambler called Maxie Mumm who impersonates Xabiski, a chief of the Yellow Shirt gang rivalled by the No-Shirts, and so on. All those musicals were written by Bolton. What is depressing about that fact is that Bolton's American period had essentially ended with the 1920s. In the aftermath of the Wall Street crash, American musical comedies became more serious and satirical. Bolton (and his clones) kept writing the same plot, unimaginative management kept presenting it and British audiences kept accepting it.

The 'dancing musicals' which began in 1922 with *Battling*

Butler seemed generally less hard-working than such shows, possessed of more *savoir-faire*, thus ideally more 'English'. This was partly because they were usually written by Douglas Furber or Austin Melford, who were free of American experience, but mainly because they starred Jack Buchanan.[10] Buchanan had made his reputation as an open-faced comedian and smooth dancer – he could even make drunk-dancing and dope-dancing palatable – in Charlot's revues between 1918 and 1921. Throughout the inter-war years, through nine productions sandwiched between successful stints in British and American films as well as radio work, Buchanan, partnered in dance by Elsie Randolph, was able to project onstage the atmosphere of the cabarets and hotel ballrooms.

Jack Buchanan was also superbly casual and impossibly well dressed: his entrance in *Battling Butler* was in the traditional driving gear of his day – cap, leather coat and huge fur gauntlets – which he removed, saying, 'Take these out and give them each a saucer of milk.' Tales circulated that the Prince of Wales adopted Buchanan's preference in evening wear, thus making white tie and tails the era's style, even before Astaire could stake a claim. That style was international, as F. Scott Fitzgerald noted: 'something subtle passed to America, the style of man'. Buchanan also proved himself from the first an astute theatrical businessman, rather along the older actor-manager lines, and like Jack Hulbert, another casual dancing comedian and graduate of Charlot's talent factory, usually produced his own shows in partnership with some money-man. Although Buchanan's musicals continued on and off throughout the inter-war years, they frequently met competition from closely modelled imitators, including a series produced by Laddie Cliff straddling 1930 and featuring an Australian pair – Cyril Ritchard and Madge Elliott – who, except for their own considerable talents, might have been Buchanan's and Randolph's stand-ins. It is notable that once sound came to motion pictures, it was the 'dancing musicals', especially Buchanan's, which were most successfully adapted.

Despite the reliable fare provided by Leslie Henson, Jack Buchanan, Jack Hulbert and Cicely Courtneidge, the 'big (book) musicals' of the London 1920s were not British. For example, the embattled

impresario Butt was able to fill the vastness of Drury Lane only by sac-
rificing its traditional pantomimes and staging British versions of
American operettas – *Rose Marie, Show Boat, The Desert Song* – starring another American expatriate who stayed on, the bird-voiced Edith
Day, subsequently Queen of Drury Lane. Aside from the Kern and
Gershwin shows previously noted – the latter often starring the
Astaires – there were originals by Rodgers and Hart, new shows by the
lately arrived American producer Lee Ephraim, and later importations
of several 'snappy' American shows by DeSylva, Brown and
Henderson. Most notable of all was Youmans' *No, No, Nanette* (1925),
in advance of its New York premiere.

Still, the critics often asked 'Where are the fresh British musicals?' Perhaps a better question would have been 'When are we going to
turn our hands to essentially British material?' The first response came
from intimate revue. In 1926 *Riverside Nights* achieved 238 performances at Nigel Playfair's Lyric Theatre, off the beaten track in
Hammersmith. *Riverside Nights* was partly inspired by the Russian
'bat theatre', Chauves-Souris, which Cochran had been importing for
several years. The Russian troupe drew heavily upon their own folklore
and literature; flamboyantly exotic settings 'à la Bakst' helped ease
these unusual demands upon audiences. *Riverside Nights* was largely
written by A. P. Herbert, a polymath destined for Parliament. Herbert
later collaborated with the composer Vivian Ellis on a variety of
musical ventures.[11] As we have seen, the genial revues characteristic of
Charlot never ventured very far into social or political commentary
and contemporary musical comedy certainly did not – but such were
Herbert's meat and drink. In his revue, Herbert also felt free to call
upon the works of Wordsworth and Walter Savage Landown and to
write sketches lasting for up to 25 minutes. He pondered the tone
of lugubrious Russian drama as if it were set in contemporary
Hammersmith. He staged vast historical spectacles in 5 minutes with
three characters. There was a small cast and little dancing.

So *Riverside Nights* had, among other innovations, laid down a
marker for the return of 'English' subject-matter – at least in revue.
Still, where were the fresh British book musicals? Eventually they
arrived, and their arrival was essentially accomplished by revue

veterans. Chief among these were Noël Coward and Ivor Novello, men who had digested the musical theatre of their time. Coward, who during wartime had failed a performing audition for Charlot, collaborated in 1923 with Ronald Jeans on songs and sketches for Charlot's *London Calling*, probably the best revue of the decade. Coward had learned during his 1921 sojourn in New York that Americans took light entertainment seriously, and 'cheap music' has incredible potency. Completely untrained in music, Coward somehow created melodies and *tempi* to match that languidly mordant world view which appealed so much to the jaded and battered of his generation. In *London Calling* he showed his versatility; as well as appearing in the show, he displayed an ability to write for Gertrude Lawrence which later resulted in some of the era's most memorable theatre. *London Calling* began with the show's first sketch, 'Early Mourning', in which Lawrence receives a phone call informing her of her husband's suicide. With only a telephone for an onstage partner, she gradually invites all her friends to meet her at Ciro's. Her plans are dashed by one final call: the suicidee actually lived in the flat above; Lawrence's 'husband' would be home shortly. Coward also parodied an eccentric literary family modelled upon the Sitwells, gave comedienne Maisie Gay a robust song sending up an ageing soubrette ('There's Life in the Old Girl Yet'). Jeans' sketch for Gay, 'The Old Lady Shows Her Muddles', was a simultaneous malapropistic anthology of contemporary slang and parody of the popular sentimental variety turn, '. . . Her Medals'. Lawrence also performed the first Coward-esque hit song, the haunting 'Parisian Pierrot'.

Coward's association with Charlot did not last long and when Charlot's *London Revue* (essentially the fusing of *London Calling* and the 1921 *A to Z*) took New York by storm in 1924, Coward's contributions were distributed among Lawrence, Buchanan and Lillie. The impact of Charlot's *London Revue* was historical; it heralded the decline of the massive American genre favoured by Ziegfeld; it also marked the turning of the import–export tide. Lawrence and Lillie spent most of the rest of their careers in the States, where they were eventually joined by Coward. By the time *Charlot's Revue* returned to London, Coward was also enjoying success as the author of controversial plays about sexual morality. When he turned his hand once more to revue, it was for Cochran.

Cochran's conception of revue regularly included notable dance elements. Significant dance had even infiltrated cabaret – Quentin Tod's choreography to Gershwin's 'Rhapsody in Blue' made its debut in a 1926 edition of the *Midnight Follies*. Coward's *On With the Dance* (1925) for Cochran included choreography by Leonide Massine. Coward's *This Year of Grace* (1928) also for Cochran, was notable for the debut of the fiery Viennese dancer Tilly Losch. Cole Porter's original London book musical *Nymph Errant* (1933) for Cochran was choreographed by Agnes B. de Mille. In the early 1930s Cochran employed the choreographer George Balanchin, a Diaghilev graduate who later added another letter to his last name and transformed American ballet.[12] In the same years, when the new native ballet pioneered by Ninette de Valois and Marie Rambert was struggling in its new homes, short serious ballets choreographed by Frederick Ashton and William Chappell could be found in most West End revues.

It was while *This Year of Grace* was being readied for its New York production that Coward heard a new recording of Strauss' *Die Fledermaus* and determined to write a new kind of musical play for Cochran. This was *Bitter Sweet*, a bold gamble on the premise that Coward's versatility could revive the tradition of nostalgic and escapist European operetta. It should have been the tonic needed for a musical stage now beset by a general malaise in the wake of the 1926 General Strike, not to mention the twin demons of the Depression and all-singing, all-dancing movies. *Bitter Sweet* (1929) possessed the kind of unity which later critics somehow believed to have been invented by American musicals beginning with *Oklahoma!* It is first and foremost a play, extended by music and character-based lyrics. Coward's tale flashed backwards from the present to 1880 – the tale of Sari, now the Marchioness of Shayne, who eloped at 16 to Vienna with her singing teacher Carl Linden. The doomed romance of Sari and Carl, who became leader of a fashionable orchestra only to be killed in a duel with an Austrian army captain, was handled with restraint and embedded in a varied score which blended ironic satire and sentiment – the latter particularly in 'I'll See You Again', which proved to be Coward's most enduring musical work. Perhaps most importantly, Coward had understood something about the changing public mood: *Bitter Sweet* renewed the lavish, beautiful and generally uplifting sort of entertainment which was the book musical's domain before the First World War. It ran for a gratifying year and a half. Although for the next two decades Coward continued to experiment with full-length musical plays, none excepting *Cavalcade*, a shameless 1931 patriotic pageant – another apt reading of public mood – filled with other people's songs, measured up to *Bitter Sweet* in acceptance. On the other hand, Coward's plays-with-music, always with Lawrence and including *Private Lives* and the *tour-de-force* series of nine short plays *Tonight at 8.30*, quickly achieved major status in America. In one of these plays, 'Red Peppers', Coward wrote a love letter to the seaside concert parties of his youth.

If *Bitter Sweet* marked a return to one familiar type of musical escapism, another 1929 production, *Mr Cinders*, marked a different type of return to British tradition. This was a reworking of the panto-mime version of *Cinderella* by Clifford Grey and Greatrex Newman, reversing the sexes and benefiting from the tunes of Ellis. 'Spread a Little Happiness', with Grey's lyric, was the show's major hit and proved to be an uplifter in the 'mustn't grumble' vein for the unfortu-nate generation stumbling towards the Second World War. *Mr Cinders*, which brought the poignant Bobby Howes to stardom, whereupon he, too, was launched into a predictable series,[13] was also imitated by *Mr Whittington* (1933), a Clifford Grey–Johnny Green adaptation of *Dick Whittington* for Jack Buchanan. *Bitter Sweet* was certainly the best of its era's various attempts to combat the first wave of American film musicals – these largely written by Bolton, Wodehouse, Thompson and Grey. Attempting to do what film could not yet do, London built new theatres and opted for greater stage effects. Cochran added a huge revolving stage at the Adelphi and starred Jessie Matthews in the Rodgers and Hart *Evergreen* there in 1930. At exactly the same moment, Charlot was transforming the Savoy Theatre into Sam Wonder's cabaret for *Wonder Bar*: its audience would be literally part of this dark tale, responding to its onstage performances whilst privy to its backstage machinations. With these productions, Cochran and Charlot almost perfectly cancelled each other out and soon Charlot was bankrupt.[14] There were large-scale successes – running for a year and a half in such times was a major accomplishment – but they did not advance the art of the British musical. These major successes were largely adaptations of German operettas – the extravaganzas *White Horse Inn* and *Waltzes from Vienna* (both in 1931) and *Casanova* (1932). As the technology of the musical film improved, in tandem with the worsening of the world economy, London musicals experienced more and more difficult times. Such was not the case for musical performers, who as we have seen could now ply their trade on stage, screen and radio. During the 1930s, however, only Jessie Matthews – the protagonist of a series of highly successful British films for Basil Dean – was entirely absent from the West End. In the face of 'continuous showings' in cinemas, even Cochran adopted the Variety strategy: play two shows daily.

Momentary relief came in what proved to be the era's most shameless example of escapism. An ideal counterpoint to Coward's (at least superficial) cynicism was the work of another homosexual son of an overpowering mother. The breadth of Ivor Novello's theatrical career is simply astounding. His song 'Till The Boys Come Home' (usually 'Keep The Home Fires Burning') became the First World War's emblem (although Nat Ayer and Grey's 'If You Were The Only Girl In The World' was its popular favourite.) In the later war years Novello launched a successful career of writing revue songs, the highlight of which was Charlot's *A to Z*. Shortly thereafter Novello blossomed as both playwright and brooding matinee idol on stage and screen on both sides of the Atlantic. By 1935, with scores of credits behind him, he was sufficiently at liberty to take up the sad case of the Theatre Royal, Drury Lane, whose fortunes had sunk badly after the departure of American operettas and was now under the stewardship of H.M. Tennant.

For Drury Lane Novello created six astonishing extravaganzas – beginning with *Glamorous Night* (1935) (a show which might have run forever except the traditional panto had been revived and booked), which recapitulated virtually every type of musical theatre. A Novello extravaganza always contained a show within a show – here a small opera, there a peppy musical comedy. A Novello show – he starred, wrote the music and book, often collaborated on the lyrics – always contained the exotic; here an excursion into Chinese legend, there the imagined glories of pre-Columbian America. Everything was included;

earthquakes and sinking ships onstage, and nothing was to be taken seriously. But the waltzes! No one wrote bigger, swoonier, or less musically orthodox waltzes than Novello – they were never successfully negotiated by non-Novello performers – and this 'glorious tosh', so memorably identified by one critic, was exactly what a nation sliding towards a second world war wanted. Inevitably, a Novello repertory company was formed, headed by Novello as king, prince, inventor, brigand – whatever was necessary – and with expatriate Americans such as Dorothy Dickson, Walter Crisham and Mary Ellis. A Novello show – and make no mistake, they were *shows* and not plays – was even bigger than the movies; in *The Dancing Years* (1939) there was even a touch of political awareness for the cataclysm about to occur. Though fondly remembered by those who saw them, these portmanteau musicals did not outlast their creator, who died during the run of *King's Rhapsody* (1953). Novello finally exerted even less influence than Coward, whose work could be revived by later generations. The work of Coward and Novello recapitulated the inter-war years. Yet, mordant and crisp or outrageously over-the-top, it was ultimately brilliant and sterile and generally devoid of meaning. Novello's escapism was in part imitated in pseudo-Hungarian musicals such as Eric Maschwitz's and George Posford's *Balalaika* (1936).

It remains to note a final instance of recovering 'English' material for the book musical. In 1934 there began a series of Gaiety 'sporting musicals', generally teaming the pianist–composer of frilly songs Billy Mayerl with the astutely hearty librettist–lyricist Stanley Lupino. *Sporting Love* and its horsy successors echoed the appeal of old-time melodramas, appealing to a working-class audience while patronising it for its belief in the 'main chance'.[15] Ultimately the series mattered because in *Twenty To One* (1935) there surfaced a wise and principled Cockney called Bill Snibson, portrayed by Lupino Lane. 'Snibson' Lane reappeared in Lupino and Noël Gay's *Me and My Girl* (1937), the phenomenon of the inter-war years, yet another switch on *Cinderella*. *Me and My Girl* single-handedly saw the book musical through the Second World War; though interrupted when its original theatre was bombed out, it eventually played more than 5,000 performances.[16]

Despite the sentimental attractiveness of *Me and My Girl* and the increasing popularity of such surreal variety theatre headliners as the 'Crazy Gang',[17] as the inter-war years approached their apocalyptic close it was revue which pointed the way forward. Although Charlot's comeback revues beginning in 1934 retained much of the old bonhomie – an entertainment for a party of long-time friends – none, however, was able to buck the economics of Depression. Charlot's tradition of discovering talent continued; he took on as director the lighting wizard and future mainstay of spectacular revue Robert Nesbitt, whose first attempt at writing revue was *Ballyhoo* (1932), a production one critic described as 'smart with the lackadaisical gloom which is the dominant quality of British youth today'. By 1937 Charlot was presenting 'non-stop revue', a continuous showing in response to round-the-clock cinema. As with others of the 'non-stop' genre these featured near-nudity. But revuedeville as practised at London's Windmill Theatre had already cornered the near-nude market. In mid-1937 Charlot left for America never to return.

Revues like *Ballyhoo* were part of a new direction in production, but more important was the influence of what Norman Marshall later named the 'other theatre' – particularly the regional companies in Liverpool, Northampton, Oxford and Cambridge – where experimental plays had been taken seriously for years. In university cities shows influenced by Herbert's *Riverside Nights* found favour. Innovative revues such as those produced at the close of the 1920s at the Cambridge Festival Theatre were, at least in part, responsible for the intellectualisation of revue which took 'intimacy' one step further.

When in 1933 the Festival Theatre's sometime director Norman Marshall took over the Gate, a small membership house in London's Villiers Street, he took with him several Cambridge Festival Theatre personnel, including composer Geoffrey Wright, choreographer Hedley Briggs and the author–comedienne Hermione Gingold – 'out of whose grey detachment application appears' – and in 1934 closed his first subscription season with a revue called *This Year Next Year*. The revue orchestra comprised two pianos. There was no chorus and the cast, headed by Hermione Gingold as (among other things) the Carnival Queen of Golders Green, numbered six, including Max Kirby, outstanding in an absurdist critique of free trade. Briggs created an original

4. *The Gate Revue* (1939)

small ballet, 'The White Negro'. The critic for the *Observer*, lauding the show's 'raids upon the ridiculous' and air of 'brisk conversation in select company', noted that in 'darkening times' when triviality was rampant, 'the theatre ought to be a vehicle of sharp social criticism'. In general it was not, but in revue it started to be so.

This first of four increasingly successful year-long revues at the Gate, which introduced the sharply satirical talents of the husband-and-wife team Diana Morgan and Robert MacDermot, paralleled what had been happening at the nearby Little Theatre (both theatres were destroyed in the same bombing raid in 1941). There, with minimal staging and piano music – often by another Festival Theatre graduate, Walter Leigh, laid on a basis of razor-sharp sketches, typically by Herbert Farjeon, another repertory group focused upon Hermione Baddeley and Cyril Ritchard was wreaking havoc upon sacred cows.

The key year for the Gate and Little theatres – and the future of revue – was 1938: at the Little one could feast upon *Nine Sharp*, with its songs 'Pulling down London' about soulless reconstruction and 'When Bolonsky Danced Belushka' – putting paid to nostalgia about the days of Nijinsky. The cornucopia of Gate revues was raided, then moved to the Ambassadors, where these revues became *The Gate Revue*. This potpourri, which ran for more than two years (until the 1941 bombing), included the plaintive song 'Washing Up to Shoobert', alluding to radio's current popularisation of the classics, and a melo-dramatic dance, 'Epilogue in Vienna', for Crisham and Alicia Marlowe, a mad dance of death to the wild crashing of champagne glasses, a goodbye to peacetime and (always-gay) Vienna. As the show ran on and war came to Britain, the sketch 'Kensington Girls from Kensington Gore' became more truly biting: in order to support the war effort, these privileged girls wore only the best clothes. Before long a sketch was added that was highly critical of Brits who ran away to Hollywood. In 1939 at the Little, the successor to *Nine Sharp* was *The Little Revue*.

What is important about these 'intimate intimate' revues is their focus, which was narrower in some ways and broader in others. There was no chorus, no orchestra and rarely a song which did not make a satirical point. Dances not for their own sake but to illustrate ideas.

Above all, social and political commentary. The intimate intimate revue was simply more intellectual. Its theatres were even smaller and its audience more select. Now added to the economic slump of the 1930s which was making London theatre-in-general more inward-looking, was the fact that wartime travel would be difficult. Intimate revue – which would survive the bombings, especially when Hermione Gingold and Hermione Baddeley could be paired – was set upon a course which would set it apart from musical theatre.

As the inter-war years ended, the tide of Americanisation had once more ebbed; excepting the intimate revues, escapism was writ even larger than in the First World War. Excepting *Me and My Girl*, Second World War escapism thrived in the large and successful variety houses. Nesbitt began a glittering series for the Palladium's latest entrepreneur, George Black: *Black and Blue, Black Velvet, The Little Dog Laughed*, starring the Crazy Gang. The latter's sketches included the blunders of builders and the decline of the Imperial P(o)int as well as broad burlesque of dictators and queens (in drag). There was even, reportedly, a female performer who danced nude with artistically arranged doves perched upon her person. *The Little Dog Laughed* opened in October 1939 just five weeks after the outbreak of war: it is said that 32,000 people saw the show during its first two weeks.

Notes

1. James Agate, *Immoment Joys* (London: Jonathan Cape, 1943).
2. Liberty's was largely responsible for popularising art nouveau: it also aligned itself with William Morris's Arts and Crafts movement. Its imperialist approach was manifest in the London store's rooftop frieze, depicting goods carried by elephant and camel to Britain.
3. Huntley Carter, *The New Spirit in the European Theatre 1914–1924* (London: Ernest Benn, 1925).
4. From 1897 to 1915 Frohman's productions at the Duke of York's were so successful – including the American play *Too Much Johnson* – that the future entrepreneur Charles B. Cochran wrote a journalistic broadside, 'Too Much Frohman'.
5. Oswald Stoll, who built the London Coliseum in 1904, began his circuit in Liverpool. Horace Edward Moss's empire of Empires – though his London flagship was the Hippodrome built in 1900 – began in Greenock, Scotland. A

former Harrods' accountant, Butt's influence expanded when he took over the Palace in 1904.

6. F. Scott Fitzgerald, *The Crack-up* (New York: New Directions, 1945).

7. Keys, a temperamental veteran of Variety who could play in many comic styles, here proved himself an ideal revue performer. He was the original drawing card for *Buzz Buzz.*

8. As a useful category 'dancing musicals' implies the importance of social dancing – by couples as opposed to choral 'hoofing' – as an integral part of the show. Often the dancing started moments after the curtain rose, as in *So this is Love* (1928) where, at a millionaire's party, the American 'refugee' Hap Hazzard shouts to the assemblage 'Lets dance/any old dance/ but let's hop on your toes!' These productions found favour with audiences craving the latest styles.

9. Librettist Thompson frequently collaborated with George and Ira Gershwin. Grey wrote theatrical lyrics with Gershwin, Youmans and Kern, as well as lyrics for several of the early Hollywood-musical films. Before his career ended he astonished everyone by winning gold medals in the American winter Olympics bobsleigh team.

10. During a forty-five-year career ending in his death in 1957 the apparently nerveless – though personally anxiety-ridden – Buchanan appeared, often with star billing, in nearly forty West End productions and in almost as many films, several of them American.

11. The Herbert–Ellis collaboration began with *Tantivy Towers* (1931), a musical comedy which poked bright fun at the huntin'–shootin'–fishin' classes, and continued in Cochran's 1934 revue, *Streamline.* Herbert and Ellis created, normally from native material, the most successful British musicals of the immediate post-war period, including *Big Ben* (1946), *Bless the Bride* (1947) and *The Water Gypsies* (1954).

12. The Rodgers and Hart *On Your Toes* (1936), with choreography by Balanchine, broke new ground in the use of ballet as an element of the plot. DeMille's choreography for the Rodgers–Oscar Hammerstein II *Oklahoma!* (1943) furthered ballet's function in underlining theme and characterisation.

13. These included *For the Love of Mike* (1931), *Tell Her The Truth* (1932), *Yes, Madame* (1934), *Please Teacher* (1935), *Hide and Seek* (1937) and *Bobby Get Your Gun* (1938) – almost all written by Bolton, Thompson or Grey, all now nominally at home in Britain and recycling their American formulae.

14. Charlot, who had never recovered financially from two disastrous 1926 forays to the United States, spent lavishly on both production values and, uncharacteristically, performer salaries.

15. Both the old and new Gaiety theatres, at 354 The Strand and the Aldwych

respectively, were located precisely at the point where the London worlds of stage, turf, law and journalism converged.

16. *Me and My Girl* was revived in 1985 and once more achieved a lengthy run.

17. The Crazy Gang resulted from the fortuitous combining at the London Palladium in 1931 of several double acts; Chesney Allen and Bud Flanagan, singers and stooges; 'anarchists' Jimmy Nervo and Eddie Knox; and dialect comics Charlie Naughton and Jimmy Gold. With the subsequent addition of compère Eddie 'monsewer' Gray, the Gang specialised in surreal interruptions from the wings or from the audience. The durable, soft-shoe dancing-and-singing Flanagan and Allen were memorialised in a musical about their lives, entitled *Underneath the Arches* (1982).

5   Errant nymphs: women and the inter-war theatre

MAGGIE B. GALE

all that incredible pre-war period when things seemed in the main still settled, just moving solidly and calmly like a glacier towards all sorts of progress. But we have had the bottom of things knocked out completely, we have been sent reeling into chaos and it seems to us that none of your standards are either fixed or necessarily good because in the end they resulted in this smash up.[1]

The woman of today ... gives expression to one of the cultural tendencies of our time: the urge to live a completer life, a longing for meaning and fulfilment ... The woman of today is faced with a tremendous cultural task – perhaps it will be the dawn of a new era.[2]

The social and economic changes incurred by the First World War were, to some extent, significant for women more than for anyone else – short hair and the sporty lithesome boyish figure became fashionable as did the shorter skirt, make-up, jazz dancing, cigarette-smoking and, importantly, the possibility of economic independence. The First World War economy meant that women had joined the traditionally male workforce in large numbers, moving from 'private' service industries to public ones, working, for example, in munitions factories or on the land. When the war was over demobilised working-class women were expected to return to domestic service – there was no Unemployment Benefit Scheme arranged for them.[3] However, many women refused to return to the low-paid drudgery of the pre-war years and instead went into the new industries or into shop and office work where trade union pressure – which had removed women from engineering, printing and transport industries after the war – did not have the same impact.[4] Women were generally paid less for doing the same work but they nevertheless had a new kind of economic power unknown to their Victorian predecessors. Their new-found economic power provided lower middle-class women with more leisure pursuits and it was this, combined with the seeming popularity of theatre as entertainment among these women, which so worried numerous theatre critics of the age. For a time it was fashionable for theatre critics to adhere to the fearful view that the theatre was somehow being overtaken by women, that theatre was becoming feminised.

Flappers in the stalls and flappers on the stage

> in the War-time theatre . . . the ruler of the roost was the half-baked, over-heated flapper. Damn her . . . flappers in the stalls wanted to see flappers on the stage.[5]

For some commentators of the age it was the female audiences who were disrupting the easy flow of male hegemony in theatre. Writing of the inter-war years Ernest Short felt that the audiences had become 'dominantly feminine', a trend which had begun around the turn of the century, and that it was now the case that women 'determine the sort of play the public wants'. He was even prepared to suggest that 'By the 'twenties and 'thirties, not only did two thirds of a typical London audience judge plays from a feminine angle, but a goodly proportion of them judged them from the standpoint of very young women.'[6] Comments such as these perhaps reveal far more about the nature of the critic's own prejudices than about the actuality of audience make-up, yet Short was not alone in his analysis. St John Ervine, critic and journalist, even went so far as to suggest that the play,

> now became chiefly the recreation of women . . . women
> enormously prevail among playgoers . . . if we were to judge the
> division of the population by the people in the theatre,
> especially those of them who stand in queues, we might
> pardonably suppose that there were at least ten women in this

country to every man. This disparity is apparent in every part of
the theatre, from the stalls up to the gallery, and its effect on the
drama must be profound . . . the woman's theatre is likely to be
the recreation of a single sex and *that* will kill it.[7]

Ervine's anxiety, originally aired in the *Morning Post* during the mid-
1920s, had been absorbed by other commentators on the state of
theatre in London. After suggesting that 'broadly speaking, the theatre
lives on women', and that women's new earning capacity gave them
easier access to theatres, the *Era* then proposed that

> men are falling away from the theatre and we are faced with the
> prospect of the male playgoer becoming extinct. The Fair Sex
> are faithful and devoted adherents of the theatre, but with every
> appreciation of their support an all-woman audience is not
> conducive to the interests of the drama.[8]

And some six years later, again in the *Era*, we find the comment, 'the
theatre has obstinately survived because women like going to the
theatre. And they always will.'[9] Yet by 1935, the 'dawn of the feminine
influx', was once again seen to have 'altered everything in the
theatre'.[10] For some, women used theatre as an 'uncritical escape from
their daily lives', a 'regular dream-hour off'.[11] Certainly it would not be
too cavalier to suggest that the large numbers of plays which used
women's lives as the narrative drive – and these were written by men as
well as women – were written with a female audience in mind. Even
less commercially oriented intellectuals and modernist writers, like
Nathalie Barney and Virginia Woolf, were to some extent aware of an
emerging women's market.[12] Certainly, St John Ervine would have us
believe that during the late 1910s, and early 1920s, 'Gallery Girls'
caused havoc by way of showing their appreciation of their female
idols. For Ervine:

> their capacity for emotional excitement was almost
> inexhaustible. Wild eyed young women, hysterically greeting
> favourites on the stage or in the auditorium, threatened to make
> every first night in London a riot . . . These girls, ignorant of any
> art of the theatre, worked themselves into a highly nervous

state on seeing an actress fling herself violently about the stage or roar her head off in an attempt to portray passion . . . Briefly but disturbingly, they agitated the theatre . . .[13]

The female enthusiasm for star actresses like Tallulah Bankhead was matched by the numbers of young women wanting to enter the stage profession as actresses and performers. Auriol Lee, who directed a number smash hits in the West End during the early 1930s, remarked that she had, when first moving into production, been 'absolutely devastated by the enormous crowd of girls with stage aspirations . . . tempted into schools of dramatic art and then let loose with nowhere to go'.[14] Similarly, in 1928 Sybil Thorndike is reported as giving a warning to young actresses not to be attracted by 'mushroom success' or by the 'Spirit of The West End', but to go instead for a variety of work, training 'on the road'.[15] This aspiration to perform that prevailed among women did not, it would seem, limit itself to the so-called 'legitimate' theatre but encompassed variety and musical theatres. One critic complained that 'the stage is now invaded by young ladies who can sing a little and dance a little in the all-pervading revue'.[16] There were numerous all-female orchestras as well as 'special acts', such as female ventriloquists, among the performers who frequented the stages of London's theatres during the inter-war years, and although, like many of the female playwrights of the era, these women were often accused of being 'oncers', many of them found continued success with their audiences. Whether or not these audiences were as predominantly female as the popular press of the time suggested is not verifiable. Such suggestions of 'womanised' audiences may simply reveal more about the fear of female economic power and social independence than anything else. Nevertheless, just as 'woman' as signifier was culturally problematised during the 1920s and 1930s, there seems to have been a significant amount of gendered disturbance to the male hegemony and status quo in the various theatres of the day.

Disappearing women

Kerry Powell has suggested that Victorian actresses such as Elizabeth Robins, Cicely Hamilton and Harriet Jay, all of whom moved into playwriting, were able to do so because of their close connection with 'powerful men in the theatre'.[17] He also points to the fact that during the 1890s playwriting became a more remunerative and therefore attractive trade. Similarly, many of the women who found success in the West End theatres of the inter-war years as playwrights had begun their professional theatre careers as actresses: I am thinking particularly of Clemence Dane, Dodie Smith, Gertrude Jennings, Joan Morgan and G. B. Stern. This is not the only thread which links women working in the inter-war theatres with those of the Victorian and Edwardian eras. Many whose early careers involved them with 'radical' organisations such as the Actresses Franchise League (AFL), or with small independent theatres, women like Gertrude Jennings, Auriol Lee and Irene Hentschel, later found success in mainstream commercial theatre. So we have a new generation of playwrights, trained as actresses, with significant experience of performance in professional theatre, who used playwriting as a vehicle for expression. Thus, in a market economy where a woman's position as actress set her in competition with other out-of-work actresses all looking for employment in a newly popular and lucrative trade, the move into a position of actually writing roles and not having to compete for them was a wise one. That many of the women playwrights had begun their professional lives as actresses may also have been a contributing factor to the predominance of female characters in their plays – why write more roles for actors when there were already many more for them than for actresses. Similarly, for these playwrights the move from enactor of text to creator of text represented a challenge to existing traditional roles for women in the process of making theatre: women playwrights were not a new phenomenon, but during the 1920s and 1930s they seem suddenly to have appeared in large numbers.

We only ever find brief mentions of such women in theatre histories of the time – often they are grouped together as 'women' rather than through an analysis of the nature or quality of individual achievement.[18] Even theatre historians of our own age continue to ignore the enormous impact which women's creative work had on theatre between the two world wars. Contemporary critics continue to privilege male dramatists over female: the positioning of the woman playwright as exception promotes what John Stokes has called 'an underestimation of the effect that sheer success – popular, commercial – was to have in changing women's status in theatre in the 1920s and 1930s'. As Stokes goes on to remark, 'Introduce the names of Dodie Smith and Molly Keane . . . and women's contribution to twentieth century theatre begins to look rather different'.[19] Recent feminist theatre critics have been too quick to assume the non-existence of 'important' plays by women during the 1920s and 1930s, the argument being that there were only 'occasional' plays which dealt with the 'women's question' and that theatre which 'linked feminism and aesthetics ceased to command its own space'.[20] There has been a tendency to look only to the cultural margins where it has been assumed that women are more likely to flourish, certainly in terms of play-writing. Of course, cultural production within a commercial system has inherent problematics and this is significant for the feminist historian. Even so, re-marginalising the already marginalised is equally problematic. Either way, in order to avoid what Sue-Ellen Case has named the 'suppression of the tradition of women playwrights',[21] the context of cultural production needs to be taken into account but should not necessitate automatic dismissal.

Although the overtly feminist AFL had disbanded by the beginning of the inter-war period, its professional membership continued to seek and to find work in theatre, both commercial mainstream and independent alike. Similarly, feminism changed in both context and shape after the First World War and yet the 'women's question' was an ever-present one during the inter-war years: it fuelled discussion in the popular press of the day and among theatre critics and playwrights alike.

In 1933, St John Ervine claimed that at least fifty women had had plays performed in London since 1900. It is likely that the number is higher in the light of the fact that there was an explosive increase in the numbers of new plays or adaptations produced on the London stage during the early decades of the twentieth century. Over the period from 1918 to 1939 there is a considerable variation, ranging from around sixty-six plays and/or adaptations in 1918 to around 307 in 1931. The maximum is at least three and a half times the minimum. The average percentage of plays by women or female/male teams (it was very popular for plays to be co-authored in this way) over the whole 22-year period is 16 per cent – figures for the London season of 1989–90 set the average at just over 10 per cent.[22] Over the 22-year period as a whole, the percentage is 18 per cent or more. Over the same period the percentage of female or female/male team-authored plays which ran for 101 performances or more is higher than for male authored plays on ten out of the total of twenty-two years. Just as with male playwrights of the era, critical reception did not always correlate with box-office success. But with the women, critics often alluded to the fact that they were 'amateur' or 'one-hit wonders': they were merely dabbling in the world of the professional playwright. If the critics and historians saw the inter-war women playwrights as some kind of 'breed', it was also assumed that they served the interests of a certain type of audience. The woman playwright, and by implication the female audience member, was usually referred to as having a penchant for sentimentality and domestic plots: the woman playwright was 'renowned' for the humour with which she treated the machinations of middle-class life, for the wealth of romance in her plays and for her seeming lack of social critique. Ervine makes the claim that most of their work took the form of comedy, claiming that women 'are less apt at drama than men, and they cannot cope with tragedy', and that having 'forced' their way into an essentially male domain, they have created a theatre which men 'have no wish to enter . . . and increasingly abstain from'. Ervine also alludes to the collapse of tragedy as a dramatic form, blaming this on women's penchant for writing comedies.[23] Wherever the truth lies on this matter, women playwrights held a fairly consistent place during the period in question, and there is no overall drop in the figures for the number of plays by women that were produced in the West End until the late 1950s.

It was relatively unusual for any playwright to have his or her plays first reach production in the mainstream commercial theatre during the inter-war years. A less historically obscured playwright like Dodie Smith, who first wrote plays under the name C. L. Anthony, provides one of the few exceptions to the general rule, as all her plays saw their first productions under commercial West End managements. Smith had a sequence of West End hits in the 1930s, but had fewer

London productions of her plays than a number of other female playwrights of the time, many of whom had their plays produced in independent theatres later transferring into the West End. Taking into consideration the female and female/male, to male ratio of productions, women actually fared proportionately rather well in a theatre system where there was an influx of new plays by new playwrights. Over the period, for example, three or more of the plays by Clemence Dane, Gertrude Jennings, Margaret Kennedy, Aimée Stuart, Dodie Smith, Fryn Tennyson-Jesse and Joan Temple, ran for fifty-one and in many cases, more performances – and this does not include the many West End stage successes of their American female contemporaries. Many plays by women were made into films or later, into television dramas. Other novelists and playwrights such as Gordon Daviot, Dorothy Massingham, G. B. Stern, Dorothy Brandon, Vera Berringer, May Edgington, Naomi Royde-Smith, Kate O'Brien and Margot Neville also had numerous London productions of their plays. The limitations of periodisation inhibit the inclusion of figures such as Esther McCracken, Molly Keane (M. J. Farrell) and Lesley Storm who found great success with London productions of their work from the late 1930s into the early 1950s. Plays by women did not 'dominate' the London stage during the 1920s and 1930s as the fearful critics would have had us believe, but they have a fairly consistent and significant place, which may be the reason behind the male uproar – for a good number of the women in question were not simply what St John Ervine had named 'oncers', and appeared to be fast becoming permanent fixtures. Plays by women appear on average to have run as long as those by men and thus were 'safe' investments for managements. Interestingly, during the Second World War there were fewer productions of plays by women but they were more popular. If one can assume that there were fewer men around leading up to and during the war, it is possible to assume that the women left behind who went to the theatre were more inclined to go and see plays by women.

Woman as problem

The so-called 'woman question' underpinned many of the narratives within plays of the era, whether authored by men or women. The

1920s and 1930s witnessed what for some was seen as a crisis in femininity and masculinity – social gender roles were no longer clear, economic power within the domestic sphere was no longer necessarily held by the male and marriage was not the only alternative for a woman living at home with her parents. The popular press at times seemed to be obsessed with the 'flapper' – in general terms an independent young woman with 'loose morals' labelled as 'selfish' because of her wish to fulfil her own desires rather than to find immediate satisfaction through marriage and family. At the same time the papers were full of articles about the problem of 'surplus' women, originating from the fact that for a time the population was predominantly female because of the numbers of young men killed in the war. The press also periodically carried articles about the impending 'petticoat government', both revealing and fuelling an overt cultural fear of women receiving political power.[24] This was not new – any possibility of extending the franchise to women had always created waves of anxious and misogynist journalism – nor was it at this point particularly an attack aimed at 'feminists' but more an attack on women's independence in general.

During the 1920s and 1930s psychoanalysis and the more populist sexology hosted and procured debate on the 'nature' of man- and womanhood.[25] Rooted in these debates are justifications of perceived gender differentials – males as active and females as passive. It is in the work of sexologists like Havelock Ellis and Edward Carpenter that we find such notions as 'female frigidity' and 'manly women'.[26] Women psychoanalysts joined in the debate, but challenges to such suppositions were rare. One such challenge came from of Karen Horney, labelled by a number of contemporary feminists as biologically essentialist, whose work on feminine psychology challenged the 'phallocentric metapsychology that dominated in the 1930s'.[27] Horney emphasised the sociological causes of sexual difference and 'feminised' psychoanalysis by reflecting the 'wounding of the devalued daughter and the hope for a new woman . . .'. [28] It is this emphasis on the sociological and cultural which can be found in many plays by women of the era: playwrights like G. B. Stern, Aimée Stuart and Clemence Dane placed a heavy significance on social and environmental causes of sexual difference, following on from their Edwardian counterparts like Elizabeth Baker and Githa Sowerby. Equally, playwrights of the age, both male and female, picked up on new ideas and trends around the issue of sexual and marital relationships that were popularised by writers like Marie Stopes.[29] One new trend was that marriage should be an equal partnership in which both men and women had a right to expect sexual and emotional fulfilment. One of Marie Stopes' biographers has suggested of the critical reception of Stopes' overwhelmingly popular *Married Love* that although,

> the chapters on sexual love naturally provoked the most interest and comment, Marie's attitude to freedom in marriage was just as radical . . . [she] advocated that both husband and wife should be free . . . and asserted that marriage could never reach its full stature 'until women possess as much intellectual freedom and freedom of opportunity within it as do their husbands'.[30]

Stopes was heavily criticised by the press and the medical profession for the openness with which she discussed sexual matters in her early work. Yet she was besieged by letters from both men and women thanking her for the way in which she had helped them to understand their own and each other's needs with more clarity.[31] Whether or not professional bodies disapproved of her work, questions of sexual and marital relationships became very much part of popular discussion.

Many playwrights of the age picked up on this new cultural mood. In her hit play of 1926, *The Constant Nymph*, based on her best-selling novel, Margaret Kennedy's heroine Tessa Sanger is a very young woman who is in love with her father's composer friend Lewis Dodd – played in the original production by Noël Coward.[32] When, after the death of her own 'musical genius' father, Dodd leaves the Sangers' bohemian homestead to be married to her socialite cousin, Tessa is heartbroken. She is sent to a boarding-school from which she escapes to find Lewis unhappy in his new relationship with a woman who wants to parade him as a 'catch' rather than to share in the making of his work. Tessa, in contrast to her cousin Florence, does not want to mould Lewis but loves him as he is, sullen, broody and musically talented – just like her father before him. To a modern audience, this narrative seems somewhat old-fashioned, especially when Tessa's tragic death occurs after she and Lewis 'elope' at the end of the play. In context, however, Kennedy clearly proposes two different kinds of relationship, one which bears all the hallmarks of middle-class respectability, the other based on free love and artistic bohemianism. The latter proposition is all the more acceptable to an audience because it is at one and the same time romantic, modern and yet tragic. Miles Malleson's discourse on modern relationships in *The Fanatics* was in fact far more radical for its day, and it was with some amazement that critics noted its licence by the then all-powerful but rather inconsistent censor. Malleson's play, which ran in the West End for 313 performances, included, among other things, indictment of the church, frank talk about birth control, sex outside of marriage and a 'disrobing' scene. The play is an open critique of the generation who fought the war and points the way to a new generation for whom the battle is different. As the son tells his father:

> Because I don't want to live as you've lived, I'm lazy; because Gwen wants to live, not exactly as her mother and grandmother lived, she's mad or wanton! Good God in heaven!! If there's one way that's been proved wrong it's your way! If we lived exactly as you lived, it'll all happen all over again.[33]

The transformation of modern domestic (heterosexual) relationships brought discussions of sexual and emotional fulfilment for both sexes into the popular press and the public domain. In 1935, Michael Egan's *The Dominant Sex*, which ran for more than six hundred performances, has two couples experimenting with their relationships. One couple have lived together before marrying, the other try an 'open relationship' which ends in divorce. Egan's couples are ordinary lower-middle to middle class, not the bohemian artists of Kennedy's play. Here the relationships are born of a desire to be modern and equal and although in the end the couple fail to agree as to whether they should move to a farm (his ambition), or the 'all-electric' estate of Blissboro (her wish), much of the play is spent pondering gender difference in terms of the needs and expectations within marriage.

DICK: ... the problem between every pair of people is to – to – help fulfil each other's needs ... most women go wrong to-day, trying to imagine they have the same needs as men and forgetting their own real needs. Every man ... wants *his* woman to fulfil herself completely –

ANGELA: (*smiles*) 'His' woman. Possessive case.[34]

In contrast, authors who dared to broach the subject of same-sex relations between women did not fare as well as Miles Malleson, who suffered just a few imposed cuts to his text – their plays were simply banned. Aimée and Philip Stuart wrote numerous hits for the West End during the inter-war years, yet their play *Love of Women*, about two women writers who live together in Sussex and create a hit play which brings them and their relationship into the public eye, was banned because of supposed intimations of a lesbian relationship. The Lord Chamberlain's reader reported:

> Lesbianism is never mentioned but it is obvious that this is what the gossip implies and Brigit's parents fear ... The girl Jaqueline's advance is lesbian, but that could easily be cut out ...[35]

The play was independently produced by Margaret Webster for the Repertory Players at the Phoenix Theatre in 1935, but it remained banned, even though the authors wrote to the censor with the comment that their intentions fell 'entirely on the side of conventional morality'. Lady Violet Bonham Carter's letter to the censor's committee points out that cutting references to lesbianism within the play would undermine the plot, and considering the censor had freely licensed Mordaunt Shairp's *The Green Bay Tree* it would appear that there was a lack of clarity as to whether all plays which mention or imply homosexuality should be automatically banned.[36] Aimée and Philip Stuart's plays invariably privileged female over male characters, and the development of overt discussion of women's relationships in terms of their own sex is an interesting one, because it acknowledges women's non-heterosexuality as well as 'non-stereotypical sexuality' in terms of contravening the boundaries of family relationships, as when Nicky discovers that his mother is also a *sexual* being outside of her relationship to the family in Noël Coward's sensationalist play *The Vortex*.[37]

During the inter-war years women's relationship to the economy, to history and to culture in general changed with vehement speed. The war had enforced very real changes in the social–economic position of middle-class women, for whom work now took place in the public as opposed to the private domain. When the franchise was granted in 1918 to men over 21 and selected women over 30, 5.5 million women remained without the vote until 1928 – and it was these 'disfranchised women who haunted the public imagination'.[38] Social attitudes to marriage and partnership and to the nature of the family unit also changed beyond recognition. Many plays of the era reflect the need to process these changes in women's lives, the problematising of womanhood, through the placing centre-stage of those changed lives – albeit in the form of the well-made, essentially middle-class, play.

Organising and producing the show

I think that one can say that women mean more in the theatre today than ever before. Women have mustered up the courage and energy to get out and work . . . Rejane, Bernhardt, Ellen Terry and in recent years Lena Ashwell have done so much for the theatre. Not only were they great artists but they were managers with policies of their own and a great understanding of business . . . There was a time when women met on the stage only as actresses, competitors . . . now they are getting into the business side; they understand stage-management, producing and décor and there is a greater spirit of camaraderie about.[39]

Women's position within the power or ownership structures of theatre, especially the commercial theatre, did not change greatly during the inter-war years; it was a system largely controlled by men – men were at the centre of the power bases and at the centre of the decision-making processes in most cases. But a significant number of women were in secondary or tertiary positions of power. So, for example, Kitty

Black, who had worked for the theatre giants H. M. Tennent Ltd, alludes to the fact that successful women literary agents were not uncommon, naming women such as Margery Vosper, Joyce Weiner, Helen Gunner and Dorothea Fasset who 'were all leading figures on the London scene'.[40] The *Era* carried an article in 1928 announcing the appointment of Miss Violet Fairbrother to the directorship of the Royal General Theatrical Fund, praising the powers of women's administrative capacities and pointing out that the Actors Association had made use of women as administrators long before the franchise and that it was from their ranks that 'many of the leading spirits of the Actresses Franchise League emanated'.[41] Thus, even within the gender hierarchies of the mainstream commercial system, there was room for mobility from secretarial to management roles within the administrative areas of production.

Prior to the First World War a number of women had been instrumental in setting up the successful management of the early repertory theatres; Annie Horniman in Manchester, Lady Gregory in Dublin and Madge McIntosh in Liverpool are particular cases in mind.[42] A number of women had been instrumental in the establishment and running of small theatre companies effectively part of the circuit of independent or Little Theatre Movement which thrived in London and elsewhere, especially between the wars. Beatrice de Leon's work at the Q Theatre in Kew, London, was integral to the developmental shape of the London stage. She encouraged and taught young actors and new playwrights – many of whom went on to later stardom – as well as those who were already finding work in the London theatres. New plays often opened at the Q Theatre or ended their performance run there after a long run in the West End. Because of the nature of the theatre system during her time at the Q Theatre, her management skills required a great sense of adventure and willingness to take risks. Just as de Leon had originally been an actress, so too Lena Ashwell began her career as an actress, was a very active member of the Actresses Franchise League and was instrumental in the formation of the British Drama League. After working with a company of actors during the war, producing 'concerts at the front', she returned to the

London theatre scene with her company, the 'Once a Week Players' which then became the Lena Ashwell Players. In an 'effort to establish civic recognition of the theatre', she and her company played town and church halls around the country and in East London before settling at the Century Theatre in Notting Hill.[43] The company organised a society, the Friends of the Players, which at one point had 2,160 members, branches in several centres and a small magazine that out-lined future events. One feminist historian has criticised Ashwell for her comment, when promoting the necessity and establishment of a National Theatre, that 'in this country there are a number of men who could write remarkably fine plays did they see the slightest possibility of their production'.[44] For Hirshfield, Ashwell's choice of wording is a sign of the 'surrender' to the 'truism' that 'playwrighting was a *male* vocation'.[45] However, this diverts our attention away from the validity and historical significance of Ashwell's prolific production of plays by both sexes. Ashwell, like many of her colleagues, moved away from overt gender issues in theatre production toward class and social issues after the First World War.

There were numerous other women who managed theatres during the inter-war years, among them Violette Melnotte, who owned and ran the Duke of York's Theatre, and Gladys Cooper who ran the Playhouse as actress-manageress in association with Frank Curzon, in the early 1920s.[46] When these women are mentioned by their contemporary (often male) theatre chroniclers it is rarely to praise the quality of their work, but rather to make some comment about personality, or quirky and unusual living arrangements. Thus Melnotte is consistently called 'curious' or 'unsavoury' by one com-mentator,[47] or de Leon is called 'tough and unsentimental' – there is always some way in which their behaviour is framed as somehow 'unfeminine', untypical of a woman. Practitioners like Lilian Baylis at the Old Vic and Edith Craig at the Leeds Arts have been reclaimed to an extent by feminist historians.[48] Others, such as Nancy Price, are beginning to re-emerge as important and innovative figures in theatre history. Price was another actress-turned-manager who began her acting career in 1899 and played literally hundreds of roles, directing some eighty-seven plays during her lifetime. With J. T. Grein she founded the People's National Theatre (PNT) in 1930. The PNT was based successively at the Fortune, the Duchess, the Little and the Playhouse theatres. Through her theatre and its members' magazine Price disseminated many of the ideas and influences of innovative European theatre practitioners, encouraging experiment and the production of plays by foreign authors (which were unlikely to bring commercial gain), as well as catering to current West End tastes and vogues for such things as historical costume dramas. She produced more than fifty plays in seven years.[49] There still exist very few detailed studies of the work carried out by such women as de Leon, Ashwell and Price who, through their desire to have some kind of control over the sort of theatre work with which they were involved, and their desire to expand the repertoire of British theatre, moved from the position of employee to that of employer.

Women directors whose work was achieved either inside mainstream commercial or outside political categories of theatre history are also poorly documented. This is partly because 'director' as a term was not as familiar as the nomenclature 'producer' – women (along with men of the day) are often listed as having produced a play when actually they were, in all probability, doing the same tasks as we might expect of a director today. So, for example, we know that Dodie Smith coproduced with Basil Dean, and as she trained as an actress it is likely that she took on a directorial role – this is suggested in her autobiography and may be the reason that the two seriously fell out.[50] However, some women directors have managed to sustain a presence through time: Irene Hentschel, for example, trained at the Royal Academy of Dramatic Art and joined the Lena Ashwell Players as actress and director after 1918. Her many West End productions included Priestley's *Eden End* (1934) and *Time and The Conways* (1937), and Aimée Stuart's *Jeannie* (1940). She worked in both the mainstream commercial theatre and on the independent circuit, was known for her direction of classics, and also at one point worked at the Shakespeare Memorial Theatre in Stratford-upon-Avon. Hentschel identified the value of women as directors and producers claiming that women had a more suitable psychological disposition to bring to the work, especially with regard to working with women.[51] Margaret Webster, another actress turned director, appeared on the stage as a young child performer in the famous 1924 production of *The Trojan Women* alongside Sybil Thorndike, and worked in both Ben Greet's and J. B. Fagan's companies. Productions of classics such as *Othello* (1943) starring Paul Robeson, which broke box-office records for a Shakespeare production on Broadway, made her reputation as a director. Webster's two autobiographies reflect, albeit in a very personalised and anecdotal manner, the depth and range of her prolific directing career and her strong desire to take theatre into new venues to audiences for whom theatre was ordinarily a luxury, but she has not as yet been reclaimed to any great extent by feminist theatre historians.[52]

Another of the great unsung women directors of the age was Auriol Lee, who had worked as an actress for Edith Craig. Lee not only played an enormous number of stage roles, but was one of the most prolific directors of her time. She directed many West End hits during the 1920s and 1930s and was praised in particular for her productions of John Van Druten's plays. For Van Druten she was a very fine director, from whom he learned a great deal.[53] Engaged as a director by Hitchcock at Elstree studios in 1932, Lee spent her later years in America and became an American citizen. She died in a car crash in 1941. In his autobiography *Playwright at Work*, Van Druten praises Auriol Lee but gives us little insight into her style or method of direcing. Unfortunately, this is the case with the work of many of the theatre women of the period who, although seemingly feared by those critics who saw them as taking over the theatres of the day, have left only vague traces of their work as directors, whereas many women playwrights of the age have their work preserved through publication, and by performance in both commercial and amateur sectors. As play-reading and play-acting had become popular pastimes, prolific playwrights like Gertrude Jennings fared well from the amateur market and copyright income. Their success and achievements went far beyond what A. B. Walkley had once claimed was work typical of women who intend to write a play on the 'very next wet afternoon'.[54]

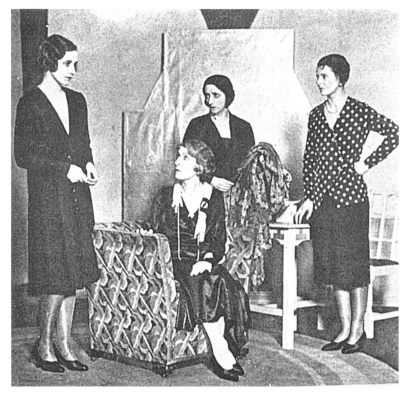

5. Auriol Lee's production of Aimée and Philip Stuart's *Nine Till Six* (1930)

The inter-war years saw women strongly influence the development of both British mainstream and independent theatre movements.
Many women were involved with both, finding success as performers
in the West End, and producing plays within and outside London. It
would appear that women flocked to the theatres of the day both as performers and as audience members. This was not especially because the
theatre suddenly became a more 'respectable' trade than the middle-
classes had once perceived it. Rather, a cultural shift which enabled
women to move further away from the private sphere also relied consistently on an active discourse around the question, meaning and significance of woman as a sign. The theatre appeared, alongside the
novel, to be a location in which this cultural shift could be played out,
but live on stage as well as in the imagination.

Notes

1. Naomi Mitchison quoted in Joanna Alberti, *Beyond Suffrage* (London: Macmillan, 1989), p. 222.

2. Carl G. Jung, *Aspects of the Feminine* (London: Ark, 1989), pp. 56–75.

3. Robert Graves and Alan Hodge, *The Long Weekend: A Social History of Great Britain 1918–1939* (London: Hutchinson, 1989 (1940)), p. 44. Deidre Beddoe notes that it was considered an outrage that middle-class women should go without servants when there were plenty of women newly out of work after men had returned from the war wanting their jobs back. Deidre Beddoe, *Back to Home and Duty* (London: Pandora Press, 1989), pp. 48–51.

4. See Miriam Glucksman, 'In a Class of Their Own? Women Workers in the New Industries in Inter-War Britain', *Feminist Review* 24 (1986), pp. 7–37, and Robert Graves and Alan Hodge, *The Long Weekend.*

5. F. Vernon, *The Twentieth Century Theatre* (London: Harrap & Co. Ltd., 1924), pp. 220–1.

6. Ernest Short, *Sixty Years of Theatre* (London: Eyre and Spottiswoode, 1951), p. 325.

7. St John Ervine, *The Theatre In My Time* (London: Rich and Cowan, 1933), pp. 127–39.

8. 'Applause and the Audience', *Era*, 24 February 1926, p. 11.

9. 'Women Are Loyal to the Stage if the Stage is Loyal to Women', *Era*, 1 June 1932, p. 20.

10. James Bulloch in interview with Margaret Rowland, *Era*, 11 December 1935.

11. John Carey, *The Intellectuals and the Masses* (London: Faber and Faber, 1992), p. 87.

12. Bonnie Kime Scott, *Refiguring Modernism: the Women of 1928: Vol. 1* (Bloomington: Indiana University Press, 1995), p. 232.

13. St John Ervine, *The Theatre in My Time*, p. 140.

14. Auriol Lee, 'Women in the Theatre: Talk with Miss Auriol Lee, *Era*, 12 March 1930, p. 9.

15. 'Fame at the Footlights', *Era*, 25 April 1928, p. 11.

16. 'Applause and the Audience', *Era*, 24 February 1926, p. 11.

17. Kerry Powell, *Women in Victorian Theatre* (Cambridge University Press, 1997), p. 81.

18. Ernest Short, *Sixty Years of Theatre*, pp. 325–37.

19. John Stokes, *Theatre Notebook*, vol. LII: 1 (London: Theatre Research Society, 1998), pp. 53–5.

20. Michelene Wandor, *Carry On Understudies* (London: Routledge, 1986), p. 3.

21. Sue-Ellen Case, *Feminism and Theatre* (London: Macmillan, 1988), p. 44.

22. Ellen Donkin, *Getting into the Act* (London: Routledge, 1995), p. 188. For full details of inter-war production runs see Maggie B. Gale, *West End Women: Women and the London Stage 1918–1962* (London: Routledge, 1996), p. 12.

23. St John Ervine, *Theatre in My Time*, p. 136.

24. Billie Melman, *Women and the Popular Imagination in the Twenties: Flappers and Nymphs* (London: Macmillan, 1988), pp. 15–37.

25. Lisa Appignanesi and John Forrester, *Freud's Women* (London: Virago, 1993). For a succinct synopsis of the basic arguments with Freud over the 'question of woman', see the chapter 'The Dispute Over Woman', pp. 430–54.

26. See Sheila Jeffreys, *The Spinster and Her Enemies: Feminism and Sexuality 1880–1930* (London: Pandora Press, 1985); Sheila Rowbotham, *A New World for Women: Stella Browne, Socialist Feminist* (London: Pluto Press, 1977), Jeffrey Weeks and Sheila Rowbotham, *Socialism and The New Life* (London: Pluto Press, 1977).

27. D. H. Ingram, ed., *Karen Horney: Final Lectures* (New York & London: W.W. Norton, 1991), p. 124.

28. Marcia Westkott, *The Feminist Legacy of Karen Horney* (New Haven: Yale University Press, 1986), pp. 64–5.

29. Marie Stopes, *Married Love* (London: A. C. Fifield, 1918). For a discussion of Marie Stopes play *Our Ostriches* (London: Putnam, 1923), see Maggie B. Gale, 'Women Playwrights of the 1920s and 1930s; A Lost Generation and the "Woman Question"' ed. Elaine Aston and Janelle Reinelt, *The Cambridge Companion to British Women Playwrights* (Cambridge University Press, 2000).

30. June Rose, *Marie Stopes and the Sexual Revolution* (London: Faber and Faber, 1993), p. 117.

31. See Lesley A. Hall, 'Impotent Ghosts from No Man's Land, Flappers' Boyfriends, or Crypto-Patriarchs? Men, Sex and Social Change in 1920s Britain', in *Social History*, 21:1 (London: Routledge, 1996), pp. 54–70.

32. Margaret Kennedy, *The Constant Nymph* (London: Samuel French, 1930). The play, adapted from the novel by Margaret Kennedy by Basil Dean, ran at The New Theatre for 387 performances from August 1926. See Basil Dean, *Seven Ages* (London: Hutchinson, 1970), pp. 313–31.

33. Quoted in Hannen Swaffer, 'Should *The Fanatics* Be Banned', *Sunday Express*, 20 March 1927, p. 5. See Miles Malleson, *The Fanatics* (London: Ernest Benn, 1924). The play ran for 313 performances from March 1927.

34. Michael Egan, *The Dominant Sex*, in *Famous Plays of 1934–1935* (London: Victor Gollancz Ltd, 1935). pp. 184–185.

35. Lord Chamberlain's Collection, 'Love of Women' 1934/14, The British Library. The script of *Love of Women* had been removed temporarily from the file at the time of writing.

36. *Ibid.*

37. Noël Coward, *The Vortex* in *Coward: Plays One* (London: Methuen, 1995), pp. 95–175.

38. Billie Melman, *Women and the Popular Imagination in the Twenties: Flappers and Nymphs*, p. 1.

39. 'Women in the Theatre: Talk with Miss Auriol Lee', *Era*, 12 March 1930, p. 9.

40. Kitty Black, *Upper Circle* (London: Methuen, 1984), p. 219.

41. 'Actresses and Administration', *Era*, 28 March 1928, p. 11. Interestingly, the article also calls for the Variety Artists Association, as the only society without women on its Executive, to open their doors to them in haste.

42. See S. Gooddie, *Annie Horniman: a Pioneer in The Theatre* (London: Methuen, 1990); Augusta Gregory, *Our Irish Theatre: a Chapter of Autobiography by Lady Gregory* (London: Colin Smythe, 1972); R. Pogson, *Miss Horniman and The Gaiety Theatre Manchester* (London: Rockliff, 1952) and G. Wyndham-Goldie, *The Liverpool Repertory Theatre 1911–1934* (London: Hodder & Stoughton, 1935).

43. Lena Ashwell, *Myself a Player* (London: Michael Joseph, 1936), p. 243. See also Ashwell's *Modern Troubadours* (London: Gyldendal, 1922).

44. Claire Hirshfield, 'The Woman's Theatre in England: 1913–1918', in *Theatre History Studies* 15: (June 1995), pp. 123–37.

45. *Ibid.*, Hirshfield is quoting from *Era*, 18 June 1919, p. 13.

46. W. Macqueen-Pope, *The Footlights Flickered: the Story of the Theatre of the 1920s* (London: Herbert Jenkins, 1959).

47. *Ibid.*, p. 37.

48. See Katherine Cockin, *Edith Craig 1869–1947: Dramatic Lives* (London: Cassell, 1998) and Roberta Gandolfi, 'Edy Craig and Community Theatre in the 1920s', *Women and Theatre Occasional Papers 4* (University of Birmingham, 1997), ed. Maggie B. Gale and Viv Gardner, pp. 18–34. See also Gandolfi, 'Edy Craig and The Suffrage Theatre' in *The Open Page: Theatre, Women, Politics* (Denmark: Odin Theatret, 1998), pp. 54–9, and Vera Gottlieb and Robert Gordon, 'Lilian Baylis: Paradoxes and Contradictions', in *Themes in Drama 11: Women and Theatre*, ed. James Redmond, (Cambridge University Press, 1989), pp. 155–77.

49. See J. P. Wearing, 'Nancy Price and the People's National Theatre', *Theatre History Studies*, 16 June 1996, pp. 71–89.

50. Dodie Smith, *Look Back with Astonishment* (London: Allen, 1979).

51. *Daily Express* (Theatre Museum London, cutting dated August 1937).

52. See Margaret Webster, *The Same only Different* (London: Gollancz, 1969) and *Don't Put Your Daughter on the Stage* (New York: Knopf, 1972).

53. John Van Druten, *Playwright at Work* (London: Hamish Hamilton, 1953), p. 5.

54. Mrs Patrick Campbell, *My Life and Some Letters* (London: Hutchinson, 1922), p. 237.

6 Blood on the bright young things: Shakespeare in the 1930s

TONY HOWARD

One theatre in London – called the Old Vic – gives performances of Shakespeare's plays constantly. Some of these are done well, and many of them are done badly. The people who keep the commercial theatre going give it the miss – dont care a damn about it; and the theatre is always in a bad way financially. The bare truth is that Shakespeare is nor wept nor sung nor honoured in his own country. As for the workers, it may be said that they never come into touch with Shakespeare from the cradle to the grave.

(Sean O'Casey: letter to the Writers Union of the USSR, 31 May 1939)[1]

Though not yet dead, the Victorian Shakespeare tradition was collapsing. Tyrone Guthrie, brought up in Northern Ireland, said people in the regions felt 'contempt' for mainstream English Shakespeare – 'Nothing in it but empty ranting and roaring'[2] – and when Oscar Asche revived *Julius Caesar* (His Majesty's) in the old Beerbohm Tree style as late as 1932, the revue writer Herbert Farjeon was appalled by the Lawrence Alma-Tadema sets and 'vestal virgins', the melodramatic tableaux starring Portia and Calpurnia, and the starry cast 'mesmerised by the sound of their own voices'. It was 'awful Shakespeare' personified.[3] Taste had changed too much for younger men to reinvigorate the actor-manager system; in the early 1930s Ernest Milton and Baliol Holloway both built West End seasons around their bravura performances in the traditional outsider roles – Shylock, Othello, Richard III – but lost small fortunes.[4] However, the vogue for radical experiment which in the 1920s had led to Barry Jackson's modern-dress Shakespeare at Birmingham and Terence Gray's iconoclastic Cambridge productions was also threatened. The Wall Street stockmarket crash of 1929 created an insecure society with little space for self-conscious games with classical drama, and even companies run, like Gray's and Jackson's, by idealists with private fortunes felt the pressure.[5]

The Old Vic was the only year-round classical theatre. Given its philanthropic origins, founded to fight drunkenness and cultural poverty in South London, there was, as O'Casey said, a tendency to patronise it. Its charter called for inexpensive performances (cheap seats at the price of a pint of beer) 'suited for the recreation and instruction of the poorer classes'[6] – lectures, music and 'high-class drama, especially the plays of Shakespeare'. Since the outbreak of the First World War its legendary manager Lilian Baylis had run a three-weekly Shakespearean repertory company to meet 'the crying need of working men and women who want to see beyond the four walls of their offices, workshops and homes into a world of awe and wonder'.[7] But it was chronically underfunded, successes were not exploited, and houses were often thin. During the Depression the Vic's loyal public was especially vulnerable – for instance, audiences shrank when teachers (a key element) had their wages cut after the 1931 financial crisis – and, on the other hand, fashionable support was untrustworthy. When John Gielgud's electrifying first *Hamlet* transferred from the Vic to the Queens Theatre in 1930, the cheap seats were full but the stalls were empty. Later transfers were equally unsuccessful, like Tyrone Guthrie's famous 'Victorian' *Dream* (1937), which attracted huge press interest when the young princesses Elizabeth and Margaret saw it (part of the post-Abdication drive to publicise their family's common touch), but failed disastrously in the West End.

Despite all this, in 1930 there were brief hopes for a revival of commercial Shakespeare. Gielgud's was one of three *Hamlet*s running simultaneously in the West End, and this vogue was directly linked to a taking-stock of the First World War's legacy. The producer C. B. Cochran, who had just presented O'Casey's devastating *Silver Tassie*, invited Alexander Moissi's *Hamlet* from Germany, while

Maurice Browne funded a series of classics out of his profits from *Journey's End*, including Gielgud's anguished young prince, who became as much a symbol of a lost generation as the shellshocked youths of R.C. Sherriff's play.[8] One of Browne's 1930 productions towered over the other tentative attempts to connect Shakespeare to modern concerns: this was *Othello*, with Paul Robeson, at the Savoy. However, the problems Robeson experienced shed light on the difficulty of relating Shakespeare to the contemporary world in 1930s London.

Robeson hoped to use Shakespeare to make a bold call for equality: 'Othello is a tragedy of racial conflict',[9] he said; the Negro in modern America was Othello's brother, his sudden psychological collapse was caused by racism and alienation. But whereas Robeson was lionised here in Eugene O'Neill's plays and in *Showboat*, he found himself confronting English racism when he trespassed on Shakespeare. He was disconcerted when the press asked 'how the public will take to seeing a Negro make love to a white woman and throw her around the stage'. 'Ever so many people have asked me whether I mind being kissed in some of the scenes by a coloured man', said Peggy Ashcroft (Desdemona), 'and it seems to me so silly. Of course I do not mind! It's just necessary to the play. For myself I look on it as a privilege to act with a great artist like Paul Robeson.'[10] But Robeson's confidence was thrown. He was incompetently directed (by Browne's wife, who specialised in puppet shows), badly supported (Browne cast himself as Iago), and hampered by underlit, misconceived sets which tied the actors to the very back of the stage. Robeson was objectified and expected to play the Primitive – they wanted him to enter singing – and although his unique popularity attracted a new audience it was unwelcome: 'One London editor walked out during *Othello*', Hannen Swaffer reported, 'because there were Negroes around him in the stalls.'[11] Unconscious racism littered the reviews: Herbert Farjeon praised Robeson's 'intelligent' comments on the play – plus his authentic 'thick lips' – but said he must know he was unfit for Othello: 'Shakespeare wrote the part for a white man.' James Agate described Robeson's hands hanging below his knees, his aura of apology ('the inferiority complex'), and called it 'Nigger Shakespeare'.[12]

Actually Agate believed white actors (e.g. Ernest Milton) were too intelligent to convey the 'childish' mind of this African 'King of Beasts', whereas Desdemona proved her own 'fragility of intellect' when she decided to 'choose a darkie'.[13]

Shakespearean stereotypes would come to stalk the thirties: in 1937 London papers carried stories that Franco paid his African mercenaries by 'letting them loose', with the horror headline 'Moors and White Women', while Jewish refugees from Hitler found the English expected them to be 'noisy and hysterical, shouting and wheedling like Shylock'.[14] Meanwhile, the metropolitan Establishment did not know how to cope with Paul Robeson precisely because his very presence jolted Othello out of the safety of aestheticism and into their unstable world.

British theatre generally worked hard to insulate the plays from off-stage realities. O'Casey said: 'The Bright Young Things . . . found . . . [Shakespeare] heavy going, and kept him at a safe distance; while the sober group, the Angry Young Men, blew themselves up into a tapertit revolt against capital and convention, and so had no time to pluck a leaf from Shakespeare's laurels.' He claimed he wandered across England, fruitlessly searching for productions worth telling Russia about.[15] Meanwhile, English fascists had their own complaints: Mosley himself liked to quote *Henry V* on the betrayal of heroes, and his disciple A. K. Chesterton railed against the 'Nancies' who were fouling British theatre. He shuddered to think of 'the English beauty of a Shakespearean play translated into Esperanto and acted by stuttering Levantine Jews'.[16] It was a time of great developments in Shakespearean acting, direction and design, but the results were as contradictory as the divided age itself. As Malcolm Muggeridge wrote, 'Every generation gets, as well as the statesmen, the Shakespeare it deserves.'[17]

'It's no distance from the Savoy!': Granville Barker and the Old Vic inheritance

Where British Shakespeare is concerned, the thirties began on 27 August 1929 when Harcourt Williams began rehearsals for *Romeo and Juliet*, his first production as director of the Old Vic.

There was catching up to do. Williams wanted to realise the ideas Edward Gordon Craig and Harley Granville Barker had developed long before, relaunching the revolution that stopped when the Great War ended Barker's Savoy Theatre experiments. Craig and Barker were Williams' backstage mentors. Craig encouraged him – 'The producers are going to save the English stage, and have already begun . . . all we need is unity' – while Granville Barker warned him it would be difficult: 'The Old Vic has been too highly praised.'[18] On a modest scale, Williams combined Barker's attention to Elizabethan theatrical values (the *Prefaces to Shakespeare* began to appear in 1930) with Craig's sense of space, form and metaphor: for the *Dream* (1929), he ditched Mendelssohn and used the English folk-song settings from Barker's production while Craig designed a key element of the set, a horseshoe rostrum – Puck's 'dimension in space'. The whole design was defiantly stylised, including a bunched-curtain forest, a silver sky, and an immense flight of steps for the lovers to race on. Craig's son Edward Carrick co-directed a *Macbeth* (1932) with masked witches and giant shadows.

Barker provided constant advice and criticism, insisting that the priority was to develop 'a common method of speaking verse' – 'Don't be so damned explanatory'[19] – and the breakneck verse-speaking in *Romeo and Juliet* provoked baffled outrage. After the second unpopular production Williams offered to resign, but Baylis supported him and the response improved with the swift lyricism of the *Dream* and the emergence in *Richard II* of John Gielgud as an extraordinary classical star. Gielgud (Craig's cousin) praised Williams' 'Elizabethan productions which preserved the continuity of the plays by means of natural and speedy delivery of the verse, and light and imaginative settings allowing quick changes of scene'. They were practical, economic – and 'revolutionary'.[20]

Harcourt Williams' Old Vic was an actors' theatre and an historic forcing-house of talent. Helter-skelter, Gielgud played Romeo, Oberon, Hotspur, Prospero, Macbeth, Richard II, Hamlet, Antony and Lear. He stayed for two years and was succeeded by Ralph Richardson (1930–2: Caliban, Enobarbus, Bottom, Iago, Brutus, Henry V) and Peggy Ashcroft (1932–3: Imogen, Portia, Rosalind, Juliet). Lyrical, intense and passionately spoken, Gielgud's Hamlet and Ashcroft's Juliet, which she also played in two Gielgud productions, became the most iconic Shakespeare performances of the early 1930s. Like Richardson, Gielgud regularly contributed casting and production ideas and in 1932 Williams invited him to direct *The Merchant of Venice*. This was a defining moment, first because Williams wanted to introduce a guest-director policy, reducing the pressure on himself and allowing for more distinctive 'conceived' productions, and secondly because the *Merchant* established Gielgud as a major director. Theatrically speaking, indeed, this became the Gielgud decade; he and his revolutionary design team Motley would dominate British Shakespeare until the late 1950s.

It was not easy to launch revolutions in an impoverished theatre where one 1935 production allegedly cost precisely £10. At Stratford-upon-Avon the budget for Theodore Komisarjevsky's 1932 *Merchant*, including his fee, was £800,[21] whereas Gielgud worked for nothing so that everything went into the production; even so, *Romeo*'s design budget was only £90 and he could only afford to attend five rehearsals.[22] But graceful and inventive poverty became Motley's hallmark. Literally creating clothes and sets out of rags, rope and hessian, they put 'a sort of Three Arts Revel' on a virtually bare stage: 'Portia comes now as an eighteenth-century Arcadian shepherdess, now as a Victorian sylphide. Bassanio comes as a jockey.' Visually, an actor in bright magenta dominated the scene: the fact that he was playing Solanio, notoriously one of the feeblest parts in Shakespeare, was a typical in-joke.[23] 'Here for the first time in my limited experience', said Tyrone Guthrie,'was a Shakespeare comedy which was not heavily and boringly trying to be funny, but was instead elegant and witty, light as a feather, and so gaily sophisticated that beside it Maugham and Coward seemed like two Nonconformist pastors from the Midlands.'[24] Catching the escapist spirit of the time, it was hugely influential. Guthrie echoed it with a masque-like *Love's Labour's Lost* (Westminster Theatre 1933) – spoken and almost danced before a simple background of tents and wrought iron – which also prompted Noël Coward comparisons. It led Baylis to invite Guthrie to take over the Old Vic.

There was an intriguing crossover. Gielgud's matinée-idol status allowed him to take his aesthetic into the West End. Working with the producer Bronson Albery and the strongest possible casts, he mounted increasingly ambitious projects: his 1934 *Hamlet* made £50,000 profit and led to a record-breaking Broadway production; in 1935 he alternated Romeo and Mercutio with Olivier; and *Richard II* and the *Merchant* (1938) were part of his legendary Queens Theatre ensemble season.[25] Reflecting Gielgud's own skills and temperament, their success helped to ensure that in the thirties' imagination 'Shakespeare' meant youth and lyricism. Meanwhile, however, Tyrone Guthrie's approach at the Old Vic was not at all what Baylis had expected.

The Old Vic's reputation was based on nurturing talent, but Guthrie built the 1933–4 season around established young stage and screen stars – many of them startlingly anti-romantic, like Charles Laughton – and a remarkably strong group of women including Athene Seyler, Flora Robson and Elsa Lanchester. Across Britain, working-class audiences were abandoning theatre and the third-rate experience of 'the gallery' for the cinema; to Baylis' distress, Guthrie was the first to exploit the movies as a source for talent, publicity and a broader public. He later brought in Olivier, Robert Donat and Emlyn Williams – the latter already famous for *Night Must Fall* – who all effectively subsidised the theatre in exchange for training and prestige. In 1929 Gielgud earned £10 a week at the Old Vic, a fifth of what the West End paid him; by 1937 Olivier (£20) was used to £500 a week in Hollywood. The Old Vic's traditional way of attracting new audiences was through 'missionary work' (regular performances in the East End) and London County Council schools matinées (which Harcourt Williams insisted must feature the regular casts, not understudies),[26] but Guthrie thought the Vic was dowdy – 'animated pictures in a Shakespeare lesson book' – and was determined to increase the audience through quality and excitement. Yet what really underlay these casting choices was Guthrie's pursuit of emotional realism.

Guthrie was a rationalist and a Freudian. His programme note for the Laughton–Robson *Macbeth* was a modernist manifesto: 'Surely the grandeur of the tragedy lies in the fact that Macbeth and Lady Macbeth are ruined by precisely those qualities which make them great . . . All this is undermined by any suggestion that the Weird Sisters are in control of the events.' So he cut Scene One. Guthrie was fascinated by the unconscious (he was annoyed by Laughton's reliance on inspiration not technique, but it was why he cast him) and his actors kept pushing the Macbeths into states of mental distortion. She seemed drunk before the murder; in the Cauldron scene he babbled like a possessed medium. Agate protested that Laughton and Robson were unfitted for tragedy although, or rather because, they were 'fiercely intelligent' – once again analytical thinking was seen as anti-Shakespearean[27] – and they were also emotionally, physically and socially outsiders to the Grand Tradition. Guthrie's choice of Olivier was equally controversial because his Romeo – whom he called a boy with conkers in his pockets – had been condemned for bad verse-speaking. Olivier's startling behavioural realism is obvious in Paul Czinner's *As You Like It* film (1936) where he physicalised Orlando's love with tiny details; for example his fingers took on their own life, toying obsessively with Rosalind's locket. Olivier's twin careers in classical theatre and film exemplify the unique double training which members of his generation experienced. This and the sudden impact of Chekhov, Stanislavsky and Freud equipped them to dominate Shakespearean theatre all their lives.[28]

Guthrie and his actors made Shakespeare sexual. Emlyn Williams' Richard III was a 'pervert whose senses faint with ecstasy' at the thought of each new crime. Olivier's Oedipal *Hamlet* (1937) was the most famous Freudian performance of the century. Guthrie also (and he was not alone here) suggested connections between 'evil', 'tragic weakness', and homosexuality: he and Olivier adopted Ernest Jones' reading of Iago as a suppressed homosexual, and *Richard II* (George Hays; Stratford-upon-Avon, 1933) became 'weak, effemi-nate'.[29] Guthrie's repertoire was fairly adventurous: whereas Harcourt Williams thought audiences would reject *Measure for Measure*, Guthrie made it the Old Vic's keynote play. In 1933 Laughton's 'horri-ble'[30] Angelo was his greatest success, and T. S. Eliot told *The Times*, 'Even those whose principles prevent them from approving either the subject matter or the profoundly Christian spirit of the play might profit [from] seeing it so well performed.' But Guthrie's dearest faith was iconoclasm and in 1938 he travestied Eliot's reading by surrounding Emlyn Williams' golden-haired, angelic, 'effeminate'[31] Angelo with grotesque religiosity. Vienna was a cathedral square populated by tiers of nuns wearing bizarre conical wimples and mock-Reinhardt crowds throwing up their hands in orchestrated pleas for mercy. In both productions of his *Measure for Measure* Guthrie downgraded the Duke; throughout, the stress was psychological, emphasising Angelo and Isabella's horrified awakening to 'corruption'.[32]

Masques and pastorals

Guthrie's innovations seemed peripheral – they were usually called 'stunts' – because most mainstream Shakespeare was about escapism. In 1936 alone, Edith Evans (*b.* 1888) played Rosalind triumphantly, the filmstars Anna Neagle and Jessie Matthews both played actresses playing Rosalind (in *Peg of Old Drury* and *First a Girl*), and *As You Like It* became the first full-length British Shakespeare film, with script supervision by J.M. Barrie. Paul Czinner and Elizabeth Bergner (Rosalind) were refugees from Hitler's Germany; in an English studio they constructed a fantasy haven packed with medieval palaces, some geriatric acting styles, Olivier, and sheep. Shakespearean comedy took audiences out of time. The Vic's 1934 *Much Ado* was a collage of Elizabethan men, Gainsborough ladies, piratical villains and a backcloth of chimney pots and cats with watches (for the Watch): 'These mixed costumes remove the play from any definite time and place and make it what it really is – a masque.' At the new Shakespeare Memorial Theatre (opened 1932), Theodore Komisarjevsky made actors move like clockwork toys in carnivalesque versions of *The Merchant*, *The Taming of the Shrew*, *The Merry Wives of Windsor* and *Comedy of Errors*. Launcelot Gobbo led a harlequinade through a Venice populated by today's 'dissipated, fast, bright young people'.[33] His Ephesus was a polychromatic Toytown with comic policemen and pink nuns, and wardrobe-loads of period-annihilating costumes wrenched the plays out of any social reality. Stratford expanded its season to fill the summer – in the thirties Shakespeare meant summer – and the *Dream* became a permanent fixture there and on an another new Shakespearean stage, the 3,000-seat Open Air Theatre, Regent's Park (1933).

Regent's Park opened with Robert Atkins' stylised 'black and white' *Twelfth Night*. Farjeon mocked the idea that lolling in a deckchair listening to voices blaring out of loudspeakers was somehow a return to the Globe experience: 'I feel myself further away from Shakespeare than I do indoors', he said. 'The characters seem more like puppets than people.'[34] But Atkins had staged the entire canon at the Old Vic and was genuinely searching for ways of recapturing what he saw as the plays' original directness and popularity. He deliberately included urban and political plays (*Henry VIII*, *Richard III*, *Julius Caesar*, etc.), so the Park's early repertoire was more ambitious than it has ever been since. He included rarities like *Pericles* and went outside Shakespeare for verse drama from Jonson's masques and Milton's *Comus* right up to Goethe's *Faust*. The credo was a kind of poetic patriotism: here was 'Beautiful English – beautifully spoken', and some critics called it the National Theatre in all but name.[35]

Shakespeare meant music there, often courtesy of Phylis Nielsen-Terry singing interpolated ditties – whether as Viola, Olivia or Oberon in a flower-like tall crown and huge cloak. And Shakespeare meant continuity – Neilsen-Terry, Baliol Holloway and others kept traditional acting styles alive next to interesting newcomers like Jack Hawkins and Vivien Leigh (Anne Boleyn). The quintessential Regent's Park actor was Leslie French, whose Puck and Ariel symbolise the Park's inter-war spirit more than any other performance. Puck became a witty and seductive faun, summer carnival incarnate. He parodied the lovers, entwined himself between them, leaped and dived miraculously (courtesy of hidden trampolines), and popped out of the ground. Ariel, at the opposite extreme, was an alien spirit that moved too slowly for the eye to register. French's inspiration was Njinsky, and balletic interludes were the last vital ingredient of Regent's Park's success. In fact the entire decade tried to marry Shakespeare and dance. At the Old Vic there were eurythmic battles for *Cymbeline* and *King John*; Ninette de Valois provided a full *corps de ballet* for the Vic's pastiche Victorian *Dream*, which launched Robert Helpmann's career as a Shakespearean star; and Benjamin Britten scored second elaborate masques for *Timon of Athens* (Westminster Theatre, 1934). The dancer Nini Theilade was the star of Max Reinhardt's only English Shakespeare, an open-air *Dream* at Oxford University, and Guthrie's comedies too were about choreography, pace and pattern.

The triumph of Shakespearean pastoral was Stratford-upon-Avon's emergence as one of the world's great tourist centres. The old Stratford theatre had burned down in 1926; the governors, led by the Flower family (the Vic was founded to fight drunkenness, its rival was built by brewers) raised sufficient international funds to replace it in six years. Designed by Elizabeth Scott, the modernist 'British Bayreuth' opened on Shakespeare's Birthday/St George's Day, 1932. It was instantly a patriotic symbol. At the ceremony Stanley Baldwin quoted *The Times'* claim that the building heralded a new dawn 'at a moment when England herself seems to be waking anew to a consciousness of her own worth and a confidence in her own future', and shamed those Leftists and intellectuals 'abnormally inarticulate about our country' and 'too proud to fight'. The BBC broadcast the events and followed them with a 'special' production of *Henry V*, and the Prince of Wales flew in to proclaim 'Shakespeare was above all an Englishman'.[36] (He left half way through the play.) The building itself has blighted British Shakespeare ever since.

It had a badly designed picture-frame stage in a clinical, cinema-style auditorium. The distant circle and gallery did not curve to meet the stage, there was only a tiny forestage and the actors were cut off from the stalls by a gaping orchestra pit. Stratford's director W. Bridges Adams rejected a thrust stage as 'insanity' – there must be a 'normal' stage,[37] which in the event was framed by a monumental ribbed wooden proscenium arch that visually imprisoned every scene. Baliol Holloway's complaint became famous:

> The acreage of blank walls between the proscenium arch and
> the ends of the circles, coupled with the immense distance
> between the lower edge of the stage proper and the front row of
> the stalls . . . completely destroys all contact between actors and
> audience. It is doubly hard on the actors that the audience does
> not realise this, and is aware only of the actor's comparative
> ineffectiveness.[38]

It was a stage for pictorial Shakespeare, with the most elaborate new scenic resources in Britain; Bridges Adams wanted a 'box of tricks' equipped to satisfy every director from Poel to Reinhardt, but it was incompetently executed. There were rolling stages for rapid scene changes, but not enough wing space for them, and spectacular hydraulic stages, but when they were used the actors on them became invisible from the balcony.

One artist did know how to use the theatre and free the actors. Again the Granville Barker influence is crucial. Norman Wilkinson, who designed Barker's 1914 *Dream* with the golden fairies,[39] was now a Stratford Governor and he returned to the *Dream* for the opening season. His work fused reality and fantasy, past and present in a practical demonstration of the complex possibilities open to modern Shakespeare production. Wilkinson dressed Theseus and the lovers in ornate white Elizabethan costumes, and the palace was a giant engraving of Charlecote Great Hall. He resurrected the 1914 fairies but made them more lyrical – blue and silver – yet up to date, even futuristic, for now they were made of perspex. When the mortals entered the moonlit wood their white garments shone as if they were ghosts or memories of lost innocence, yet the wood itself, a huge tree on a mound, was also unashamedly a set in a theatre in Stratford: the fairies could change the scene in full view by dragging the tree and the rolling stages from side to side. Wilkinson was the greatest Shakespearean designer of the century. Realising the new theatre's drawbacks, he worked to counterbalance them: for *Romeo and Juliet* (1933) he covered the orchestra pit with a forestage and built a tiring-house façade which brilliantly incorporated Elizabeth Scott's proscenium arch and matched her modern decor exactly. Elizabethan streets and formal gardens could be seen in the far-off distance, and thus the actors literally trod a borderline between the audience's world and Shakespeare's. In private, Wilkinson was a desperate alcoholic, shattered by the First World War, but his theatre work celebrated the intricate continuity of beauty across the ages. In 1934 Wilkinson died while designing *The Tempest* and Bridges Adams resigned.

Adams was frustrated by the Governors' refusal to pay higher salaries, to rehearse the plays properly (seven plays always opened in one week, after five weeks' preparation), or to welcome major guest directors: 'As Stratford has decided to go local rather than national, it must stew in its own juice.'[40] Rejecting Bridges Adams' ambitions but without any idea how to make his theatre work, the Board settled for merrie-Englandism. They hired the virtually unknown Ben Iden Payne, whose ambition was to try out archaeological staging ideas inherited from William Poel. He had left British theatre for an academic career in America (to which he would return ten years later, granting Stratford only a page or two in his autobiography) and *Theatre Arts* called him 'a professional amateur'.[41] Payne liked to turn the stage into an imitation Globe Theatre, fill the upper stage with 'Elizabethan' spectators, and have pages open or close a traverse-curtain. Lacking his own theatre, Poel had to work like that in the 1900s; at Stratford now, it was a reactionary and dull approach, but Payne's visual credo was defiant: 'We become corrupted and we lose our real capacity for responding to and appreciating a Shakespeare play if our attention is diverted and concentrated upon scenic investiture.' Shakespeare 'scorned' scenery – 'a shackle to the imagination'.[42]

Which Shakespeare?

Meanwhile there was a counter-revolution at the Old Vic. Baylis had also built a brutalist new Shakespearean theatre, Sadler's Wells (1930), and it was equally disappointing: 'The auditorium looked like a denuded wedding cake, and the acoustics were dreadful . . .'[43] After the huge expense of construction work, both Stratford and the Old Vic wanted to reduce running costs during the Depression, and both fought shy of expanding their small-scale local operations or ending the tradition of parsimony and production-line schedules. So in 1934 they both retreated and brought in low-profile artistic directors whose productions were mostly remarkable for their modesty. Guthrie's contract was not renewed; Henry Cass from Croydon Repertory promised to replace flashiness with 'modern simplified production, good verse-speaking, combined with sincerity and understanding'. Cass and Payne both opened their regimes with *Antony and Cleopatra* as a sign of loyalty to Barker, whose *Preface* established it as the ultimate example of Shakespeare's stagecraft, stretched almost to breaking-point: 'the essential thing' was to 'relate it to the theatre of its nativity'.[44] At Stratford, Bridges Adams' close collaborator Aubrey Hammond disobeyed instructions by designing 'charming pictures' and never worked at Stratford again. Payne then introduced his 'modified Elizabethan staging' but, as Farjeon said, the problem was not the designers: 'The company is mediocre, the acting uninformed by any original or individual force.'[45] The difference between Stratford and the Old Vic was that Baylis recognised her mistakes. She quickly accepted Sadler's Wells' unsuitability for Shakespeare and instead based her opera and dance operations there. Then in 1936 she invited Guthrie back with authority to transform the company's working methods. He ended the three-weekly repertory system so successful plays could run for six to eight weeks and/or transfer, and though Guthrie continued to nurture talent – Alec Guinness rose from Osric to Hamlet – he rarely cast actors for whole seasons. Guthrie's companies looked virtually identical to Gielgud's commercial ones.[46]

In 1937 the philosophical gulf between the Vic and Stratford was symbolised by two productions of *Henry V*. Payne's was an unimaginative celebratory pageant, with Clement McCallin as a type of pre-Raphaelite king with bobbed hair. The designer Herbert Norris copied details from heraldic sources to present 'Henry as he appeared to his countrymen' – affecting such 'fantastic' and 'fashionable eccentricities' as golden bells on his armour as if leading a nation of playboys on a bloodless galliard through France. Bold English scarlet outfaced Gallic peacock blue. With the histories, Payne relaxed his Elizabethanism and became a medievalist instead. This was in keeping with the patriotic spirit of a coronation year (H. V. Neilson's touring company offered the Grand Theatre, Luton, a 'Special Patriotic Night and Coronation Performance' of *Henry V – Henry VII*, the usual choice for royal events, was inappropriate after Mrs Simpson), but the Old Vic offered 'a more adult aesthetic'. A national symbol itself, Stratford embraced colourful patriotism, whereas the Old Vic was always cautious. In the wake of the 1931 crisis Harcourt Williams revived *King John*, a study of bad leadership, and cast Ralph Richardson as a deliberately unpoetic Henry V: 'He was not the Henry that the hero-worshippers wanted. He put a certain hard, almost cruel quality into it.'[47] The theatre was catching up with the critics' attacks on Henry V's moral poverty and especially with Yeats' dismissal of his language as the 'resounding rhetoric' of a 'newspaper editor'. A few months later, when the Oxford Union voted not to fight for King and Country (March 1933), Richardson's restraint might have provoked real controversy.

So when in 1937 Herbert Norris wrote an article calling for orthodoxy – 'No Stunts with the Histories' – Guthrie rejected it: 'As for the question of "stunts", it seems to me excessively timid not to have the courage of one's own ideas.'[48] He initially chose *Henry V* to attack jingoism: Olivier recalled, 'I fought against the heroism by flattening and getting underneath the lines, no banner-waving for me.'[49] They debunked the Church and the Salic Law and underlined Henry's conscience ('He was prowling about the stage trying to make up his mind about the war, and all along thoughtfulness kept breaking in. When Fluellen says, '"As long as your majesty is an honest man", Henry replied, "God keep me so," in low anxious tones'),[50] but they could not find a theatrically valid way to downplay the rhetoric, and when 'bunting started to go off for the coronation, neither of us had the guts to go through with it'. But the creative tensions produced Guthrie's finest pre-war production, a fusion of realism, stylisation, uplift and gravity. Flag-waving actually became the defining image: Motley provided a mass of huge blue, red, and silver banners set at various angles throughout the evening. They moved to reflect and propel the action, folding themselves before Agincourt into tents which dissolved to evoke a 'ragged, hungry army, the nervous "flux and flow" of unattached soldiers . . . a wonderful impression of the bustle and stir of an army breaking camp in the night: with only a handful of actors, a shifting light and no visible scenery Guthrie suggested a whole body of men on the move'.[51] The opulence of France was staged with equal economy: Katherine and Alice were carried shoulder-high in a palanquin. *Henry V* inspired Olivier's film, Guthrie's experiments in open-stage Shakespeare, and a generation of post-war directors for whom narrative values transcended poetics.[52]

'Why doesn't one come here oftener?' Agate reported a 'perfumed' intellectual saying in 1933. 'It's no distance from the Savoy!' Old Vic Shakespeare became fashionable, and then thrilling. But Guthrie's aims went deeper: the home of 'Shakespeare for the People' should now grow into the National Theatre. Stratford-upon-Avon's 1938 season was especially weak. Stratford's greatest leading actor, Randle Ayrton, had retired and his heir Donald Wolfit left to be an actor-manager. Payne himself directed the overworked young company in seven plays out of eight. The *Daily Telegraph* began a campaign against Stratford-upon-Avon's standards and the governors' parochial under-spending. At the Stratford Birthday lunch Guthrie suggested a merger, which would create the National Theatre. In the circumstances it looked like a takeover bid, or the forced marriage of the Vic's talents and Stratford's cash reserves.[53]

'There is a world elsewhere': offstage storms

In 1933 both Bridges Adams and the BBC marked Shakespeare's Birthday with productions of *Coriolanus*. Stratford's version was the first since 1926, when it coincided with the Great Strike and the mysterious fire, and it was spectacular. Anew McMaster's Coriolanus berated the plebs, a battering-ram crashed through the gates of Antium towards the audience, saluting crowds poured up from the bowels of the pit (a common image in English productions of the Roman plays), the hydraulic stages created mountainous stairs down which warriors and eagle standards paraded in triumph. *The Times* wondered why the BBC bothered – 'Wireless is a medium even less kind to this piece than the stage,'[54] – because despite the power of Sybil Thorndyke's Volumnia, it was dreadfully hard to take an interest in battle scenes and the incomprehensible grievances of a 'mutinous Roman mob'. But actually no play offered fiercer comment on the growing schisms in European Society. On 23 April 1933 the trial began in Durham of demonstrators against the means test ('rioters') baton-charged by the police, and in the Midlands Prince George toured refuges for jobless workers. The workers entertained him with calisthenics, allotment-digging, and 'Dear Old Pals', 'the unemployed men's anthem'; he was delighted by the 'cheerfulness of the unemployed' and that night at the dinner of the Society of Saint George, Winston Churchill toasted England, 'Still the best country for the duke or the dustman to live in' (Cheers).

At that moment in a Munich rally Hitler demanded a new German world. The Nazis of course understood the ideological power of art – German radio had just celebrated another birthday, Hitler's, with a day of First World War dramas, including a biographical play presenting Hitler as an *über*-Coriolanus returning from the battlefields to cleanse the nation.

In Paris *Coriolanus'* supposed fascism provoked riots. In Britain its political relevance was self-evident to literary figures on the Right like Yeats and Eliot, but the perceived function of Shakespearean theatre was to proclaim national unity – especially after the 1931 victory of the 'National Government' and the marginalisation of the parliamentary Labour Party – not to analyse conflict. When the veteran William Poel directed *Coriolanus*[55] in 1931, he did evoke the Irish Civil War by casting Abbey Theatre actors in key parts (e.g. Sarah Allgood as Volumnia, Barry Fitzgerald as a Tribune), but as usual destroyed the political debates by making immense cuts, by turning the Tribunes into nasty clowns (Robert Atkins had made them 'hebraic scarecrows'), and by endorsing Coriolanus' heroic self-image: the play ended with him hammering on the gates of Antium, demanding martyrdom. Soon after, Ramsay MacDonald who knew about changing loyalties offered Poel a knighthood. Poel costumed *Coriolanus* in the fashionable kaleidoscopic style with images from the Paris Directoire, society magazines, and military history – the hero appeared both as a Guards officer and a warrior in a leopard skin. Poel's version of the play was dismissed as eccentric. Time and again, Shakespeare seemed not to belong in any real world.

The Old Vic marked Shakespeare's Birthday in 1933 by celebrating its own place in theatrical history. It staged scenes from *The Merchant of Venice* in the styles of 1898, 1933 (Gielgud's production) and an imagined 1999. The skit '1898' featured 'realistic scenery, including a movable (spasmodically so) gondola and a view of the Grand Canal all complete'. The young parts were played by elderly gentlemen whose 'speech was as slow as the "business" was laboured, stage crosses were prevalent, and the "my" was always the short "me"'.[56] Then '1999' was futuristic – a revolving stage, a lift, steel furniture, Ralph Richardson as Shylock doing somersaults, and the Trial rewritten into 'Hollywood-ese'. Harcourt Williams jokingly warned of a future dominated by foreign directors ('1999' parodied Komisarjevsky's *Merchant*) and the American cultural menace, but his choice of *The Merchant* for lighthearted satire was unfortunate.[57] The press was already packed with accounts of anti-Semitic brutality in Germany and Goebbel's 'boycott' of the Jews. Jewish actors were being expelled and a new Aryan repertoire was emerging – including twenty German productions in 1933 alone of *The Merchant of Venice*, now hailed as Shakespeare's 'prophetic' denunciation of Jewry.[58] That week scientists and artists from Julian Huxley to Dame Ethel Smythe wrote to *The Times* calling on the UK to intervene and offer refuge, but the naivety of many British theatre workers was symbolised five months later when anti-Nazi protesters disrupted the first night of Werner Krauss' London debut and his co-star Peggy Ashcroft defiantly shouted them down. Krauss went on to act out the most obscene antisemitic fantasies in *Jew Süss* and (Vienna 1943) to play Shylock as a racial degenerate.

The one Shakespearean director who was palpably aware of the connection between the theatre and the new ideologies was Ashcroft's then husband, the Russian émigré Theodore Komisarjevsky. Bridges Adams hired him for Stratford-upon-Avon directly against his Board's wishes and despite Iden Payne's misgivings he stayed till the war, creating uniquely adventurous bravura productions with minimal rehearsal – he justified them as 'artist's sketches'.[59] His 1933 *Macbeth* confronted the First World War's legacy directly and made the play a Vorticist nightmare with, as in the *Silver Tassie*, a ghastly battlefield dominated by howitzers and peopled by dehumanised steel-helmeted men. The Sisters robbed the dead and read palms, the Ghost was a reflection on scroll-shaped aluminium walls which shone like the actors' oiled skin, and the Apparitions were Macbeth's nightmare. Loudspeakers blared out his voice as he spoke the incantations. Fabia Drake's gypsyish Lady Macbeth slowly froze into horror while George Hayes – 'a soldier under neurotic stress', his face a rictus snarl – rattled out the text like a machine gun. 'I have been accused,' Komisarjevsky said, 'of interpreting Shakespeare's plays from the point of view of a modern man' – but 'the business of digging artistic corpses out of cemeteries doesn't interest me'. He demanded disruptive experiment:

> The quick, impatient modern mind with its syncopated, jumping rhythm is bored by the old 'expositions', 'developments' and 'conclusions' of situations . . . We need, sometimes, in the midst of a scene a flash into the past or the future. We need different actions happening simultaneously in various places on the stage – on the right, on the left, somewhere

high above – accompaniments of 'expressionistic' noises, and of moving lights . . .[60]

So *Macbeth* became a heightened expression of the traumas of war; madness was the product of modern history, and the design, sound and lighting were all meant to forge a direct connection with the subconscious of the spectators who, he said, 're-create in their minds the creative work of my irrational self'.[61] Critics complained that in this labyrinth of horror' Macbeth shrank into a puppet, but that was Komisarjevsky's political statement: he condemned the 'mercenary', 'money-grubbing' society that had created the 'huge-scale human butchery'. Unfortunately, writing in 1934, he also set the corrupt 'liberal' era against the 'all-penetrating genius of Mussolini', the artistic vision of Dr Goebbels, and the brave, violent will-power of the dictators – the 'great individualists' whom he explicitly compared to the director, another 'idealist' who transcended common ethics.

Komisarjevsky called himself 'neither a Jew nor an anti-Jew', but his book *The Theatre in a Changing Civilisation* seemed obsessed with Shylock. He attacked the nineteenth-century German-Jewish actor Bogumil Dawison 'who transformed Shakespeare's comedy . . . into a tragedy and acted Shylock as a leading character . . . Dawison transformed the twisting, comic devil outplayed by Portia into a deceived, noble and emotional Jew, thereby upsetting the whole balance of the comedy and introducing a false social motive.' He condemned Irving for making Shylock a 'refined Jew' and said Charles Coghlan's Shylock was correct – a mere 'Whitechapel Jew'.[62] In his own Stratford *Merchant* he ordered Randle Ayrton to forget the Shylock he had always played ('with pulsating power; here was a man intellectually superior to his adversaries'),[63] and make him an insignificant comic villain to be beaten and forgotten. Other directors might not have understood the political implications of this, but Komisarjevsky did: the engraver Eric Gill's cover design for *Theatre and a Changing Civilisation* showed 'Man, fighting with the twin snakes of War and Usury. These are the powers of evil with which man in the twentieth century will have to settle, or perish.' Komisarjevsky conceded it was 'very sad' that 'many Jews were forced to seek exile or confined in concentration camps. But there has never yet been any mass progressive movement in the history of humanity without bloodshed and injustice.' He dismissed the 'insignificant cruelties': totalitarianism stood for 'youth' and its victims condemned themselves by clinging to outdated beliefs.

Komisarjevsky's folly was an extreme case – Gielgud called his personality inspiring but strangely cruel – but even Gielgud, as late as 1938, played Shylock as a balding, squalid, gummy-eyed wretch, crouched in servility at the noble Christians' feet. He seemed unaware that by rejecting a theatrical tradition (Irving's heroism) he was perpetuating appallingly real racist images which journalists then recycled, itemising his 'ghetto' Jew's 'whining intonations, shuffling gait and snarling venom . . . a mean creature, rancorous and greedy . . . cringing, vengeful . . . he creeps away from the court like a beaten cur, execrated by all' (*Theatre World*). 'At a time when Jews are being driven to mass-suicide by unsurpassed brutalities,' the *New Statesman* commented, 'the spectacle of Shylock's baiting becomes almost unbearable.' It seemed the height of myopic aestheticism, but Gielgud was actually obeying the instructions of Granville Barker, who told him that revealing Shylock as a 'contemptible', 'sordid little outsider' was the only reason for staging the play – which was a fairy-tale, irrelevant to what Barker called '*the Semitic problem*'.[64]

Perceptions sharpened slowly yet the Shakespearean stage began to emerge as it always should be, a public forum. Guthrie kept *The Merchant* out of the Old Vic until the war, when another German-Jewish actor, Frederick Valk, made 'Hath not a Jew eyes' a titanic attack on fascism. In 1935, in a Westminster Theatre season dedicated to 'theatre as a social force', the Group Theatre resurrected *Timon of Athens* and warned its savage 'ideology ' was 'relevant to the present'. The Westminster's adventurous policy constantly linked classics and experimental work: here, alongside Wystan Auden's anti-capitalist *Dance of Death*, was 'Shakespeare's comment on a world which was then beginning, and is now at an end'. Even so, Nugent Monk's neo-Elizabethan staging blurred this message, and in 1936 Ben Iden Payne seemed determined not to make his Renaissance-costumed *Troilus and Cressida* seem too disturbing: this play, 'essentially anti-war in its bias', was 'of *almost* topical interest'.[65] At the time the arguments for patriotism, nationalism, socialism and pacificism were profoundly confused. Unsurprisingly, the work of some artists who did confront the national debates became schizophrenic. Olivier's *Coriolanus* (Old Vic 1938) was a study of 'arrested development' embodying all the military pride and anger he had censored out of *Henry V*: deciding that Coriolanus' sympathetic modesty was out of character, he cut it. The plain production in Renaissance–classical peasant mode was directed by the old socialist Lewis Casson; but a few weeks later, in startling contrast, Casson directed Ivor Novello's tub-thumping and eye-stopping *Henry V* (Drury Lane, 1938) with a cast of 200, and such Irving-esque images as Henry's armoured Court actually sailing from Southampton. Casson believed in continuity, he hoped to marry 'the old school' and 'the new' so, although there was a catalogue of sets in the programme, Craig's son designed them; but Novello's *Henry V* was the last Shakespearean spectacular and the end of an age. Munich killed this 'stirring production that unfortunately centred round the one topic most people were trying to forget'.[66]

Michael MacOwan, who had run the Old Vic School, chose 1938 to stage *Troilus and Cressida* in modern dress at the Westminster. Ulysses became a monocled diplomat, Thersites a bedraggled radical journalist in a mac, and Pandarus, the revue star Max Adrian, tinkled his white baby grand as Trojan Society posed against an empty sky and their twenty-year cocktail party staggered to an end. It had shattering force. In *The Times* Dorothy L. Sayers hailed it as 'the great "war-debunking" play, whose savage bitterness has never been equalled before or since' – 'Modern-dress productions frequently have the merit of restoring the emphasis to the place where Shakespeare put it.' The same year the BBC broadcast the first full-length television Shakespeare production, sensationally it was *Julius Caesar* set in a fascist state. At the Vic, Guthrie directed a modern-dress *Hamlet* with Alec Guinness. Now Hamlet's fight against profound corruption was the core of Guthrie's repertoire (he directed it in 1937, 1938 and 1944) and in January 1939 Shakespeare became central to a pioneering act of modern soft diplomacy when the British Council for Cultural Relations toured *Hamlet* and *Henry V* to Egypt, Greece – and fascist Italy.[67] Many interpreted the Italian visit as abject appeasement. There were protests, leaflets, even suicide threats, but Lewis Casson defended it onstage by appealing to the Old Vic's founding traditions: the plays were 'an offering from the people – not the government – the people who had given the world Shakespeare to the people who had given the world Dante and L. da Vinci (loud prolonged cheers)'.[68] In fact, the pairing of *Henry V* (now starring Anthony Quayle) and *Hamlet* sent out a carefully balanced political warning. Guinness's Hamlet was a quiet intellectual who personified the 'King and Country' generation, summoned to fight by his father's great-coated ghost. Watchful and reserved until the play scene, when blinding arc lights were turned on Claudius, this saddest and gentlest of Princes gradually accepted his role in a just struggle, and was now sent out on to the world stage.[69] When the war began, Henry Cass moved into the West End with another modern-dress Caesar (originally at the Embassy Theatre): Brutus symbolised common humanity revolted by 'the superman', Casca hid behind a languid Bertie Wooster persona, and Eric Portman's opportunist Antony was the true Nazi. *The Times* thought the umbrellas and field telephones helped 'the mind's eye along its natural course' – ' Shakespeare knew what there is to be known about the problem of the dictator.'[70]

In 1940, just before France fell, Guthrie and Casson joined forces to direct Gielgud in a dark and beautiful *King Lear* masterminded by Harley Granville Barker. Harcourt Williams played Albany. Briefly Granville Barker, the so-called 'lost leader', secretly returned from his French home to work with the cast. It was the logical culmination of a long decade. Throughout the 1930s, Shakespeare had crystallised the idea of transition – a hope that to be English was to be in touch with living, lasting values versus a fear that it was to drift between a dead past and a terrifyingly unclear future. Now as the bombs began to fall on Lambeth, it became clear: Shakespeare was their contemporary.

Notes

1. David Krause, ed., *The Letters of Sean O'Casey: 1910–1941* (London: Cassell, 1975), p. 801.
2. Tyrone Guthrie, *A Life in the Theatre* (London: Hamish Hamilton, 1960), p. 85.

3. Herbert Farjeon, *The Shakespearean Scene* (New York: Hutchinson, 1948), p. 128.

4. Edith Evans' *Shrew* (1937) and even Ivor Novello's *Henry V* (1938) failed. The casting of George Robey as Falstaff (1935) was the West End's only major attempt to find surprising talent and a broader public. For reasons of space this chapter concentrates on professional London theatre and Stratford-upon-Avon. This is not to denigrate the importance of, say, Birmingham Rep. and Liverpool Playhouse, the thriving amateur scene, some serious work in schools (O'Casey praised Guy Boas' productions in his essay 'Shakespeare Lives in London Lads'), or the influence of Neville Coghill and George Rylands at Oxford and Cambridge. Both Max Reinhardt and Theodore Komisarjevsky directed for Oxford University Dramatic Society, and Giles Isham and William Devlin's Oxford *Hamlet* and *Lear* were reported as national events which respectively made them Stratford-upon-Avon's and the Old Vic's leading men. (Though Michael Redgrave, who went to Cambridge, said Oxbridge Shakespeare was seriously over-praised.)

5. Barry Jackson's most famous modern-dress Shakespeare productions, the *Hamlet* in plus-fours (1925) and *Macbeth* (1928) which both visited the Court Theatre, had aspired to make them as prosaic, rational and familiar as Shaw. At the opposite extreme, Terence Gray ran the Cambridge Festival Theatre from 1926 to 1933 as an assault on realism inspired equally by Gordon Craig and dance. He honoured Shakespeare's theatre as the pinnacle of imaginative freedom while mocking reverence for the Bard – most notoriously when the Duke in *The Merchant of Venice* yawned and played with a yo-yo during the 'Quality of mercy'. In 1934, a year after Gray gave up, Birmingham Rep. also almost closed when Jackson announced he could no longer support it single-handed; in 1935 it passed to a less adventurous Trust. Graduates of both companies became key figures in the 1930s, from Olivier to Ninette de Valois; Guthrie can be seen as Jackson's heir, Komisarjevsky as Gray's.

6. Quoted in Tyrone Guthrie, *A Life in the Theatre*, p. 100.

7. Lilian Baylis quoted in Felix Barker, *The Oliviers* (London: Hamish Hamilton, 1953), p. 117.

8. For Sean O'Casey the fact that Sherriff did not know *Hamlet* symbolised British cultural poverty.

9. *Observer*, 18 May 1930

10. *Daily Sketch*, 21 May 1930

11. *Variety*, 4 June 1930. However, Robeson remarked that he could not yet play Othello in America. When he did so in the 1940s the director was Margaret Webster, a member of the 1930 Old Vic company.

12. See James Agate, *Brief Chronicles* (London: Jonathon Cape, 1943), pp. 285–7.

13. James Agate, *First Nights* (London: Nicholson and Watson, 1934), p. 91.

14. Austin Stevens, *The Dispossessed* (London: Barry and Jackson, 1975), p. 220.

15. Sean O'Casey, 'Looking Back in 1964', in *Blasts and Benedictions* (London: Macmillan, 1967), p. 31.

16. A. K. Chesterton, *Oswald Mosley* (London: Action Press Ltd., 1937), p. 46.

17. Malcolm Muggeridge, *The Thirties* (London: Collins, 1967), p. 194.

18. Granville Barker quoted by Harcourt Williams, *Four Years at the Old Vic* (London: Putnam, 1935), p. 89.

19. *Ibid.*, p. 15.

20. John Gielgud, *Early Stages* (London: Falcon Press, 1948), p. 126.

21. Initially – but the governors insisted on lowering it.

22. Williams took other rehearsals. He attacked Komisarjevsky's *Merchant* because it only had eight rehearsals (or five – accounts differed).

23. Herbert Farjeon, *The Shakespearean Scene*, p. 53.

24. Tyrone Guthrie, *A Life in the Theatre*, p. 83.

25. Gielgud and Motley searched for increasingly sophisticated and beautiful equivalents to Elizabethan stagecraft, devising composite settings that could lay bare the physical dynamics of each play – e.g. a stepped hieratic set for *Hamlet*, a magic box for *Romeo and Juliet* with hinged walls to create different streets and households. Elegant eclecticism and slim silhouettes marked all Motley's Shakespeare work – and so did a sense of sophisticated revelry, from Capulet's ball in a sort of striped marquee, to a wry, pseudo-Victorian *Twelfth Night* (Stratford 1939: director Irene Henschel) with Olivia and her ladies in prim mourning black.

26. Children saw two-hour versions. Williams tried to get County Hall to vary the set texts and tear up 'the hackneyed list headed by *The Merchant of Venice*'. Gielgud sparked a controversy by arguing that all school trips killed the love of Shakespeare and should be abolished.

27. James Agate, *First Nights*, p. 300.

28. Michael Redgrave wrote earnest articles about Stanislavsky, John Gielgud tried to use emotion memory as Richard II (Queens Theatre) and gave Michel St. Denis sufficient rehearsal time to create a great *Three Sisters* in the same season (St. Denis could not fit his methods into the Old Vic's schedules, causing the near-débâcle of the 1938 Olivier *Macbeth*). St. Denis's *Twelfth Night* with Redgrave and Ashcroft was the first Shakespeare to be shown in full on British television. Theodore Komisarjevsky, another pioneer of British Chekhov, insisted that Shakespeare was an ensemble dramatist and that *King Lear* demanded the same approach as *The Seagull*.

29. *The Times*, 22 April 1933.

30. *Ibid.*, 24 April 1933.

31. Herbert Farjeon, *The Shakespearean Scene*, p. 101.

32. Thirty years later at the Bristol Old Vic Guthrie made the Duke God – he carried a cross and showed Isabella the stigmata. Whether this was serious in intention or elaborate parody was unclear.

33. Theodore Komisarjevsky in the *Birmingham Mail*, 7 July 1932.

34. Herbert Farjeon, *The Shakespearean Scene*, p. 72.

35. See *Theatre World*, September 1937. When the season was financially threatened in 1936, a public fund was set up to support it.

36. In the same ceremony Frank Benson welcomed the internationally financed theatre as a shrine to peace, a guard against world war.

37. *Observer*, 14 January 1928. The 'normal' configuration was a 'Picture Stage' with a 4-foot apron and an 8-foot wide orchestra pit. A temporary 'Elizabethan Stage' could be built over the pit, which could also be turned into a stepped area for a so-called 'Greek Stage': Shakespeare Memorial Theatre, Stratford-upon-Avon: *Competition for Designs for a New Theatre* (privately printed, 1927), p. 4.

38. Quoted in Norman Marshall, *The Other Theatre* (London: John Lehman, 1947), p. 176.

39. Norman Wilkinson was trained in the Arts and Crafts tradition; his aesthetics embraced everything from medieval art to Chelsea Power Station

40. Letter quoted in Sally Beauman, *The Royal Shakespeare Company: a History of Ten Decades* (Oxford University Press, 1982), p. 147.

41. *Theatre Arts*, February 1935.

42. See Ben Iden Payne, 'The Elizabethan Theatre', *Play Pictorial* (April 1936), p. 6. The only advantage he granted modern theatres was 'the suggestive power' of lighting. He hoped to make Stratford an academy for Shakespearean actors, but this was impossible given low investment, cramped rehearsals and no winter season.

43. John Gielgud, *Early Stages*, p. 142.

44. Granville Barker, *Prefaces to Shakespeare* (illustrated edition, London, 1963). vol. III, p. 5. Both productions were transitional. Cass's Antony was played by the idiosyncratic character-actor Wilfred Lawson, who would have thrived with Guthrie but left after a bad press.

45. Herbert Farjeon, *The Shakespearean Scene*, p. 24.

46. For instance Redgrave was Horatio for Gielgud, Laertes for Guthrie, then Bolingbroke for Gielgud again.

47. Harcourt Williams, *Old Vic Saga* (London: Winchester, 1949), p. 116.

48. The influential debate took place in the pages of *Amateur Stage*, 1937.

49. See Laurence Olivier, *On Acting* (London: Weidenfeld and Nicolson, 1986), p. 60.

50. Gordon Crosse, *Fifty Years of Shakespearean Playgoing* (London: A.R. Mowbray, 1941), p. 108.

51. Audrey Williamson, *Old Vic Drama* (London: Rockliff, 1948), p. 90.

52. The toughening-up of Shakespeare was also evident when Robert Atkins staged *Henry V* in a boxing-ring at Blackfriars, close to the Old Vic, in November 1936.

53. As part of his complex intervention in the British drama scene, Granville Barker relaunched the National Theatre project with a book in 1930. He called for a new building with a permanent company and two stages. Gielgud (*Observer* 17 March 1935) said the best scheme would be to endow the Old Vic, Sadler's Wells and Stratford together as the National Theatre: productions could be properly rehearsed, run for a month at each venue, then tour. He linked this to 'the great South of the River Embankment Scheme': the Old Vic should be rebuilt and 'arise, phoenix-like, from its own ashes, on its old site, or near its own site, as the corner-stone of the scheme'.

54. *The Times*, 27 April 1933.

55. Chelsea Palace Theatre (matinees).

56. Harcourt E. Williams, *Four Years at the Old Vic*, pp. 228–9. Granville Barker was appalled by the cultural threat of the American mass media, and by Hollywood Shakespeare. He and Alfred Hitchcock debated this heatedly in *The Listener*. Hitchcock mocked the pretentiousness and little-Englandism of British Shakespeare in *London Calling* (1930), where a pompous stage actor (Donald Calthrop – Granville Barker's Puck) spends the whole film trying to do some Shakespeare. Hitchcock turns 'To be or not to be' and 'Once more unto the breach' into ludicrous conjuring acts packed with rabbits and Union Jacks and the *Shrew* into a custard-pie fight. More typically, Warner Brothers paid lip-service to English cultural superiority by sending out busts of Shakespeare to be displayed in cinemas showing the Reinhardt *Dream*, and the British romantic film melodrama *Men Are Not Gods* (1937) reaffirmed it by showing a wisecracking American journalist falling rapturously in love with an English actor the moment she hears him speak Shakespeare.

57. That same day the Jewish Congress in Warsaw denounced Nazi atrocities and begged Britain to ease emigration to Palestine.

58. John Gross, *Shylock* (London: Chatto and Windus, 1992), p. 294.

59. 'Those conditions make me feel keen on doing my incomplete "sketches" there and saying through them what I think I ought to say to the public, as an

artist and a citizen of the commonwealth.' Theodore Komisarjevsky, '"Russian" Productions', *Play Pictorial* (April 1936), p. 10.

60. Theodore Komisarjevsky, *Myself and the Theatre* (London: Heinemann, 1929), p. 150.

61. Theodore Komisarjevsky, *The Theatre and a Changing Civilisation* (London: John Lane, 1935), p. 23. He sought a subliminal blending of 'meaningless elements' and 'elements which were rationally real, and even familiar to the spectator' to make the tragedy 'stand firmly on a basis of real life' but project 'into the eternity of time'.

62. *Ibid.*, p. 102.

63. The phrase is from T.C. Kemp, the *Birmingham Post* critic.

64. Quoted in Granville Barker, *Prefaces To Shakespeare, Vol. 4*, p. 119. Barker made the 'sordid outsider' comments in a 1937 letter to Gielgud; see pp. 323–4 of the 1963 edition. See *New Statesman*, 7 May 1938.

65. *Play Pictorial*, April 1936, p. 16 (a Stratford issue prepared with Payne's co-operation). [Emphasis mine] 'This, doubtless, was the basis of its popularity in Germany during the years of disillusionment prior to the advent of the Nazi regime.' *Play Pictorial* implied the play – a study of 'wantonness' – was less relevant in a clean post-Weimar world.

66. *Theatre World*, November 1938.

67. The elaborate tour also included some modern English plays – set texts – and classic comedies (e.g., Shaw, Priestley).

68. Letter written by Guthrie on the eve of the tour, quoted in James Forsyth, *Tyrone Guthrie: a Biography* (London: Hamilton, 1976), p. 169. Ironically, conservatives feared that showing a modern-dress Hamlet abroad would prove England's decadence.

69. In return Greece sent a *Hamlet* to London, and the Old Vic's next exchange was with the Comédie-Française. The Vic now was the national theatre.

70. *The Times*, 30 November 1939. After the war Henry Cass made a shortened *Julius Caesar* film for schools. In the 1960s he directed propaganda for Moral Rearmament.

7   The religion of socialism or a pleasant Sunday afternoon?: the ILP Arts Guild

ROS MERKIN

In June 1925 the Independent Labour Party (ILP) launched 'one of the most promising developments' in its history, the ILP Arts Guild, 'a revolt against the ugliness and monotony of modern industrialism and a seeking after beauty and a fuller life'. In truth, much of the party's work, since its foundation in January 1893, had already shown that it saw its search for socialism as a seach for beauty, for 'the spirit of liberty' and as a 'spiritual crusade'. In the early days of the party, Keir Hardie had announced that 'socialism is much more an affair of the heart than of the intellect', and a symposium held in 1924 displayed a parade of members who defined socialism in precisely the same terms, as a 'fraternity of comradeship', as 'something greater than an economic doctrine as 'an ethical-religious mass movement', a 'true brotherhood'. In the words of one member, 'our politics may be right and our economics sound, but unless we have caught the vision we shall fail, for where there is no vision the people perish'.[1] Now, to find this vision, the actor and playwright Miles Malleson, serving as director of the Guild, was to be enlisted as a missionary touring the country, spreading the spirit of William Morris anew. More pragmatically, the Guild was to co-ordinate and extend the already existing ILP dramatic groups and offer skilled help and advice; the best societies would be invited to perform at the Strand Theatre, run by ILP member Arthur Bourchier. The skilled help was to come from those members of the acting profession who sent messages of support to the new movement, including Lewis Casson, Sybil Thorndike, Laurence Housman and Edith Craig. Support was also apparent from the National Administrative Council (NAC), most significantly from Fenner Brockway, who not only organised most of the subsequent Arts Guild national meetings and became chairman in 1927, but who was also an 'enthusiastic participant in the productions mounted in the London area and contributed two anti-war plays . . . to this attempt to broaden the spirit of the socialist movement. By 1930, the Guild could boast in excess of 130 groups nationwide.'[2]

Yet, despite such an auspicious start, comparatively little is known of the work of the Arts Guild. Writing in *Theatres of the Left*, Raphael Samuel comments that 'it is surprising . . . how little direct part theatre played in the cultural practice of the early socialist movement'. While (in this instance) he is referring in particular to the role of the Fabian Society, such assertions are common currency when people talk about the history of political theatre in Britain. For many, it was born all but fully fledged with the Communist inspired Workers Theatre Movement, with a passing acknowledgement to the work of the Actresses Franchise League a few years earlier. Little is known about the work of the Chartists, the Fabians, the Clarion movement, the Labour Party or the trade unions in relation to theatrical cultural practice (and there will be little about any of these here, although all need a fuller exploration to fill out the tantalising glimpses provided by Samuel's work). What follows is an attempt to add some flesh to the bones of at least one organisation that attempted to harness the force of theatre to the vision of a better world. As a result, it is also an answer to Andrew Davies' assertion that early socialists performed little other than the 'ubiquitous Shaw plays'.[3]

The Guild did not mark the first stirrings of dramatic activity within the ILP and the life of the party had always entailed far more than a round of politics. At its heart were the social gatherings – everything from 'at homes', garden meetings, teas or suppers and whist drives to annual fairs, the singing of Labour songs, all manner of sporting activity, rambles and charabanc outings. The sheer volume of social activities encouraged within the ILP (and listed on the pages of its press) suggests that members may indeed have found it hard to find time for the more serious matter of politics. Some were concerned that branch social life took ILP members away from politics, so Bruce Glasier, for example, was convinced that cycling, football and 'other forms of personal recreation have cost us the zealous services of many admirable propagandists'. In 1896 a meeting of Stockport members heard complaints of 'the apathy and indifference which causes members to absent themselves from Business [*sic*] meetings while regularly frequenting the Club for purposes of amusement', an argument echoed half a century later when a columnist in *Labour's Northern Voice* pointed out that the 'party has not made its mark on working class politics by running whist drives and billiard handicaps'. Yet for every voice raised in concern came numerous others justifying every type of social activity as a means of either making or keeping socialists, a point made vociferously by James Widdop, who concluded that most people refuse to stake their lives to one interest and that while they might be prepared to vote for a Labour candidate 'now and again', they were not prepared to drop their interests in exchange for the social life of the ILP branches as it now stood. The branches therefore had to extend their social activities if they wanted both to appeal to, and to hold, a wider layer of people. There is no clearer statement of this interest than the NAC advice of 1920 that all branches should aim at forming a dramatic group for members who have 'not the ability or aptitude to serve in political work but who are willing to be associated with other efforts'.[4]

Dramatic activity therefore can be seen as a simple extension of this round of social activity and a handful of branches did establish dramatic groups in the years prior to the First World War, including Halifax, Nelson and West Salford. Liverpool boasted two groups, both established in 1917 – one aided by Norman MacDermott (a branch comrade and later founder of the Everyman Theatre) and the other by Philip Snowden (at the time National Chairman of the ILP) who contributed a 'most imposing prospectus'. Yet, despite Snowden's apparent endorsement of drama only four other branches appear to have taken any notice – Gateshead (where the ILP Amateur Dramatic Club later became the Progressive Players and survived far longer than the Guild itself), Middlesborough, Shettleston in Glasgow, and Edinburgh. For a party that boasted 787 branches in 1920, dramatic activity prior to the establishment of the Arts Guild (this despite a surge of interest in the eighteen months prior to the establishment of the Guild, which led to a further eight or nine new dramatic groups) can be described as being little short of sporadic.[5]

The theatre of ideals: Sunday evenings at the Strand

A more significant development occurred not at branch level but when Arthur Bourchier put the Strand Theatre at the disposal of the Party on Sunday evenings in 1925. Organised by Reginald Stamp (and assisted by Kyrle Bellew, the actress wife of Bourchier) the purpose of the gatherings at the Strand was spelled out on the opening night by Clifford Allen's statement that they were there 'to show that Socialism meant not only an economic policy but a way of life . . . Socialism must affect their hearts as well as their minds. It was at once a scientific remedy for the evils of the world and the expression of the idealistic human spirit.'[6]

Such an idealistic human spirit was to be expressed in a variety of ways including political speeches, lecture recitals and a wide variety of performance. Dance was provided on several occasions by the ever-popular Margaret Morris and her pupils, as well as by the Cecil Sharp Folk Dancers. On one occasion, the audience were entertained by Marjorie Gullein's Verse Speaking Choir performing rhythmic movement to spoken poetry. Music was a constant feature of the evenings, with frequent performances from the West End ILP Orchestra and the Socialist Choir as well as special appearances by groups such as the Neath ILP Orpheus Male Choir and professional soloists. Drama was also performed by a combination of professionals and amateurs but plays with overt political themes were few. Apart from Galsworthy's *Defeat* and the 'Cell Scene' from *Justice*, there were two performances of Yaffle's *Foiling the Reds* (one given by the staff of the *New Leader*), two plays by Miles Malleson (*Black 'Ell* and *Young Heaven*), the Gate Theatre company's production of *Masses and Man*, Laurence Housman's reading of his play *Lord of the Harvest* (a one-act morality about famine in the midst of plenty) and George Calderon's *The Fountain*, a play about housing and charity, full of resonances of Shaw's *Widower's Houses*. Apart from these plays, the dramatic performances reflect an eclectic rather than a propagandist approach, although they all, in the eyes of Bourchier, stood 'for the highest cultural and spiritual life'.[7] This 'life' could apparently be found in many and sometimes surprising plays – in St John Hankin's one-act play about love, *The Constant Lover*, in R. L. Roy's *Chandragupta*, in Edna St. Vincent Millay's 'illusive phantasy' *Aria da Capo* and in an original play performed by the Parliamentary Labour Club, *The Tomb*, which was written by John H. Clynes (son of J. R. Clynes) and tells of a party of tourists who wander, mistakenly, into the previously undiscovered resting-place of a Pharaoh and are then forced by him to join the ranks of the dead – a play no doubt inspired by the interest in the subject awakened by the discovery of Tutankhamun in November 1922, and Lord Carnarvon's subsequent death. Less surprising is the choice of Shakespeare; in this instance both the Forum scene from *Julius Caesar* and the trial scene from *The Merchant of Venice* were performed, the latter by Arthur Bourchier and Sybil Thorndyke.

Over the two seasons the programme alternated weekly between political speeches and musical or dramatic evenings, although there were always musical items on the programme, suggesting that despite Allen's opening address the economic and the artistic were seen as separate ways of appealing to people. However, the evenings were a great success in terms of attracting both an audience and recruits. At the first six meetings 250 people were enrolled to the Party, and on the first night as many persons were left outside the theatre as managed to get in. Such popularity may well be accounted for by the fact that the tickets were free, although the *New Leader* preferred to view the success as proof that people wanted the beautiful things in life.[8]

Such success was no doubt in part a spur to the establishment of the Arts Guild, which could take such beauty to those further afield than the walls of the Strand Theatre, and it would be easy to argue that the ILP chose to organise its dramatic activity simply in response to the success of the Strand Sundays and the dramatic activity at branch level. Unquestionably, there is some truth in both of these interpretations but simply to focus on them would miss the key influence of Clifford Allen, who had become president of the Party in 1922 and who, as part of his re-organisation of the ILP, had encouraged artistic activity. For example, he was responsible for re-launching the *Labour Leader* under H.N. Brailsford (and under the title of the *New Leader*) as a paper with a wider cultural appeal, a 'mixture of perceptive comment and romantic fustian' in which four pages out of sixteen were devoted to artistic topics in the hope that the 'vaguely sympathetic reader' who began by liking the literary articles might 'soon become a convinced and intelligent Socialist'. Many also hold Allen responsible for the prominence attained by the middle-class pacifists and intellectuals who had flocked to the Party during and just after the war, of whom many were instrumental in the establishment of dramatic societies. Such developments did meet with some hostility, and in the year of the Arts Guild's formation Allen resigned, to be replaced by James Maxton. By this time the Party had very pressing matters to deal with, including the failure of the first Labour government and the 'poaching' of its left wing by the Communist Party. The immediate response to the former was to rethink the relationship of the ILP to the Labour Party and to sharpen its role in bringing 'to the public a realisation of the urgent need for fundamental changes which socialism represents'. Here, drama could play a role, as Malleson made clear in his discussion of the unnecessary misery which still existed 'largely because the mass of people are ignorant of the facts of the society in which they live', an ignorance which drama could help to dispel. The ILP could also help to stem the flow to the Communist Party by distancing itself from the failure of Labour in office and by offering a clear, ethical, educative (and sociable) path to socialism, distinct from the perceived violence of Bolshevism. In this aim too drama could play a role. An understanding of the intersection of all these elements offers a clearer understanding of the Party's willingness to establish a more organised approach to artistic work.[9]

Organising the work of the Guild

The Guild did not, however, limit its work to drama. From the outset it embraced music, dance and arts, and handicrafts as well. Each subgroup had the same initial aims, but each also had its own identity. It was hoped, for example, that the art group would 'produce really beautiful posters for electoral purposes' and after a somewhat shaky start this section of the Guild attempted to align itself to the dramatic work by concentrating on the production of sets and props. The dance section set out to encourage the study of traditional folk dances, folk-dancing being the most 'natural and inevitable expression of the desire for rhythmic movement'. For a while (and with the encouragement of the playwright Evelyn Sharp) it became a 'very live branch of the work of the Guild' but, in the end, the folk dances were discontinued in favour of the more popular 'Margaret Morris' dance classes. The musical work started on a firmer footing, as choirs were already a familiar feature of ILP branch life, and the Guild aimed to extend this work through the organisation of a national ILP musical festival. By 1926, with the help of Rutland Boughton and Leonard Pearce, the leader of the West End ILP Orchestra, this section of the Guild boasted fifty affiliated choirs and orchestras.[10]

Drama unquestionably showed the most rapid development of the four areas. Within six months the Guild, which had been formed with the definite knowledge of the existence of ten groups, received sixty applications for affiliation and was in the process of dealing with another thirty enquiries. Malleson had already traveled 'several hundreds of miles' helping groups and conducting rehearsals. By April 1926 the number had increased to 115, with twenty-five groups in London alone. After this date no figures appear to have been published, but the NAC reported that notices of activity from 'all parts of the country' showed a 'live artistic movement growing slowly but surely', suggesting that if the growth of groups was not outstanding it was still increasing. In 1927 and 1928, the Guild organised a number of successful weekend schools to train members and to share experiences, and in 1926 the London groups formed the Central ILP Players to offer three performances at London theatres.[11] However, in 1929 the Party had to report that development, although slow, continued, and at its annual meeting, which had been held every year during the annual conference since 1926, the Arts Guild agreed to dissolve the national committee. Its place was taken by a voluntary secretary (a post filled by Marguerite Louis). By this time, the number of new drama groups was declining annually (six were reported in 1930 and only three in 1931) and Marguerite Louis had little time to make any changes before the 1932 Conference decided to abandon attempts to organise artistic work separately and to seek to develop them in future as part of the ordinary cultural activities of the branches.[12]

More than bread and butter: towards a theory

Such a sketchy history of the Guild tells us little about the work undertaken in the groups, least of all about what was performed or how drama served the cause of the ILP; neither does it explain what the Guild groups were trying to achieve. Were they an extension of the Little Theatre movement with its sociability, or were they led by a belief that theatre could indeed make socialists of its audience? Guild members did try to develop theories of the role that drama could play on the path to socialism. One starting-point for the formation of the Guild (as with the Little Theatre movement) was a reaction to the debased art of commercial theatre, where all that was on offer were shows 'which are to be enjoyed by leaving one's brains in the cloakroom'. In contrast, the Guild set out to give those denied access to the 'treasures of art and literature' at least a small glimpse of these delights. The desire for access to all art – and it was not, as Arthur Ponsonby explained, an attempt to force footballers to appreciate Renaissance art or bookies to read Shakespeare – was in part an argument about accessibility and in part a feeling that there was something inherently of value in 'great art' which could 'provide a ladder out of the conditions into which people are condemned some of the time'. At times the argument was couched in ethical terms, as in Ethel Snowden's belief that people needed culture to 'banish hate from our hearts' and to 'plant therein righteousness and the love of humanity' or in the characterisation of the Guild as the 'reincarnation of the spirit of William Morris'. But behind the flowery language there was also a hard attack on a world that deadened and cramped people's potential by forcing them to work in drudgery and to live in poverty. As the *Northern Democrat* pointed out, 'in this modern and systemised world, creative and artistic impulses are warped, cramped and distorted to an alarming extent'. The Guild believed that by offering art to people they would begin to see the reality of the world in which they were forced to live. 'A knowledge of good art, literature and music,' said Comrade Lewis Jones at a lecture to Cheetham Hill ILP, 'would help to raise the workers against the squalor of their conditions and make them revolt against the ugliness of it all'. Artists could also indicate the sort of life that might by shared by everyone. Whilst economics explained what needed to be changed in order to achieve socialism, 'it only explains part of the way along which we must travel to reach it and tells us very little of why we want it or what it will be like. The artist has to be called in to give vision, form and content . . .'[13]

Others believed that by showing workers were capable of appreciating and understanding the higher life the Guild could show that 'aesthetic emotion' was not the special attribute of a small professional or cultured class, but that it was common to all. And if workers could be aesthetically cultivated, surely they were capable of attaining power and fitted to be in control? Sometimes, however, such arguments were couched in terms that were far from aesthetic, as in the *New Leader*'s pronouncement that while 'some people are fond of saying that Labour could not govern because it has no training, no experience', the 'finest possible training in dealing with men and women and crises is to be gained by organising a dramatic club'.[14]

None of these ideas was watertight, and throughout the history of the Guild arguments continued as comrades tried to resolve their dilemmas. For all their belief in the capabilities and potential of the people, there were many who believed the working class got the art it 'deserved'; as E. G. Barlow, in a lecture on 'Art and Democracy', told members in Gorton: 'the lives of the working classes seemed devoid of any beauty, partly owing to . . . their own apathy with regard to these things'. There were others who began to question whether it was possible to achieve any real beauty under the present system. 'We cannot conduct our economic life according to one system, and possess a theatre that belongs to another', declared Bourchier. It was only under socialism that art and culture could truly begin to flourish, and Bourchier cited Trotsky to back up his argument.[15]

Trotsky's name was also used by John S. Clarke to provide ammunition in another argument raging in the Guild – an argument concerning access to bourgeois culture. There were those who questioned the validity of highbrow art and who believed bourgeois art worth only consigning to the rubbish bin. In reviewing Trotsky's

Literature and Revolution, Clarke used the opportunity to return the attack, spending much of the two-part article arguing against those who championed 'Proletcult' and explaining in detail Trotsky's argument about why access to bourgeois culture was important in the development of the working class. Culture, in Clarke's view, 'is not something that can be manufactured like a pound of sausages. Neither can it be wiped out wholly as one erases a pencil mark'. Quoting Trotsky directly, he goes on to argue that a new class does not begin to 'create culture from the beginning', but 'enters into possession of the past' which it 'touches up' and then builds on, and concludes with Trotsky's arguments that the 'main task of the proletarian intelligentsia in the immediate future is not the abstract formulation of a new culture . . . but definite culture-bearing, that is systematic, planful and of course, critical, imparting to the backward masses of the essential elements of the culture which already exist'. Thus, the most important job the Arts Guild could undertake was 'to ground the Socialist working class in bourgeois culture', for the more this could be achieved prior to socialism, the 'more rapidly will the work of cultural reconstruction occur after they have won political power'.[16]

But where's the propaganda?

While this argument raged, another debate over propaganda also ran through the history of the Guild. Many attacked the Guild for not being propagandist enough, for being too sentimental, too ethical. It is a label which has stuck. Raphael Samuel argues that propaganda was 'subordinate to the more general aim of making great art available to working people'. Ian Saville speaks of Malleson considering drama primarily as a means of 'cultural enrichment', worthwhile 'for its own sake no matter what the content'. Alongside comments from Philip Snowden, for example, who described drama as a force for 'moral teaching', such conclusions would seem to be correct. Yet, if simply left there, we would miss a part of the story and a part of the argument that raged through the life of the Guild.[17]

Throughout the pages of the ILP press and in the ILP's writings on the Guild there are numerous mentions of propaganda. For example, the NAC report for 1928 welcomed the fact that the Guild was developing a new method of propaganda which was more effective than 'the street corner work' but any mention of propaganda is equally balanced by comments attacking the notion that the aim of the Guild should be propagandist. The *Socialist Review* attacked 'didactic' drama as being as 'great an abomination as the war propaganda cinematograph' and the *Bradford Pioneer* proclaimed that the ILP Arts Guild 'is not propaganda breaking out in fresh places', warning its readers that the function of plays was not 'to enforce morals' but 'to deepen and broaden your sympathies'. The contradictions were even embodied within individuals. Malleson, writing in his launch pamphlet for the Guild, spoke ('of course') of the fact that the Guild would not *just* do propaganda plays, but neither would they be scared of the word. Harold Scott, in an article entitled 'Propaganda in the Theatre', was incapable of making up his mind. If propaganda had a place in the theatre, he concluded that it was allowable in the work of a good dramatist, but not in the work of a bad one, and ended the article with his discovery that there were 'no general principles' from which to lay down laws for revolutionary dramatists. 'There appear to be two distinct elements at work', declared W. C. Raffe, when summing-up the division, 'one of which believes dramatic productions should be "cultural" and the other which aims at propaganda of a very direct kind.' And it was a debate that was never resolved during the lifetime of the Guild but if we look at two examples (and then at the plays produced by the ILP Arts Guild) we can begin to see both the potential and the problems the Guild faced.[18]

In June 1922 the *New Leader* carried an article about the spectacular success of one branch which, on finding that speakers were able only to fill half of their hall, had introduced a playlet. Demand proved so great that the piece was performed three times to full houses. The branch in question was Shettleston ILP and the sketch was *The Fear of the Factor*. Written by a socialist magistrate (and performed with the help of music provided by the Clyde Workers' Silver Band), it deals with issues close to the heart of the working class in Glasgow – the factor, rents, unemployment and eviction – and is full of blatant propaganda and class politics, including a speech from Jock, the out-of-work father, which is an indictment of the social system where 'I an' mine own nothing but a wheen o'sticks an' the claes that cover us.' While 'ma class produces everything, your freens tak' everything . . . The mansions and motors, slums and palaces were built by us, and are owned by idlers. They control land and sea, hill and dale, the waters 'abin and the metals below. They control me and mine – I live by their leave, ma weans are infant slaves. I work when it profits them, I starve when it suits them.'[19]

The success of their first attempt encouraged the group, who had by now named themselves the Shettleston ILP Propaganda Party, to produce a second sketch. *What Tommy Fought For* was written in much the same style as their first play, but the breadth of its political propaganda was extended to include a wider scope of ILP politics. In the course of the short piece, the characters discuss under-consumption theory, why Black Tam, the mine-owner, is given a pit by his father but he will not give one to Tam's son and why Tam, during the war, was promised 'woodbines and chocolate, banns [*sic*] playin' and flags wavin'', only to be forgotten with his 'weans staivin' an' I'm an al pauper'. Inspired by Mary, who constantly asks her husband why he and the 'ither simple sowls' do not join together to get 'the wurld's wealth for the wurld's workers', Tam begins to realise he can do something. By the end, Tam declares he will join the ILP and 'fecht the system that creates poverty'.[20]

In comparison to the work in Scotland, Bradford ILP chose for its performance in February 1930 a comedy of the Italian Renaissance based on the life of artist Benvenuto Cellini, Mayer's *The Firebrand*. Although described as 'no mere conversation play', it was clearly far from being propagandist and was described by Fenner Brockway as a 'gaily costumed' and 'irresponsible' historical comedy. As such he found much to recommend it for any group 'who cares to forget for one production the necessity of stimulating the intellectual life and social consciousness of its audience' and who wished instead to 'revel in . . . fun and gorgeous dressing up'. Whilst Brockway may have been recommending the piece only as a part of a more serious repertoire, its production in Bradford started a debate on the pages of the *Bradford Pioneer*. Some wanted to know if the Arts Guild just viewed itself as a few 'ILPers having fun' and warned of the danger of finding it had been overtaken by the growing amateur movement in the city. Others took up the question of why propaganda plays were not being produced. One correspondent was clearly incensed to be told that 'members aren't keen on such' and that 'they want to laugh, that their lives are not jolly, so they look to get fun and amusement out of the Guild'. Others valued the 'excursion into another world', seeing the role of the Guild as saving members from 'the narrow outlook which makes our lives a routine of preparation for the next election' and one member mocked those who looked for propaganda in the Guild's work, asking if the 'handicraft section embroider the ILP motif on all its work?'[21]

Shettleston and Bradford represented two extremes of the work of the Arts Guild which, although separated by eight years – a period during which the Guild was established and run by many influenced by the professional theatre as well as the burgeoning amateur and Little Theatre movements – begin to show that there was no real cohesion in the attitude that members of the Guild took to their work. Rather, the life of the Guild represented a series of debates and disagreements as they attempted to work things out. And the two extremes also begin to show that the plays the Guild chose to perform were drawn from a much wider spectrum than the 'fairly conventional diet of Galsworthy, Shaw and Malleson' suggested by Ian Saville.[22]

Finding the right plays

The question of repertoire was one of the key and most persistent problems. Most letters asked for advice on the choice of plays and Malleson made several practical suggestions concerning sources, including recommending the British Drama League list and translations of plays performed in the Little Theatre Movement abroad which groups could familiarise themselves with through the formation of play-reading groups.[23] While Shaw *was* one of the most popular writers (twenty-five of his plays were produced), he was by no means the only writer looked to. In terms of popularity, Galsworthy and Chekhov were a close second, as were the plays of Miles Malleson. The latter numbered at this point some eleven plays that are incessantly concerned with two connected themes: war (or rather arguments against war) and sex. The two themes are connected as they are seen to be the prerogative of the young who are in revolt against the mess the older generation has made of the world and who spend much of the plays arguing about the need to do better. Many of Malleson's leading characters are women; they either suffer loss through war or are attempting to break free from the shackles of marriage – and they are all (with the exception of the servants) the middle-class inhabitants of comfortable, suburban houses.[24]

Nearly as popular were the plays of Ernst Töller, which the ILP was instrumental in introducing to the British theatre. It was ILP member Ashley Dukes who translated *The Machine Wreckers* (a play dedicated to another ILP member Wilfred Wellock) for its first English production by the Stage Society in May 1923, and ILP member Lewis Casson produced the first performance of *Masses and Man* the following year. Given such support from leading members of the Party as well as from the pages of the *New Leader* where, as early as June 1922, Wellock was praising his work, it is not surprising many groups turned to Töller's plays, especially when we realise the political closeness of the author (a member of the German USPD) to the ILP, particularly over the question of pacifism.[25]

In terms of helping Guild members break away from this handful of dramatists, the Arts Guild provided little leadership beyond trying to negotiate a lower fee through the British Drama League and discussing the possibility of a library. The pages of the *New Leader* offered little more help. Occasional articles offered *ad hoc* advice but there were no sustained suggestions available. Instead, groups found their own plays by turning to numerous and eclectic sources that included plays produced by the Repertory and Little Theatre Movements, and to some extent the repertoire reflects that of those movements. To this repertoire was added work from further afield, including the West End, and several of A. A. Milne's and Gertrude Jennings' comedies found their place in the repertoire. Classic plays were less popular; a handful of Shakespeare productions can be found, alongside single performances of *Caste*, *A School for Scandal* and Frederick Reynolds' *The Dramatist*. But given the Guild's supposed emphasis on bringing great art to the people, classic plays made up only a very small part of the repertoire.[26] Even the productions cited above show a breadth of interest beyond Shaw and Galsworthy, but there is little to back up the ILP's claim to represent the 'rebirth of English Theatre' or even to present 'the Socialist case on a broader and deeper note'. Indeed, W. C. Raffe was moved to remark: 'we hear of *RUR* being done again and again; or an old Shaw play is dug up; and a pre-Revolution Russian play is favoured. Or a trifling one-act comedy having no bearing on Socialism will be offered and the audience wonders why better stuff is not produced.'[27] Help was at hand, however, and the search for suitable plays was aided by a timely initiative taken, not by the ILP publishing companies (the ILP ran both the National Labour Press and the Blackfriars Press in Leicester), but by a company run by Guild Socialists, the Labour Publishing Company, which, between 1925 and 1928, issued a series of plays entitled 'Plays for the People'. Under the editorship of Monica Ewer, the collection eventually numbered eighteen, mainly one-act, plays. With the exception of *The Rising Sun*, all the plays were original and with the exception of the same play (one of only three full-length plays in the series), all became staple pieces for ILP dramatic groups. Apart from dealing with suitable themes, all were simple to stage and this, combined with the small number of characters, the low fees charged and the dearth of suitable material, would have been sufficient to make the plays popular for the ILP groups.[28]

Despite their popularity with groups much of the Labour press, though welcoming the initiative, was not uncritical. The remarks of J. F. Horrabin are typical of much of the discontent – discontent which centred on the gloomy nature of the plays. 'Labour Grand Guignol' and 'shilling shockers' were the terms Horrabin employed when asking, 'need – should – must labour plays be gloomy? . . . [i]n only one of these eight plays is one allowed to laugh; and in that one – Evelyn Sharp's not very riotously funny "incredible" episode – the scene is set "in the City That Never Was" and the time, we are explicitly informed, is "Not Yet"! Which is a little discouraging.' The *Bradford Pioneer* thought the series 'radically false to our faith', echoing 'the melancholy of such second-rate bourgeois work as Galsworthy's' rather than the optimism of a socialist movement which was 'gay, militant and conquering'. In these plays 'the note of resistance, of unbreakable will, of the sunrise on the horizon, is absent'.[29]

Such accusations provoked a response from B. N. Langdon, managing director of the Labour Publishing Company, who defended the publication of tragic pieces not on the basis of their excellence (in fact, he thought that with the possible exception of *The Rising Sun* they had not discovered anything of 'particular excellence') but on the simple grounds that out of 200 manuscripts received only two or three were anything but tragic. Malleson too did not see the new plays as 'perfect pieces'. Indeed, he dismissed *Mrs Jupp Obliges* and *The Bruiser's Election* as 'slight trifles', concluding the series should be seen as the first steps in self-expression rather than finished products.[30]

A glance at the plays does show many of them to be grim little pieces guaranteed to send the audience home in a melancholy state of mind. *His Last Bread* dramatises the brutalising effect of starvation and culminates in a wife mistakenly murdering her husband for the last crust of bread. *The Street* is a bleak explanation of why women are forced to turn to prostitution. *The Best of Both Worlds* ends with a failed demonstration and two dead. *His First Money*, while starting with a clerk being left some money, ends with his murder by a workmate even more desperate to escape; in *The Forge*, the hammer crushes both the bodies and souls of the inhabitants of Hyacinth Court. Even those plays whose themes have the potential for optimism do not exploit it. *The Great Day* is the day of the clerks' expected pay-rise, a rise which, despite the hope of the opening, never comes and the Socialist who argues for some kind of resistance 'is talked over, and receiving no support from his fellow clerks, retires beaten, and the grind goes on'. In *The Founders*, Lewis shows the dangers which lay in the paths of the first trade unionists and ends with the agricultural workers under arrest, betrayed by one of their members. Lewis tries to make the most of their martyrdom, ending with the cry that '[a] spark has fired this land of ours and Kings, Dukes, Bishops and agents will fail to extinguish the flame that is kindling', but it is a small crumb of comfort in a bleak world.[31]

Yet not all the plays are sombre. Both *Mrs Jupp Obliges* and *The Bruiser's Election* are comedies at the expense of the ruling class or the parties that represent them. *A Place in the Sun* is a gentle satire on kingship which, in the words of the author, sets out to amuse. *The*

Loafer and the Loaf opens with a minstrel playing a nursery rhyme on a penny whistle and continues in fantastical vein until it ends with the cast 'stuffing cakes into their mouths and dancing wildly'. But this lighthearted feel does not mean the play has no moral and it concentrates on asking (and answering) the question of who steals more: the fat or the lean?[32]

The most popular play of the series was Yaffle's *Foiling the Reds or the Heart of the Labourer*, a piece which is anything but a naturalistic tragedy. In satirical manner it sets out to 'awaken the British working class to a sense of duty and to show how the commercial stability of the nation is being undermined by sinister Socialist propaganda'. Set in a factory run on co-operative lines which builds ocean liners supplied on an instalment system to impecunious crowned heads (the workers having eschewed all Bolshevist and Socialist theories, working instead for the pure love of serving their country), trouble begins with the arrival of a Bolshevik agent, accompanied by Lola and Trotsky, seeking to 'unsettle the peaceful minds of the British worker and bring about an incipient state of strike and revolt'. Charlie Muggup – the 'ideal working man' – succumbing to his fascination with Lola, agrees to join in the plot to stun the night watchman and steal the cashbox, but is turned from the 'wrong path' by Jenny, the factory angel, and finally defeats the striking men and the Bolsheviks in single-handed combat. Having saved the firm from ruin, he nobly refuses a reward – for he has only done his duty.

All characters are painted in broad strokes. Charlie is tall and fair and 'like all real heroes . . . wears a white shirt open at the neck'. Jennie is the 'ideal heroine' of the films, her face 'devoid of expression', reflecting 'what is most to be desired in The Girls Men Want namely that complete emptiness of mind generally known as Innocence'. Lola, by contrast, is the seductive vamp with a mouth like 'a piece of raw beef' and the Socialist is distinguished by his perpetual evil sneer and mass of black matted hair. The acting style demanded by Yaffle fits the character types, with Muggup trotting 'lightly and gracefully' around the stage, to show his athletic habit and his *joie de vivre*, and the villain crawling around in a furtive, crouching manner, comporting himself as 'typical Socialists do, in the minds of the best people'. Yaffle also builds into the play a number of set pieces using a variety of techniques including ballet 'or concerted movement form of presentation, varied where necessary with the Tableaux Vivant method'. This has two advantages; first, it points up the satirical nature of the piece, and secondly it is 'much easier for amateurs to do it like that, because if they stand in stiff attitudes and repeat the same gestures it gets over the problem of what to do with your hands when you're not speaking'. Yaffle's tongue may have been firmly in his cheek – although there was no doubt an element of truth in his assessment of the acting abilities of many of the members – but given the complex demands the play makes on the performers it would not seem to recommend itself to easy performance. However, it was precisely its style and satire that led many ILP groups and critics to greet it enthusiastically; the *Bradford Pioneer*, for example, praised it as 'a superb farce' which 'holds up the mirror to the Jix mind, and you laugh. It is more playable, more sincere, infinitely more true to the soul of the movement than any of the others.'[33]

Not everyone was completely enthusiastic about Yaffle's play and it was mercilessly criticised by Tom Thomas on the pages of the *Red Stage* several years after its first appearance. In his eyes the play was often put on the programme in the belief that 'a bit of working-class leaven . . . will justify a whole evening of bourgeois plays'. It might have been mildly amusing at times, but 'this method of exposing the "bloodstained bolshevik" propaganda' was only effective with people who are already convinced of its absurdity. For the majority of workers 'who take their views from the capitalist press', it was 'worse than meaningless', exposing nothing, and many of them would take the piece to mean 'that the players are being sarcastic at their expense in picturing them as mental deficients'. Thomas was writing in 1932, six years after the piece first appeared – and at a time when the Communist Party and the affiliated Workers Theatre Movement regarded the ILP as 'social fascists' – and while the play could lay itself open to the charge that the workers are portrayed as somewhat stupid (they either swallow the *Daily Mail*'s propaganda or are easily led by the Bolsheviks), the broad satire of the piece must have left no one in doubt that here was 'a parody of our opponents' parody of Socialism'.[34]

Another potential source of plays for the Guild was the earlier series of 'revolutionary plays' published by C. W. Daniels under the title 'Plays for a People's Theatre' and edited by Douglas Goldring.[35] Between 1920 and 1924 C. W. Daniels issued twenty-six plays including Goldring's own four-act play *The Fight for Freedom*, which focused on the impact of war and violence on personal relationships, and D. H. Lawrence's *Touch and Go*, a play which prophetically explores the defeat of a miners' strike. The rest of the series included Ralph Fox's *Captain Youth*, a 'romantic comedy for socialist children', Eleanor Gray's *The Image Breaker*, a one-act tragedy about a socialist MP who gives his life for the revolution, and several plays by Margaret Macnamara including *Mrs Hodges*, a 'comedy of rural politics'. This short play opens at a council meeting about the finance of a new housing scheme. The members of the committee are shown to be unqualified to discuss the matter, none more so than the architect Feathergill and Mrs Clam-Digby, who is happy only when she is 'patriotically' saving money from being spent on erecting 'palaces' for the poor. Present too is Mrs Hodges, co-opted as the one person who has experience of living in the kind of house under discussion. When she is all but ignored she takes matters into her own hands, tricking the architect into staying with her family and thus, through a number of comic contrivances, to dispose of his useless plans.[36] It is worth noting the existence of this second series to see the number of plays available to the Guild, yet from this list they chose to perform only one – Margaret Macnamara's *Mrs Hodges*. Members were possibly unaware of the existence of these plays; they were published a few years prior to the Guild's formation and are not referred to in any detail in the *New Leader*. On the whole, apart from *Mrs Hodges*, they make more complex staging demands and the series includes numerous full-length pieces, while the Guild favoured shorter plays, but many of the issues dealt with are reflected in the plays the ILP did produce.[37]

Malleson, however, was not simply content with reproducing plays by others; his great hope was that as the movement grew new writers would emerge. From the first he argued that the *real* importance of the ILP Dramatic Groups lay in the fact that from them might eventually come a new school of playwriting and over time local writers did begin to appear – albeit sporadically. In Chigwell in 1927, for example, the Players performed three short plays by C. Lewton Brain: *Darkwater Bridge, The Morning After The Night Before* and *The Miracle of Swanleigh Village.* The following year Brain wrote (and performed in) *The Right of Way*, a play about a village's successful resistance to the threatened closure of an ancient right of way.[38] Scottish groups found a prolific writer in James Robertson, producer of the Kirkcaldy group, who in four years produced four plays, including a play about mining, *King O' Men*, and a tragedy about the intolerance of the strictly religious. In West Salford, the society's drama coach made several contributions to the repertoire including *The Fiery Cross*, 'a serious attempt at the presentation of historical propaganda'. His talent was also in evidence in both *The Wheel* – a tragedy in which the wheel of the title is life itself which 'comes round and crushes them as they cannot get out of its way' – and *Bill Smith Explains*, an optimistic comedy in which an electrician gives the members of the Egocrats Club 'more light than they anticipated'.[39] Alma Brosnan, a leading member of the ILP Arts Guild in Bath, contributed four popular plays, including *Scrapped*, performed by the Central ILP Players in 1926, an 'unexaggerated piece of real life, culminating in minor tragedy' when 'one after another members of a family become the victims of unemployment or the other oppressions of our present capitalist system'.[40]

In Gateshead, the Progressive Players had an impressive record of encouraging local playwrights, for alongside 'rejuvenating old masterpieces' the club made a commitment to developing new writing. Best known of the Gateshead writers is Ruth Dodds, one of the mainstays of the Players from 1919 until her death in 1976. Of her three plays the most successful (and the clubs 'greatest venture') was *The Pitman's Pay*, dealing with the first miners' union and its founder, Thomas Hepburn. This was followed by an industrial comedy *The Hilltop*, which tells the story of Bill, Secretary of the Lewers Society (a trades union), who inherits £100,000. He intends to spend it on building a new Labour Hall, but the constant arguments and people's distrust of him now he is rich drive him away. For a while he is seduced both by the good things in life and by Lucy, the banker's daughter, but finally decides that if he and Lucy find 'it so good to come out into the sunshine and the green world, wouldn't it be good to give it to those others, to bring them out of the smoke and grime onto the hilltop?' and he goes back to the town to carry on the fight. Underlying this plot is a story of trade unionism and the need for unity in the face of the employers: particularly the need for political unity between men and women. This was followed in 1928 by *The Pressed Man*, a romantic comedy about press-gangs set in Northumberland during the Napoleonic Wars. Ruth was not the only new dramatist at the Progressive Players, and she was joined on the boards by her sister Hope, by Agnes Johnson and by the Gateshead journalist Fred Chadwick.[41]

On to the Masses Stage and Film Guild

It is clear from even such a brief survey of the Guild's plays that their repertoire displays a breadth and eclecticism far beyond the generally held picture. Nor did the ILP stop with the formation of the Guild in its attempts to use drama, but in 1929 it embarked on 'a very gallant piece of work', the formation of the Masses Stage and Film Guild (MSFG) with the objective of 'bringing modern plays and films of democratic significance within the reach of working class audiences'. The new organisation was not intended to supersede the work of the Arts Guild, which was, in the words of Harold Scott, production secretary of the MSFG, doing 'extraordinarily valuable work . . . towards creating a drama by means of amateur groups', but was to work with professionals to create large performances and 'initiating a policy for working class theatre' to promote a more 'public-spirited attitude' to playgoing. The scheme was financed by means of a subscription society, at the cost of one shilling per member, to avoid the 'vicarious' help of the business world.[42]

In the event, the MSFG made only a small contribution to this ideal. Although membership peaked at 2,300 in 1931, the Guild only managed to stage three plays of one performance each starting with Upton Sinclair's *The Singing Jailbirds*, produced by Edith Craig at the Apollo Theatre on Sunday 9 March 1930. This attack on the Californian prison system that tells the story of the growth of the group Industrial Workers of the World was chosen because it was different from those plays performed both in the bourgeois theatre and by amateur theatre companies such as the Stage Society. The ILP stamped its own identity on the play by changing the ending, much to the displeasure of Frank Horrabin, who thought 'the ending as Sinclair wrote it, with . . . the curtain coming down on the jailers terrified at the rising swell of the "wobblies" singing', was 'infinitely more effective' than the 'rearranged version with its Passing-of-the-Third-Floor-Back flavour'. *Jailbirds* was followed in April by *Brain*, in which man is moving towards destruction as 'the beast' in him takes control. The only way out is co-operation, a solution which comes from a group of the intelligentsia, who decide to create a mechanism resembling the human brain which is to be infused with the capacity for 'directing the activities of mankind'. All goes well until the mechanism loses its connection with humanity and takes dictatorial control. The world is destroyed, and the curtain comes down on 'a terrific explosion, a blazing flash of light' followed by 'total darkness' and silence; the 'world has disappeared'. *Brain* can be read both as a critique of science – a not-uncommon theme following the First World War – and of Stalinism, but what is most interesting is the experimental style and the demands for complex staging – an ambitious project for a company brought together for one performance.

The third and final Guild production was somewhat less ambitious in style than *Brain*, but no less significant, as it is claimed to be 'the first play by a Negro author' to be played in the West End. Paul Green's *In Abraham's Bosom* was set in the Deep South at the turn of the century and told of Abraham's battle with the whites, a battle ending in tragedy as Abraham is shot by a lynching party. *The Times* reviewer declared the play to be gloomy and unimpressive, and beset by production problems. If the review is to be taken literally it was a rather inauspicious end to the theatrical ventures of the MSFG. What is also apparent is that the MSFG did not appear to have solved the problem of depressing the audience; all three plays were of a somewhat gloomy nature and the Workers' Theatre Movement went on to attack *The Singing Jailbirds* in particular for its 'profound pessimism' and 'defeatism' – and this without the re-arranged ending.[43]

On the film front, the Guild was more active, showing both Russian and French films, but it soon ran into legislative problems as the London County Council tightened up the regulations that governed film societies, particularly those charging low subscription rates. Although the MSFG led a spirited fight against these changes, by the end of 1930 it found itself unable to continue to show films.[44] The death of the MSFG was all but ensured by changes in theatrical legislation when the 1781 Act prohibiting Sunday performances was resurrected in 1931. Coupled with the cost of hiring theatres, the Guild 'soon had to abandon its aspirations of forming a People's Theatre'.[45]

As well as these pragmatic considerations, political changes are also of central importance to understand the demise not only of the MSFG but also of the ILP Arts Guild in the early 1930s. As Stephen G. Jones points out, it was likely that the demise of such artistic endeavours was 'intimately linked to the political difficulties faced by the ILP, which disaffiliated from the Labour Party in 1932'.[46] Such political considerations left those with a dramatic bent to face the choice of joining the blossoming Workers' Theatre Movement, which many had already opted to do, or finding a less political niche with an amateur group.

Notes

Much of the research for this chapter was undertaken for a Ph.D. thesis. Ros Merkin, 'The Theatre of the Organised Working Class 1830–1930' (unpublished: University of Warwick, 1993).

1. For the 1924 symposium, see Dan Griffiths, ed., *What is Socialism?* (London: 1924); *Labour Leader*, 30 March 1924, p. 163; Geoffrey Foote, *The Labour Party's Political Thought: A History* (Beckenham: Croom Helm, 1986), pp. 34–5.

2. *New Leader*, 12 June 1925, p. 7 and 3 June 1925, p. 14; *Clarion* 19 June 1925, p. 7; Arthur Marwick, *Clifford Allen: The Open Conspirator* (Edinburgh: Oliver & Boyd, 1964), p. 89. The provisional list of experts co-opted on to the advisory committee which was to run the Guild included Kyrle Bellew, Arthur Bourchier, Lewis Casson, Edith Craig, Ashley Dukes, John Goss, Laurence Housman, Oswald Mosley, Irene Rooke, Milton Rosmer, Evelyn Sharp, Horace Shipp, Sybil Thorndike and Harcourt Williams.

3. Raphael Samuel, 'Theatre and Socialism in Britain 1880–1935' in Raphael Samuel, Ewan MacColl and Stuart Cosgrove, *Theatres of the Left 1880–1935* (London: Routledge & Kegan Paul, 1985), p. 11; Andrew Davies, *Other Theatres* (London: MacMillan, 1987), p. 100.

4. *Stockport ILP Minute Book*, 6 December 1896; *NAC Memorandum to Social*

Secretaries 1920; Labour's Northern Voice, 13 November 1925, p. 3, 27 November 1925, p. 7, and 12 March 1926, p. 3. Glasier is quoted in Tony Mason, *Association Football and English Society 1863–1915* (Brighton: Harvester, 1981), p. 236.

5. *Labour Leader* 21 November 1912, p. 758; 16 January 1913, p. 14; 13 February 1913 p.14, 11 January 1917, p. 11; 8 February 1917 p. 12; 29 March 1917, p. 10; 6 September 1917, p. 12. For the second Liverpool group, see Jerry Dawson, 'Unity Comes of Age', *Labour's Merseyside Voice*, August 1957, p. 5 and Len Jones, 'The British Workers Theatre' (unpublished Ph.D. thesis, Halle, 1964), pp. 29–30.

6. *New Leader*, 16 January 1925, p. 18, and 23 January 1925, p.14.

7. Quoted in *New Leader*, 23 January 1925, p.14.

8. *New Leader*, 16 January 1925, p. 18 and 13 February 1925, p. 18. All details of the Strand Theatre performances can be found in the pages of the *New Leader* between 23 January 1925 and 26 March 1926.

9. ILP conference Report 1926, p. 28; Malleson, *The ILP and Its Dramatic Societies*, London, n.p., 1925 pp. 4 and 6.

10. *New Leader*, 3 July 1925, p. 14; 13 November 1925, p. 14; 8 January 1926, p. 14; 2 April 1926, p. 15; 16 April 1926 p. 14; 17 December 1926, p. 14; *ILP Annual Report* 1925, p. 25 and 1926 p. 25.

11. *New Leader*, 13 November 1925, p. 14; 16 April 1926, p. 14; 23 October 1926 p. 15; 19 November, 1926 p. 18; *Town Crier*, 23 April 1926; *ILP Annual Report 1928*, p. 16. The Guild ran seven weekend schools in total, starting in Golders Green in October 1927. See *New Leader* 17 February 1928, p. 15; 2 March 1928, p. 15; 27 April 1928, p. 23; 9 November 1928, p. 15; 29 March 1929, p. 14 for example. The Central ILP Players performed: Alma Brosnan's *Scrapped*, Blackfriars Theatre, December 1926 and *Grand Guignol Evening*, Blackfriars Theatre, February 1927; Elmer Rice's *The Adding Machine*, West Central Hall, March 1927. See *New Leader*, 19 November 1926, p. 13, 7 January 1927, p. 15; 4 February 1927, p. 15; 25 February 1927, p. 15; 18 March 1927, p. 18.

12. *ILP Annual Report 1932*, p. 4. See also the annual reports for 1929, p. 22, 1930, p. 30, and 1931, p. 25.

13. Arthur Bourchier, *Art and Culture in Relation to Socialism* (London: ILP Publications Dept, 1926), p. 12; *Bradford Pioneer* 23 October 1925, p. 4; Arthur Ponsonby, 'Socialism and the Arts', *Socialist Review*, September 1922, p. 108–9; *Labour's Northern Voice*, 13 November 1925, p. 3, 21 January 1927, p. 8, 15 March 1929, p. 7; Ethel Snowden is quoted in Raphael Samuel *et al*, *Theatres of the Left*, p. 6; *New Leader* 12 June 1925; Rutland Boughton, 'Socialism and Song', *New Leader* 28 September 1923, p. 12.

14. *New Leader*, 8 October 1926, p. 14.

15. *Labour's Northern Voice*, 4 February 1927, p. 7.

16. *Forward*, 27 June 1925; 4 July 1925.

17. Raphael Samuel et al., *Theatres of the Left*, p. 29; Ian Saville, *Ideas, Forms and Development in the British Workers' Theatre 1925–1935*, unpublished Ph.D. thesis, City University, 1990, p. 25.

18. *NAC Report 1928*, p. 25; *New Leader*, 4 February 1927, p. 18 and 29 March 1929, p. 5; *Socialist Review* Oct.–Dec. 1918, p. 325 and January 1930, pp. 163–4; *Bradford Pioneer* 20 May 1927, p. 6.

19. *The Fear of the Factor* was published in *Forward*, 5 November 1921.

20. *Forward*, 11 February 1922, p. 7.

21. *Bradford Pioneer*, 21 March 1930, p. 5 and 28 March 1930, p. 5; *New Leader*, 14 March 1929, p. 14. Bradford were by no means alone in choosing this type of production or in instigating a row because of it. Golders Green chose Patrick Hamilton's *Rope* in 1928, prompting the *New Leader* reviewer to ask 'why . . . should Socialists choose to revive *Rope* so recently seen in the West End when there are scores of first class plays crying out for production?' See 28 November 1928, p. 15.

22. Ian Saville, *Ideas, Forms and Developments in the British Workers' Theatre*, p. 44. For the weekend school see *New Leader*, 4 November 1927, p. 18.

23. Miles Malleson, *The ILP and Its Dramatic Societies* pp. 4 and 7.

24. Malleson's plays performed by the Guild included *The Artist, Black 'Ell, D Company, Conflict, The Fanatics, Man of Ideas, Maurice's Own Idea, Merrileon Wise, Paddly Pools, Young Heaven, Youth*. For details of Malleson's life see Lady Constance Malleson, *After Ten Years* (London: Jonathan Cape, 1931).

25. For details of the ILP's involvement in putting Töller on the English stage see Richard Dove, 'The Place of Ernst Töller in English Socialist Literature', *German Life and Letters*, 38: 2, January 1985, pp. 125–37. For Wellock, see *New Leader*, 15 June 1922, p. 2. For one example of an ILP production of Töller see Green Park Players production of *The Machine Wreckers* which is reviewed in detail by Malleson in *New Leader*, 1 October 1926, p. 14.

26. *New Leader*, 19 February 1926, p. 15, 14 January 1927, p. 14; 5 September 1930, p. 15. For examples of suggestions put forward for plays made see Monica Ewer's article, *New Leader*, 20 March 1925, p. 8, or a list from the ILP publications department, *New Leader*, 31 October 1930, p. 12.

27. *Bradford Pioneer* 20 May 1927, p. 6. See also *NAC Report 1931*, p. 5; *New Leader*, 19 November 1926, p. 18; *Northern Democrat*, December 1927; *Clarion*, 19 June 1925, p. 7.

28. The full list of 'Plays for the People' comprised: H.E. Bates, *His Last Bread*;

Alma Brosnan, *The Street*; L. H. Burbage, *Jack's Quest*; Monica Ewer, *The Best of Both World's*; H. Cecil Fisher, *The Great Day*; Herman Heijermans, *The Rising Sun*; Josephine Knowles, *His First Money*, Edwin G. Lewis, *The Founders & The Forge*; Margaret Macnamara, *Mrs. Jupp Obliges*; V. T. Murray, *Bringing It Home*; Ian Rankine, *A Place in the Shade*; Stephen Schofield, *The Judge of All Earth*, *The Odour of Sanctity* and *Sir George and the Dragon*; Evelyn Sharp, *The Loafer and the Loaf*; Horace Shipp, *The Invasion*; Yaffle (A. J. Boothroyd), *Foiling the Reds* (London: Labour Publishing Company, 1926).

29. Horrabin in *Lansbury's Labour Weekly*, 25 December 1926, p. 10; *Bradford Pioneer*, 10 December 1926, p .6.

30. *New Leader*, 8 January 1926, p. 13; *Town Crier*, 31 December 1926, p. 3.

31. Huntley Carter, 'Plays for Socialists', *Sunday Worker*, 15 November 1925, p. 8; Edwin G. Lewis, *The Founders* (London: Labour Publishing Company, 1926), p. 23 and title-page.

32. Evelyn Sharp, *The Loafer and the Loaf* (London: Labour Publishing Company, 1926), p. 23; *Amateur Stage*, September 1926, p. 320; Ian Rankine, *A Place in the Sun* (London: Labour Publishing Company, 1925), p. vi.

33. *Bradford Pioneer*, 10 December 1926, p. 6. Jix was the nickname of Sir William Joynson-Hicks, Home Secretary, Conservative Party, 1924–9. See also Raffle, *Foiling the Reds*.

34. *Red Stage*, No. 5 April–May 1932, p. 3. One question however is hard to answer: although Trotsky in Yaffle's play is clearly portrayed as a mouthpiece not for Bolshevism, but for the *New Leader*, the ILP's attitude to Trotsky (and, indeed, to the Russian Revolution itself) was ambiguous, to say the least. Members of the ILP were quick to condemn Trotsky's book *Where is Britain Going?* See for example the criticisms of Ramsay MacDonald, George Lansbury and Robert Williams in *Leon Trotsky on Britain* (New York: Pathfinder, 1973), pp. 214–28. Given such an attitude, Trotsky is an unlikely 'hero' for Yaffle to choose.

35. The impetus to publish the series came from Goldring's involvement with the People's Theatre Society, a rather confused venture that started as an off-shoot of Clarté founded in conjunction with Harold Scott (among others) primarily to perform 'dawnist plays'. The original organisation quickly fell apart due to internal arguing and a new group was established with the help of a Curtain Group (a triumvirate of conscientious objectors). Once again the group was split by wrangling. See Douglas Goldring, *Odd Man Out: The Autobiography of a Propaganda Novelist* (London: Chapman Hall, 1935), pp. 247.ff.

36. Other plays that make up the list include Hamilton Fyfe's *The Kingdom, the Power and the Glory*; Claude Houghton's *Judas*; Stephen Schofield's *Men at*

War; Shaw Desmond's *My Country*; Lilias McCrie's *Let There Be Light!*; M.A. Arabin's *Yeraz*, Clifford Bax's *Old King Cole* and Jacob Scwartz's *The Golden Calf*. Margaret Macnamara's three other plays were *Love Fibs*, *The Witch* and *Dark Grey or Light*. The title-page of each edition carried the following sentence: 'The plays in this series will merit the attention of those whose eyes are turned towards the future.'

37. See *Huddersfield Worker*, 3 January 1920, p. 4. Nor was it just the ILP that seemed oblivious to these plays. Goldring's drama was performed in Hungary (and possibly also in Frankfurt) but not in Britain, and D. H. Lawrence's had to wait until 1973 for its first performance.

38. *New Leader*, 4 November 1927, p.18; 16 March 1928, p. 15; *Woodford Times*, 9 March 1928, p. 3.

39. Leaflet in G. S. Ireland Collection, Dundee Public Library; *New Leader*, 12 March 1926, p. 19; 14 March 1926, p. 14; 27 April 1928, p. 23; *Forward*, 19 December 1925, p. 14; 6 February 1926, p. 14; *Labour's Northern Voice*, 9 March 1928 p. 7, 30 March 1928, p. 7; 1 March 1929, p. 7; *Salford City Reporter*, 24 March 1928, p. 3.

40. *New Leader*, 24 December 1926, p. 12. *Scrapped*, revised by Miles Malleson (London: Sidgwick & Jackson, 1928). Brosnan's other plays included *At Number Fifteen* (London: Sidgwick & Jackson, 1927), a further indictment of unemployment, *The Street* (published in 'Plays for the People Series') and *Glittering Prizes*.

41. Maureen Calcott and Margaret 'Espinasse, 'The Gateshead Progressive Players, 1920–1980', ed. J.H. Bellamy and John Saville, *Dictionary of Labour Biography: Vol. VII* (London: Macmillan, 1972–87), pp. 67–8; *New Leader*, 16 January 1925, p. 19. Ruth Dodds was secretary of Gateshead Women's Suffrage League and from 1929 was a Labour councillor, until her resignation from the Party at the outbreak of the Second World War. She was also editor of the *Gateshead Labour Herald*, for which she wrote many articles under the byline of 'Redcap'. For details of her life see J. H. Bellamy and John Saville, eds., *Dictionary of Labour Biography: Vol. VII*, p. 63–67; *Gateshead Post*, 18 April 1974; 8 April 1976 p. 1, and an interview with Councillor Ruth Dodds (n.d.) in *Gateshead Personalia* at Gateshead Public Library. See also *A Pitman's Pay* (London: Labour Publishing Company, 1929), and 'The Hilltop' (Gateshead Central Library; typescript).

42. Harold Scott, 'What Can We Do For the Theatre?', *Socialist Review*, September 1929, p. 26–8 and 'The ILP and Play Production', *Socialist Review*, November 1929, p. 43–45. See also *Socialist Review*, March 1930 p. 33; *New Leader*, 15 November 1929, p. 3. The most often quoted account of the MSFG comes from Fenner Brockway, *Inside the Left* (London: George,

Allen & Unwin, 1942), p. 148. This seems to be a rather confused amalgamated account of the Strand Sundays, the Arts Guild and the MSFG rather than an accurate portrayal of the work of the MSFG.

43. For *The Singing Jailbird* (Long Beach, California: Author, 1924) see *New Leader*, 11 April 1930, p. 14; *Socialist Review*, March 1930, p. 14. For *Brain* (London: G.P. Putmans, 1930) see *Socialist Review*, May 1930, pp. 276–7; *New Leader*, 2 May 1930, p. 13 and 12 December 1930, p. 14; *The Times*, 28 April 1930, p. 12. The play was to have been produced by Theodore Komisarjevsky, who pulled out owing to illness. For *In Abraham's Bosom* (London: George Allen Unwin, 1929) see *New Leader*, 28 February 1931, pp. 3 and 15; *The Times*, 8 December 1930, p. 10. For the WTM's response to Sinclair's play, see Raphael Samuel *et al.*, *Theatres of the Left*, p. 48 and pp. 86–7.

44. For details of the MSFG's fight against the new legislation see Bert Hogenkampf, *Deadly Parallels* (London: Lawrence & Wishart, 1986); Don MacPherson, *Traditions of Independence* (London: BFI, 1980); Stephen G. Jones, *The British Labour Movement and Film 1918–1939* (London: Routledge and Kegan Paul, 1987); Harold Scott, 'The Law's a Hass [*sic*]!', *Socialist Review*, April 1930, pp. 325–7.

45. Andrew Davies, *Other Theatres*, p. 102.

46. Stephen G. Jones, *Workers at Play* (London: Routledge & Kegan Paul, 1986) p. 155.

8 Delving the levels of memory and dressing up in the past

MICK WALLIS

> England, England, grey walls of England,
> What can you hear and what can you see,
> Far in the dark of man's unknowing,
> Below the levels of memory?[1]

Thus the refrain with which the Narrative Chorus opens the *Kenilworth Castle Pageant*, performed 8–15 July 1939 by 1,200 locals before a daily crowd of 2,500. Eight hundred others have been involved in its production. The pageant celebrates the gift of the castle to the nation by Lord Kenilworth. Profits are to be given to charity. Regular press coverage since June, relying on photos, culminates with a four-page pull-out. In the same period come reports of smaller events – the Warwickshire Charity Carnival, and a *Pageant of Wroxall Abbey* for a girls' school prize distribution.[2]

The ruined keep of the castle has been reconstructed from theatrical flats. Greensward descends to the specially constructed grandstand through three natural levels, on which stand occasional platforms and eight knee-high microphones. Recently developed circuitry helps to keep the actors at level volume. An orchestra plays specially composed music.

The dramatic action consists of ten episodes, followed by a Triumph Song and Finale presided over by the majestic purple-draped Figure of Kenilworth. The episodes feature (I) Founding of the castle, 1123; (II) Simon de Montfort, 1265; (III) Medieval revival of the Round Table, 1279; (IV) Edward II at Kenilworth; (V) Henry V and Falstaff at Kenilworth; (VI) Eleanor Cobham, Duchess of Gloucester, 1441; (VII)

Queen Elizabeth at Kenilworth; (VIII) Slighting of the castle by Roundheads, 1649; (IX) The Golden Wedding, 1786; and (X) The Ballet of Ribbons. Entrances and exits from varied points and all other cues are given from the 'crow's nest' above the grandstand, from which the Pageant Master – a combination of producer and director – directly presides.

The Programme gives synopses of the episodes. But spectators may also purchase the *Book of the Pageant* for the entire dramatic script, historical notes, and a Preface in which Pageant Master and authors present the rationales of the event. The *Book* is both an aid to concentration – the event is outdoors, the action from episode to episode disconnected – and a souvenir.

Episode II is further divided into three scenes. Episode VIII, the republican assault of 1649, consists purely of action, during which the artificial keep is blown up. Episode X, marking the erection of ribbon-makers' looms in the castle in the early nineteenth century, is a song-and-dance number, a fusion of folk celebration and balletic masque looking over its shoulder to Hollywood. In the other episodes dialogue interweaves with large-scale action – processions, ceremonies, galloping entries, fights:

> *Enter the King and his train . . . all on horseback. From the opposite side enter the townsfolk; joyfully Falstaff and his party stand awaiting the King. He and the others dismount and he comes towards Falstaff . . .*
>
> (Parker, *Book* Episode v, p. 60)

Several episodes open with common folk discussing recognisably 'historical' events. The dialogue is robust prose, the principal author, the Senior English Mistress of Leamington High School for Girls, L. Edith Thomas, having avoided both real medieval language and 'that pseudo-historical diction so precious to the Victorians' (*Book*: Preface, p. 5). Three depressed monks walk across the arena, carrying fishing rods:

POLYCARP: Come on, brother. Be quick!
ELIAS: (*hurrying faster*): What's the good of being quick? Got nothing to be quick for.

PETER: My Lord Simon is coming, isn't he?
ELIAS: (*crossly*): Nothing to be quick for, I said. No fish – no dinner.
POLYCARP: Well, we've got some fish.
PETER: Only three. Not enough for Simon. He'll eat twice that when he's in a fury.
POLYCARP: Roaring fury, too. You'd think the man would burst.
ELIAS: I suppose it is because Prince Edward had escaped.

(Thomas, Book: Episode II, p. 26)

In her preface Thomas explains her attitudes to history and historical accuracy:

> A pageant should be an attempt not to glorify the past, but to dramatise it . . . We have been, we hope, if not photographically, at least picturesquely truthful, on the principle that a picture rather than a photograph reveals the more profound and human reality.

(Book: Preface, p. 5)

Thus, the pageant typically combines historical accuracy as one mode of fetish and the magical presence of famous or near-mythical figures as another. Episode VII both claims authenticity by being based on Laneham's account of 1575 and imagines a moment when Shakespeare, aged 11, is presented to Queen Elizabeth. This 'picturesque' does not average between scientific truth and romantic fantasy: it simultaneously claims each as full presence.

Episode III recalls a recalling: we imagine ourselves in the real presence of fictional thirteenth-century folk who are themselves reviving an ancient ceremonial form – the chivalric Round Table – that existed somewhere on the margin between history and myth. This typifies the regular assertion in such pageants that a sense of tradition is itself a valuable tradition. But it also typifies a trope of fetishistic reclamation that is managed by magical doubling and the interplay of the concrete and the poetic.

Three episodes, 'Triumph Song' and 'Finale' have been guest-written by the august figure of Louis Napoleon Parker. His Episode IX, a sentimental Darby-and-Joan narrative, celebrates the rediscovery of saline waters at the castle. This interpolation of pure fiction into a catalogue of ostensibly historical episodes is a regular feature of the historical pageant.

Much less typical is Parker's cut-and-paste reworking of passages from Marlowe's *Edward II* and Shakespeare's *Henry IV* Part 2 and *Henry V* for Episodes IV and V. This departure from the norm asserts his special status as founder of the very form which bears his name. For, as we shall see, the historical, or 'modern', pageant is also the 'Parkerian' pageant. This processional drama in 1939 claims its special place in a procession of similar events since the founding moment of Parker's own *Sherborne Pageant* of 1905.

As inventor of the form – and of the role of Pageant Master which his grandson Anthony Parker now performs at Kenilworth – the grand old man is given charge of the allegorical elements that conclude the show. Not only the Figure of Kenilworth, but also the figure of Louis Napoleon Parker, preside over and inform the majesty of the moment. The headnote to the 'Finale' proclaims that it 'will revive for many the glories and triumphs of the *Warwick Pageant* of 1906' – Parker's second pageant (*Book*, p. 96). The event not only heads an historical procession of similar events, a grand tradition; it is also a special doubling of a previous triumph. Grandfather and grandson rhyme and the latter looks back with pride and reverence to his famous ancestor. But Parker is also directly present, infusing the event with his authenticity. Sons and daughters of the gathered community are implicitly invited to turn to mothers and fathers and feel the glow of generations.

The *Kenilworth Castle Pageant* typifies the inter-war British historical pageant in many ways. It is strictly episodic; predominantly amateur; aims to unite and memorialise a community around a sense of local history; connects the consolidated local with the national, the warmth of ordinary folk to the majesty of high persons and events; avoids recent conflict; mixes historical document with romantic fantasy; incorporates masque elements as special episodes and processions as a matter of course; involves hundreds or thousands of performers, frequently representing local institutions; delivers the pleasures of spectacle, fetish, copiousness and variety. It is basically similar to Parker's founding event in 1905, except for the *Festschrift* momentum focused on Parker himself. This signals a desire to protect the 'truth' of the form from the pressures of corruption and decadence feared by Parker and his faithful followers.

Pageants old and new

Significant among those followers is Robert Withington, whose two-volume study *English Pageantry* was published in 1918 and 1926. Withington argues in favour of Parker's ideals at a time when these are already threatened.[3] Parker had wanted to emulate the Germanic *Festspiel* in the 1870s, while a public schoolmaster at Sherborne. In his subsequent theatrical career, he made the *Sherborne Pageant* to celebrate the 1200th anniversary of bishopric, school and town. As Withington records, enthusiasm for Parker's projected 'folk-play' was scant, since 'the name was not understood'. But the change of name to 'Pageant' 'suggested delightful masquerading', and 900 locals became involved (*Pageantry*, vol. II, p. 198). Both event and Parker became famous. Parker went on to make further pageants and others – such as Frank Lascelles at Oxford in 1907 – emulated him.

Withington traces the development of the pageant, strictly understood as a 'moving show' (*Pageantry*, vol. I, p. 1), from its roots in folk-mumming through to the Lord Mayor's Shows of the 1890s. Predominantly the products of the merchant class and realised through the agencies of trade guild and church, these civic manifestations are, according to Withington's categorisations, essentially 'aesthetic': they appeal to the eye, intend to entertain, and celebrate the present.

Himself a maker of pageants in the United States, Withington dedicates two final chapters to the Parkerian pageant in Britain and the United States. This new form of pageantry, he stresses, 'has no connection at all' to the older form, 'other than a mere accident of name' (*Pageantry*, vol. II, p. 197, n. 3). The modern pageant is by contrast essentially 'educational': it appeals to the sense of history, intends first to instruct and celebrates the past. Only in the twentieth century does pageantry become 'rooted to one spot' (*Pageantry*, vol. I, p. xviii). The audience are seated before a stage and arena, and the fundamental procession is a sequence of episodes enacted there. Moreover, the modern pageant is fundamentally dramatic.

The 'modern', 'Parkerian', or 'historical' pageant, then, is a form ushered in by the new twentieth century, and existing alongside the several varieties of the persisting form of processional pageant proper.

Withington likens the Parkerian pageant to the Elizabethan chronicle play, with the community rather than a single person as 'hero'. An episodic drama with popular appeal celebrates a shared past and so knits the community. Now, while Parker made *Sherborne* under his direct auspices, he also established committees for activities such as prop-making and costume. The consolidated mode of organisation between the wars was by a raft of committees, each responsible to the Pageant Master or Mistress. Not only would there be Finance, Wardrobe, Publicity, Street Decoration, Equestrian Committees and so on, but also separate Episode Committees, each centred on a local organisation.[4]

Thus, viewed as a communal activity, the historical pageant mirrors some aspects of the medieval 'Corpus Christi Cycles'. Local institutions simultaneously promote themselves and reaffirm their adherence to shared beliefs. Both forms also have elements of the beating of bounds – the community is rendered symbolically coherent by this gathering together for the rehearsal of a shared narrative. Nonetheless, the Chester British Legion or Townswomen's League, which set up Episode Committees for the *Chester Historical Pageant* (1937), are a far cry from the Water Drawers of Dee or the York Company of Mercers. Institutions participating in inter-war pageants are typically peripheral to the economic and social life of the town, not centres of mercantile or craft power but bolt-holes for petit-bourgeois worthiness and pretended influence. Moreover, both the Cycles and chronicle plays rehearse an over-arching narrative. There is both story and logic to the story. But Parker both restricted himself to events before 1642, since 'the Whig and Tory camps still exist in England, and feeling still runs high'[5] and avoided making an explicit historical argument. Indeed, very few 'historical' pageants – until the form was appropriated by the

Left – tell a history at all. The standard aim was simply the 'awakening or creation of communal historical sense'.[6] That sense is awakened and constructed by what is after all a fundamentally aesthetic procedure: the showing of and participation within a series of attractive vignettes.

Those vignettes are made attractive both by scale and by the sense of authenticity. Historical 'accuracy' further confers a sense of depth and substance, that below the surface of any community are to be found successive sediments, each bearing a rich seam. The sumptuous parade of famous personages is typically coupled with snatches of their intimate dialogue: we simultaneously gaze upon them as ideal or mythic creatures, yet also 'know' them. And we common folk are there in this authentic and splendid history too, playing our part. Not that the lives of ordinary people are usually really figured – their presence confers a sense of 'human depth', simultaneously a rhetorical guarantee and a form of entertainment commodity.

Killing modernity and the leisure principle

Parker's aims for this new 'National Drama' were reactionary. He wrote:

> the modernising spirit, which destroys all loveliness and has no loveliness to put in its place . . . is just precisely the kind of spirit which a properly organised and properly conducted pageant is designed to kill.[7]

This retreat to the past openly attempts to maintain class privilege as organic practice. According to Gilbert Hudson, who made several Yorkshire pageants, the 'awakening or creation of communal historical sense' dissolves the 'artificial restraints and enmities' between classes. He preferred 'a small old-fashioned town' as his site for ideological production, since that might retain 'a remnant . . . of the more philanthropic aspects of feudal conditions'.[8] Parker reflected that 'the classes mix for the moment' and gain a 'lasting sympathy . . . but as soon as the pageant is over, class lines are recognised'.[9]

Withington guesses that the new pageantry might be 'an unconscious development of the Puritan conscience, which will not admit pure enjoyment, but seeks to find joy in edification' (*Pageantry*, vol. ii,

p. 202) while in his Preface to the *York Pageant* (1909) Parker celebrates the 'self-sacrifice, self-effacement, surrender of leisure, on the part of thousands of voluntary workers, unnamed, unrewarded, often unthanked'.[10]

Yet while Parker detested the idea of mere display, the townsfolk of Sherborne were clearly grabbed by the very idea of 'delightful masquerading'. Whatever the ideals of its progenitor and his followers, historical pageantry between the wars was first and foremost a form of leisure – an opportunity to meet others taking part, to dress up and show off, to take pleasure. Civic pride can still be part of that pleasure, as was the case for Irene Kenyon, who repeatedly told to her children the story of her involvement in a pageant at Gawthorpe Hall, near Burnley, in 1926. Part also of her pleasure was being allowed a glimpse of the aristocrats in the big house across the river.[11]

High hopes for the future

In 1936, when the pageant was 'increasingly popular all over the country', Mary Kelly published her guide *How to Make a Pageant*. She writes that

> To the general public a 'pageant' suggests a large-scale historical
> show in a number of unconnected episodes, real crowds, mass
> movement and colour, processions and horses, music and
> dancing, on a beautiful outdoor stage: first of all an appeal to the
> eye, and then an attempt to reproduce history in a romantic
> light. The players are entirely amateur, and most of them are
> not even regular amateur players . . . The audience is large,
> uncontrolled, and ignorant: it is there to pick out its friends in
> unfamiliar clothes, to admire them or laugh at them and to
> enjoy to the full any incongruity – not to experience any
> emotion or to make any effort of understanding or imagination.
> It expects little from a pageant, and is easily satisfied.[12]

Most pageants 'resemble each other as closely as do peas. There is the Spirit of the Ages, or Father Time, or some such personage, who "narrates" (usually in rather halting blank verse)' (p. 4). The episodes are predictable:

The Roman Occupation of Britain; The Founding of an Abbey
by Edward the Confessor; An Old Englysshe Fayre; The Visit of
Good Queen Bess; The Arrival of Charles I on the Eve of a Battle;
The Stage-coach bringing the News of Waterloo.

(p. 5)

For Kelly, historical pageants are by now popular, mildly pleasurable
and pointless. They trade not in history but in nostalgia:

> if any definite idea lurks behind them, it is that for continuity, a
> vague desire to remember the days that are past . . . and to
> preserve, even if only for a little while longer, that bond which
> ties us to our country by an intimate love of some corner of it.
>
> (p. 8)

But the pageant form truly provides the opportunity to show 'the real
drama of history; the conflict between the individual and the mass, the
force of strong ideas driving men forward, the reaction from them that
pulls them back . . . the growing-pains of humanity' (p. 9). Kelly calls
for 'some original and constructive minds' to realise pageantry's 'possibilities as drama, and lift it into a fine and potent form of artistic
expression', inculcating a liberal-Hegelian consciousness in the
mass, 'to show in dramatic form . . . the slow unfolding and growth
of ideal which history reveals' (pp. 6–8). Her view of this future possibility is ecstatic: 'the raw crowds [of performers] will lose all self-
consciousness and be lifted together into a strongly felt and sincerely
acted emotion' (p. 6). The audience of the future

> will no longer sit as apathetically as possible on a wooden seat
> without a back, but will form part of the play as an audience
> should, and will be made to experience something that is
> thoroughly disturbing.
>
> (p. 6)

Yet Kelly's hopes for a 'progressive' national drama by and for the mass
and based in the pageant are made precisely in the context of the banal-
ities of content and engagement that, as she notes, predominate.

Dressing up in the past

While Hudson in 1918 looked back, and Kelly in 1936 forwards, each wanted to escape the shabbiness and dislocation they perceived in their contemporary England.

Withington notes that 'romantic' and 'historical' elements had begun to creep into civic parades from the 1880s, in his terms preparing the way for Parker (*Pageantry*, vol. II, pp. 194–5). David Cannadine has demonstrated both how Queen Victoria's waning popularity was defended and how town hall authority was symbolically consolidated by the invention of supposedly immemorial traditions.[13] While such defensive constructions of a sense of continuity with an actual or imagined past are designed to confer a 'natural' authority upon centres of power, their ideological power must to a considerable degree depend upon those demotic feelings of dislocation classically identified with modernity.

Most participants in historical pageants between the wars were mainly out for fun. But the proud lists of participating organisations in the hundreds of Programmes are not only a contribution to the spectacular dimension of those events; they are also an attempt to image a community being at one with itself. Recall Kelly's identification of a '*vague desire* to remember the days that are past', the wish 'to preserve, *even if only for a little while longer*, that bond which ties us to our country'. To participate in a pageant is to help construct the sense that the community coheres: dressing up in the past echoes and amplifies this sense of connectedness. It seems that the historical pageant offered a brief compensation from anxiety and anomie, a sense of continuity and of depth, by mobilising a vague sense of 'history' – in contrast to both Kelly's progressive struggle of ideas and Parker's reverence for tradition, and the pretensions to grand synthesis they shared.

As Augé reaffirms, modern identities have been sustained by sharing the narratives common to the place we inhabit; and by tracing a route which 'passes through the most visible signs, the most institutionalised signs, those most recognised by the social order' – a route which thus 'designates the place of the social order, defined by the same stroke as the common place'.[14] The standard historical pageant offers a shared narrative that is shareable precisely because it narrates nothing of substance. And it makes the town a monument to itself. In later modernity, the dissolution of place into non-place that character- ises Augé's 'supermodernity' was of course already under way. The his- torical pageant may for many have been a bemused response.

Preliminary mappings

In his autobiography, Parker complains of a double corruption. Rather than accept advice, his imitators 'sneaked; they spied; they stole; they vulgarised; they were absurd'. Parker's dream of inculcating 'a sense of history' through splendour and the self-sacrificial engagement of the mass had dissolved, he felt, into mere showmanship.[15] And when 'speculators began to try to commercialise pageants . . . the word Pageant was affixed to almost everything', including 'Motorcycles' and 'Lingerie' (Parker, *Lives*, p. 298). Parker's revitalisation of pageantry had unwittingly colluded with the ongoing spectacularisation of com- modity forms in the new century, and with it the commodification of cultural perception.

Precisely because 'pageant' described a very wide variety of cul- tural objects between the wars – processions, commercial, thematic and spectacular as well as historical; dramas indoors as well as out; pageant-plays; history and science books; missionary propaganda – and because their traces are scattered across many local archives – it is not yet possible to give a clear picture of the development of the Parkerian pageant. What follows here are some results of a national survey begun in 1998.[16]

Significant Pageant Masters working both before and after the First World War include Nugent Monck and Frank Lascelles. Monck (Northampton 1925, Norwich 1926, 'Cardinal Wolsey' at Ipswich 1930, Ramsgate 1934, Nottingham and Notts. 1935, Chester 1937, Manchester 1938) claimed to have evolved the historical pageant inde- pendently of Parker, as part of his general project of revitalising earlier theatrical forms.[17]

Lascelles began with Oxford in 1907 and Bath in 1909. In the inter-war period, he made pageants at Harrow (1923), Carlisle (1928), Barking (1931), Bradford (1931), Dartford (1932) and Leicester (1932). Parker recognised that his own initiative echoed the British state's revival of ceremony: Lascelles applied the historical pageant itself to imperial myth-making. In 1911 he made a *Pageant of London* for the Festival of Empire, and in 1924 the *Pageant of Empire* with Sir Frank Benson to accompany the British Empire Exhibition.[18] Edward Baring teamed up as director with a variety of Pageant Masters and sometimes led the production himself, as for instance for Newcastle and the North in 1931. While script-writers were regularly local amateurs, John Drinkwater's collaboration with Baring at Shropshire in 1934 (which included a *Masque of Comus*) offers a rare example of linkage with the literary sphere. Matthew Anderson and Edward P. Genn devised pageants for Britain's first Civic Weeks in Liverpool (1926, 1927), a *Pageant of Transport* (1930) marking the Liverpool and Manchester Railway centenary, and the *Lancashire Cotton Pageant* (1932), sponsored by the trade and development agencies.

Withington notes that historical pageants had 'not been so prolific' in 1911–14 as 1907–11, possibly because of commercialisation (*Pageantry*, vol. ii, p. 228). A revival had seemed imminent with the millenary *Hertford Pageant* in 1914, but war intervened. Meanwhile, pageantry was used for charitable and propaganda purposes, and some peace pageants (notably Berenice de Bergerac's *Pageant of Victory* at Oxford) were made in 1919.

While in the 1920s church and small-scale pageants seem to predominate, the Parkerian pageant did re-emerge with some vigour. A 1907 script was revived for the *Reading Historical Pageant* in 1920. Historical pageants were for instance given in Wells (1923), Torquay (1924), Northampton (Monck, 1925), Norwich (Monck, 1926), Bridgwater (1927) and Carlisle (1928). In 1929, Beatrice Morrell made *The Romance of King Arthur, A Pageant* at Tintagel. In 1923, Parker was on the road promoting an unrealised pageant at Croydon.

It is in this decade that Mary Kelly's pageant-making begins. While her book imagines mass-movement in the large scale, her own productions were mostly very local, intimate affairs. *Bradstone* (1929), for instance, is little more than a hamlet. Both this and her pageant for *Rillington* (1927) do much to concentrate on the domestic sphere and women's experience. While this last presents a picture of successive invasions of Britain as an enriching, albeit brutal, process, her

6. *Pageant of Bradstone* (Mary Kelly, 1929). Episode V: 'Harvest Home, 1820':
Note the specially erected grandstand; processional and festive elements; the
integration of significant buildings (Bradstone Church faces the grandstand).

Pageant of Launceston (1931) evokes the native and still active
Cornish feeling that the Anglo-Saxon overlords got what they deserved
with the Norman invasion. Kelly founded the Village Drama Society in
1918 (subsequently amalgamated with the British Drama League in
1932), working closely with various branches of the Women's
Institute.[19] It is clear also that WIs initiated and organised various
pageants, such as the *Pageant of Dorset History* (1929) and *The Spirit of
Dorset* (Lulworth Castle, 1939).

As Lascelles' busy time in 1931–2 suggests, the early 1930s
show a time of high concentration, possibly because of the trade crisis.
Kelly's observation of another surge around 1936 – sustaining itself
until the outbreak of war in 1939 – is upheld by the archival traces. A
successful pageant at a particular site frequently prompted later emulation, sometimes much later. The 1960s are marked by such revivals.
Thus the 1969 *Gower Pageant and Fair* at Penrice Castle, part of
'Croeso 69' in Investiture Year (of Charles as Prince of Wales), echoes
the 1924 *Gower Pageant*.

7. *Pageant of Bradstone* (Mary Kelly, 1929). 'The Freeing of the Serfs at Bradstone, ca 970': Bradstone Manor Gatehouse provides both scale and spectacle, and is itself 'reanimated'. Note the considerable care (including historical research) and resources invested in costumes and properties.

A pageant may be mounted principally to raise charity – for instance, the *Garscube Pageant* (1928) aided Glasgow Dental Hospital's work with the poor. Several pageants – especially in the 1930s – mark no special occasion. Many others celebrate the granting of a charter, or its anniversary. National events are marked by local pageants, such as the Bolton *Children's Pageant* for the 1937 Coronation. 'National' events include not only Lascelles' imperial pageants but also Frank Benson's *Scottish Historical Pageant* (1927) at Craigmillar Castle, attended by King George V and Queen Mary, and – at a slightly different level – Gwen Lally and Marjorie Bowen's *Pageant of England* (1935) at Langley Park, Buckinghamshire, which sported aristocrat performers.

Sediment, theme and narrative

These three terms may help to articulate rhetorical similarities and differences between pageants. Parker's avoidance of narrative and concentration on detailed local research implicitly activates a metaphor of sedimentation. While this has some connections to the later notion of 'heritage', the historical pageant typically addresses *local* sedimentation. At times this becomes an explicit concern. Charles Henderson, who helped Kelly with *Bradstone* (1929), insisted:

> The history of any English parish is the history of England in
> miniature . . . the true pageant of the normal English parish
> knows neither kings nor battles. Its task is to depict the social
> life of the place through out the ages.[20]

The individual is metaphorically placed in a rich soil which is at once deeply local and yet thoroughly integrated into the nation. In Kelly's hands this logic works largely to evoke actually lived history; in the hands of many others, it sentimentalises nationhood.

In a sense, 'history' itself is the theme of the Parkerian pageant proper: history is *reduced* to this status. At times, thematic concerns become more explicit. *Garscube* (1928) dedicates itself to searching out 'high romance' in emulation of Walter Scott; Gwen Lally's *Runnymede* (1935) celebrates the 'spirit of fair play'. Lascelles at *Barking* (1931; see below) foregrounds the agency of ordinary people. Monck and Baring in *Nottingham* (1935) advocate pride in 'the men and women who played their part in building up and preserving for us our liberties and institutions'.[21] Major M. F. Cely Trevilian's *Defendamus: A Pageant of Taunton* (1928) lays out a 'continuity of striving for the right' in various spheres of life, with a strong emphasis on 'the people'.

It is with narrative that we turn to the Left. In 1934, Anderson, Genn and Communist composer Alan Bush made the *Pageant of Labour*, tracing the development of trades unions, for the London Trades Council. The Communist Party then appropriated pageantry for propaganda means during the time of the Popular Front. Alan Bush, playwright Montagu Slater and director André van Gyseghem variously combined to make *Towards Tomorrow* (1938), tracing the development of co-operation as an anti-capitalist force; the *Pageant of South Wales* (1939), tracing working-class struggle in the hundred years since the Newport Rising; and *Heirs to the Charter* (1939, indoors) which marked the centenary of Chartism by constructing a narrative from the Charter to Harry Pollitt's leadership of the Communist Party of Great Britain.[22]

Alan Bush and poet Randall Swingler's *Pageant of Music and the People* (1939, indoors), traces a narrative of the people's struggle against oppression, illustrated by their music and songs, and uses music as a metaphor for natural, unalienated humanity.[23] This overt thematisation points to a thematic burden – of 'the People against the Exploiters' – underpinning each of the narratives in the Popular Front pageants. This in turn may be seen as an appropriation of the quasi-liberal strategies of, say, *Defendamus*.

Pageantry, urbanisation and depression

Testimony is paid to the pressures of change in the literature for both small- and large-scale pageants in the early 1930s. *An Oxfordshire Historical Pageant* (Shipton Manor, 1932) is a Right-ist romance in which, for instance, Charles II pardons a poacher and Nell Gwynn throws money around. It was part of a drive to raise £1,000 for a social club in Kidlington – identified as one of the largest villages in Britain, in a rapidly growing area. A focus for village life was now needed.[24]

In a foreword, Frank Clarke MP promises that Lascelles' *Dartford Historical Pageant* (1932) will create 'a common bond of local association' between natives and 'families from other parts'. 'Fifty years of change' have transformed hitherto 'typical Kentish communities wrapped in intense parochialism'. The now united population will win 'its collective way to a merrier and more prosperous Dartford Division'. The episodes illustrate the power of 'the ordinary natural instincts of our people', how 'in a courageous spirit smilingly expressed the resolve of a self-reliant people overcame the difficulties of their times'.[25]

This rhetoric is not just for the direct benefit of the local population. It is designed to attract local investment during economic depression. Thus, Clarke's prose lurches into one of those rhetorical disjunctions so typical of historical pageantry. Local districts have united:

to take to themselves the spirit of happy resolution and to
invoke universal attention to the unique industrial facilities
offered by vacant sites, efficient modern services and wholly
sympathetic municipal administration.

(Dartford *Book*)

For this is a twin event, an 'Historical Pageant and Industrial
Development Exhibition': more than one-third of the Official Souvenir
is taken up with statements from local industrial exhibitors.

In a broadly similar context, the *Barking Historical Pageant and
Industrial Exhibition* marked the granting of a charter to that borough
in 1931. In the message accompanying his full-page photo-portrait,
Prince George applauds Barking's determination 'to face the economic
difficulties through which our Country is now passing with a progressive policy'.[26]

The *Book* defines a charter thus:

the symbol of a procedure which has its roots in antiquity and
. . . associated with ceremonials and traditions which are not
merely superficial survivals of the past, but [which] have real
value in marking the continuity of local government and
fostering the ambitions of local authorities.

(p. 8)

Town Clerk S.A. Jewres chronicles forms of local government in
Barking from medieval times to the present, ending with an heroic
account of the planning and development of these very celebrations,
culminating in the erection of a 13,000 sq ft exhibition hall in just fourteen days by the District Manufacturers' Association, direct labour,
the borough engineer and British steel.

Enterprise and steel-framed modernity join hands with scenes of
Romans, Danes, Queen Elizabeth and the great Barking Fair of 1746.
Mediating between the two – perhaps rather prompting their collision
– is Jewres' story of local administration.

The *Book* presents panoramic cast portraits for six episodes, up
to 250 men and (many more) women, children from toddlers to teenag-
ers, all carefully costumed, neatly arrayed as if for a school photograph.

Under the name of one is printed, 'name to be added to the Costumes Design Committee'. And as part of this absolute drive for inclusiveness, this opulence of commonality, page 2 lists 'Members of the Last Urban District Council, 1931', arranged by committees which inevitably include Joint Sewerage and the Allotment Sub-Committee.

If that last detail bespeaks corporate pomposity, instantly punctured by the collision of the concretely bathetic with images of transcendence, it also marks an historical shift into a present when for most of Britain urban sanitation is seemingly natural, not a consequence of communal planning and enterprise.

Lascelles has this typical message for the audience, modern pageantry's version of the treasures of the humble:

> let your mind drift back to the early days when this new
> Borough was still a little village . . . dream of those days and the
> great characters who loved in them, of the King and Queen who
> came to this place, of the saints whose home it was, of the
> famous men who once were boys roaming in these fields. Then
> think ahead a hundred years or more, and remember that each
> one of you, however humble, can in your own short life make
> your mark upon your generation, and so upon countless
> generations of Barking yet to come.
>
> (p. 47)

Lascelles too has his full-page photo-portrait, palette in hand. He is engaged for his proven skills; but he also confers the transcendence of art. Messages from royalty meantime combine transcendence with the then active myth of the national community as family. From this distance at least, that knitting together of the aristocratic and the demotic, a fantastic yet potent throwback to feudal suppositions, comes under comic strain the more local it gets. Thus, Clarke falls into further rhetorical disjunction when he opines that

> At such a time as now confronts us, it was a timely inspiration
> that led the Dowager Countess of Limerick to rise from her
> domestic bereavements with the suggestion for such a Pageant.
>
> (Dartford *Book*)

Doubting coherence: petit-bourgeois carnival

Twenty years later, another aristocratic lady rises in an instructively more comic manner. It is the closing procession in the 'Pageant of Mangel-Wurzelton'. Mary, who plays Chorus, proclaims:

> The royal cavalcade is drawing near:
> Let every citizen prepare to cheer.
> The bells are going mad – and very soon
> I fear the band will play another tune.[27]

The crowd cheers as an apparently empty carriage is drawn on by two comedy horses. Lord Bliss follows riding a comedy hobby-horse and dressed up as a Life Guard. As the bewildered crowd quietens, '*Suddenly, the head and shoulders of* LADY BLISS *pop up from the carriage. She is dressed as Britannia*'. Surveying the crowd with a bright smile, she explains that since the Censor will not allow Victoria to be represented on stage, it has been decided that 'I, Britannia, should be the one / To bring this scroll to Mangel-Wurzelton' (pp. 90–1).

The 'pageant' is in fact Act II of L. du Garde Peach's play *The Town that Would Have a Pageant*, performed by the Great Hucklow Players in 1951. Both acts derive their comedy from aesthetic and social disjunction. Act I is a planning meeting for the celebrations in the Mayor's parlour: disruptive incursions by a charlady pair with the aristocratically vague Lady Bliss's late arrival. The Mayor is made late for this meeting to mark communal unity, by a deputation of disgruntled ratepayers. While he believes the borough has no history, Sheldon – expert because he has produced the YMCA panto for three years – insists that 'It will have, after we've done a pageant' (p. 22). In Act II, the Hucklow performers simultaneously present innocents from 'a small provincial town' (SD, p. 5) obliviously partaking in stupidities meant to typify such pageantic efforts, *and* perform a commentary on this unintended farce. But in this 'Delerium', innocent farce and lampooning commentary are folded into the same dialogue. Mary as Chorus 'fears' more band music simultaneously as she anticipates the royal procession.

The ratepayers' interests are at once seamlessly yet also ridiculously incorporated:

We're ancient Britons, and we live
In Mangel-Wurzelton;
Our lives are full of incident,
And clean but simple fun:
That we're both wise and healthy,
Our appearance indicates,
And as we always live in caves,
We don't pay any rates.

On stage is not only Mary/Chorus but also in the same person the woman from Great Hucklow playing that double role. The final procession is far more ludicrous than anything that has gone before. At this moment, all three levels of her person and those of other performers coalesce – or perhaps enter into endless circulation – as part of a gesture of generosity from these famously proficient amateurs to the amateurish burghers of Mangel-Wurzelton. And holding the fun together is the comic old female aristocrat . . . who is also Britannia, a better version of Victoria who, because of Victorian stuffiness cannot appear. Lady Bliss appears no longer as a ridiculous old woman, but as a grand old lady generously letting her hair down, joining in a celebratory bit of fun.

While it might be said that *The Town that Would Have a Pageant* celebrates innocence, it might be more accurate to say that it negotiates petit-bourgeois embarrassment by first revelling in feelings of deep inauthenticity and then basking in a sentimental glow – which manages simultaneously to be modern yet very definitely old-fashionedly fond of upper-class eccentricity. The burlesque is not ultimately satirical, but an act of sentimental synthesis.

Peach's play exemplifies the broad persistence of a structure of feeling surrounding historical pageantry. Withington (*Pageantry*, II, p. 204) cites the 'semi-ironic, semi-appreciative, view' of pageant-making in Arthur Thomas Quiller-Couch's *Brother Copas* (1911). Inhabitants of Merchester, a fictionalised Winchester, come together 'in a common pride of England and her history' and 'distort it as the performers might, and vain, inadequate, as might be the words they declaimed, an idea lay behind it all', such that 'even careless spectators began to catch this infection of nobility – this feeling that we are indeed greater than we know'.[28] Quiller-Couch helped to write F. R. Benson's *Winchester Pageant* (1908).

A synthesis of inauthenticity and transcendence marks both Quiller-Couch's fictionalised documentation and Peach's burlesque. Both manage to be generous, yet Peach's incorporation of that synthesis into the very style of his composition suggests his greater investment. While at Merchester 'the rite took possession of them, seizing on them, surprising them with a sudden glow about the heart', Peach's pretend pageant can have no more 'real' purchase than panto. And note that between 1908 and 1951 the primary focus had shifted from England to the local borough, and that the folk of Merchester met 'for a purpose in itself ennobling because unselfish', not for self-advancement or through aimlessness.[29]

Horace Sequira's 1936 comic monologue 'The Pageant Rehearsal' opens with the Producer, her briefcase bulging with paper, whistle and field-glasses slung around her neck, hollering through a megaphone for the Organising Secretary Mrs Donaldson-Wuff, whom she imagines is probably – like everyone else – still up at the town hall. Not only have key personnel gone missing: so too have the prospects of both theatrical and historical presence. Everything she addresses threatens to turn planned magnificence into bathos: 'Will the Ancient Britons kindly step this way . . . Your battle with the Romans is timed for six-fifteen, so you've only got a few minutes to get the green OFF and the blue ON'; someone has decided that a bathchair will represent Boadicea's chariot; it rains, so the Roman army go off for mackintoshes and umbrellas, Henry VIII's wives for galoshes; Donaldson-Wuff appeals for the retrieval of Miss Casting's (Boadicea's) plait, lost on the pageant ground. Parker and others later cued entrances by electric bells – at this dress rehearsal the Producer must shout: 'Will the Steward at No. 3, kindly clear those nurses, mothers, perambulators and sheep away from the entrance at once!' The sketch ends with a series of collisions and the producer marching off with Donaldson-Wuff to the town hall.[30] In abstract terms, the sketch draws its humour from the relentless repetition of ironic bathos. In cultural terms, it gently satirises theatrical amateurism as inept, over-ambitious and bureaucratic. As a sketch designed for amateur performance, the satire is self-deprecatory – at least for the performer.

While in her book of the same year, Kelly sees the pageant as a potential means for mass expression, Norman Marshall's Preface welcomes it as a means whereby the mass of amateurs might find their best potential as performers. If only the writers of 'the endless stream of one-act plays designed for amateurs' at British Drama League Festivals he adjudicates 'would realise that they have much finer material in the amateur crowd than in the amateur actor.' Yet in 1936, the 'genuine vitality' promised by the crowd is missing both there and in the pageant, which 'too often descends . . . into a pitiful waste of infinite energy and enthusiasm.'[31]

In his reminiscence of Great Hucklow, Peach insisted that the 'lack of a society, democratised by committees [was] the real secret of [its] success': he supported democracy everywhere except in the theatre.[32]

Sequira's sketch draws some interesting distinctions and connections. The pageant rehearsal, presided over desperately by a woman encumbered with conventionally male trappings, is made even more ludicrous by the self-importance, bureaucratism and ineptitude so prevalent in amateur theatrical enterprise. And matched with this is that other institution of petit-bourgeois organisation: local government. And consider how double-sided the trope of bathos might be. These amateur-theatricalists of 1936 are incapable of matching the example of, say, Louis Napoleon Parker at Warwick in 1906, or indeed his grandson Anthony at Kenilworth in 1939. But mediating between the two is the picture we might infer of life in one of the Episode, Technical or Organising Committees even of a 'proper' pageant – a realm in which committee-man-and-woman and amateur theatricalist might rule. Further, given that the bathos is structured around not only organisational chaos but also the collapse of historical magnificence, the sketch indicates doubts about pretensions to the latter *tout court*, regardless of professional competence.

Both Sequira's sketch and Peach's 'delerium' oscillate between gentle self-satire and a sort of petit-bourgeois carnival, the happy refusal of any claim to meaningful narrative, substantive presence or transcendent truth or experience (happy but also nervous; these are not the peasants of heroic Bakhtinian fantasy). If this is right, then the wettings, mild decaptitations, babies, nurses and animals (what are the nurses *doing*?) fall neatly into place.

The historical pageant between the wars was a major, if occasional, leisure pursuit for hundreds of thousands. It was also tied up intimately with the articulation of identity in terms of place and a shared heritage. Rightist in conception, it nevertheless proved a vehicle for the populist left. Michael Woods convincingly argues that *Defendamus* at Taunton (1928) mobilises discourses of continuity and community in the interests of a declining landed gentry and a rising business élite, allied in defence against a class-based – socialist – politics.[33] While this is a fairly generalisable model for the inter-war pageant, it may be too instrumentalist in conception.

While Parker and Hudson's hegemonic purposes are plain, for instance, Mary Kelly in 1919 was a quietly modernising rebel in the still secure context of her gentry upbringing. There are fractures in gentry discourse and practice. Also, while *Defendamus* may invoke conservative verities, it does so only with uncertainty – by actively negotiating class and geographical liminalities, laying them bare as much as smoothing them over. Such considerations, taken together with, say, the popular embarrassments that Kelly notes, Jewres' grand narrative of local administration, and Peach's gentrified disdain for town councils, which we may glimpse through the sentimental synthesis *The Town That* enacts, do more than point to the maintenance of a conservative hegemony – they begin to delineate the emergence of a petit-bourgeois cultural sphere, which is yet adequately to be mapped.

Notes

1. *Book of the Words of the Kenilworth Castle Pageant* (1939), p. 12.
2. *Leamington Chronicle and Warwickshire Pictorial*, June–July 1939, *passim.*
3. Robert Withington, *English Pageantry: An Historical Outline*, 2 vols. (Cambridge, Mass.: Harvard University Press, 1918, 1926).
4. Kenilworth is atypical in this respect. Doing without episode committees might be one way in which it was being 'pure'.

5. Quoted in Withington, *Pageantry*, p. 221.

6. See below, n.8.

7. *Journal Social Arts live*, p.143, quoted in Withington, *Pageantry* II, p. 195.

8. Letter dated November 1918, quoted in Withington, *Pageantry* II, p. 203.

9. Quoted in Withington, *Pageantry* II, p. 205, n. 2.

10. Cited in *ibid.*, p. 197, n. 2.

11. Judith Park, pers. comm.

12. Mary Kelly, *How to Make a Pageant* (London: Pitman, 1936), pp. 2–4.

13. David Cannadine, 'The Context, Performance, and Meaning of Ritual: the British Monarchy and the "Invention of Tradition", c. 1829–1977', *The Invention of Tradition*, ed. Eric Hobsbawm and Terence Ranger (Cambridge University Press, 1983); 'The Transformation of Civic Ritual in Modern Britain: The Colchester Oyster Feast', *Past and Present* no. 94, pp. 107–30.

14. Marc Augé, *Non-places: Introduction to an Anthropology of Supermodernity*, trans. John Howe (London: Verso, 1995), p. 51.

15. Parker, *Several of my Lives* (London: Chapman and Hall, 1928), p. 297.

16. By the author, with financial support from Loughborough University.

17. Withington, *Pageantry*, p. 226.

18. See Rt. Hon. Earl of Darnley, ed., Frank Lascelles, 'Our Modern Orpheus' (London, 1932); Deborah Ryan, 'Staging the Imperial City. The Pageant of London 1911' in F. Driver and D. Gilbert, eds, *Imperial Cities* (Manchester University Press, 1999).

19. See Mary Kelly, *Village Theatre* (London: T. Nelson & Sons, 1939).

20. Charles Henderson, 'Preface' in Mary Kelly, *The Pageant of Bradstone 970–1820* (1929), p. 7.

21. *Nottingham and Notts Historical Pageant Handbook* (1935), p.14.

22. See Mick Wallis, 'The Popular Front Pageant: Its Emergence and Decline', *New Theatre Quarterly* XI (41), February 1995, pp. 17–32; and 'Heirs to the Pageant: Mass Spectacle and the Popular Front', *Weapons in the Struggle? Essays in the Cultural History of the British Communist Party*, ed. Andy Croft (London: Pluto Press, 1999).

23. See also Mick Wallis, 'Pageantry and the Popular Front: Ideological Production in the 'Thirties', *New Theatre Quarterly*, 10 (38), May 1994, pp. 132–56.

24. *An Oxfordshire Historical Pageant. Book of the Pageant* (1931).

25. *Official Souvenir and Programme of Dartford Division of Kent Historical Pageant and Industrial Development Exhibition* (1932), unpaginated.

26. *The Book of Barking. Being a Souvenir of the Charter Celebrations, Historical Pageant and Industrial Exhibition* (1931), p. 2.

27. L. du Garde Peach, *The Town That Would Have a Pageant. A Delerium in Two Acts*, 1952, pp. 1–91 in *Collected Plays Vol. II* (Manchester and London: Countrygoers Books, 1955), p. 90.

28. Quoted in Withington, *Pageantry*, p. 204.

29. *Ibid.*

30. Horace Sequira, 'The Pageant Rehearsal' in *The Pageant Rehearsal and other Monologues and Duologues for Women with Foreword by Dame Sybil Thorndike* (London: Stanley Nott, 1936), pp. 9–16.

31. Norman Marshall in Mary Kelly, *How to Make a Pageant*, pp. vi–vii.

32. L. du Garde Peach, *The Village Players of Great Hucklow. Twenty-five Years of Play Producing 1927–1952* (Great Hucklow: The Village Players, 1952), p. 8.

33. Michael Woods, 'Performing Power: Local Politics and the Taunton Pageant of 1928', *Journal of Historical Geography*, 25(1), January 1999, pp. 57–74.

9 The ghosts of war: stage ghosts and time slips as a response to war

CLIVE BARKER

The period from 1918 to 1939 never escaped the effects of war. After a post-First World War period when the elation of victory turned into a search for answers to bitter critical questions of why the war was fought – in whose interests it was fought and whether the results justified the mass slaughter – the possibility of a further international conflict raised further questions largely concerned with how to prevent it: by swift counteraction, by appeasement or by an international movement for peace committed to avoid armed conflict at any cost. Ghosts walk the stage throughout the 1920s and 1930s. They come back in search for the answers to questions that will not let them rest in their graves; sometimes they offer hope and the illusion of a world at peace. They bring hope that there is another world beyond this world which makes death meaningless in the context of a wider spiritual vision. Sometimes they seem to be a manipulative tool which the dramatist uses to create suspense, or a sense of romance, in which love can exist somehow out of time and space. There have been ghosts in other ages of the theatre but rarely, since the seventeenth century, have they existed in such profusion.

During the 1930s, some 2,000 spiritualist churches or groups were formed. In 1940, seances became so widespread that they were banned by the government under wartime emergency powers. Within this context it is to be expected that the suffering of those bereft of loved ones in the war should provoke a search for some meaning and comfort in the mediums and seances which advertised contact beyond the grave, and the illusion of a restored wholeness to those whose bodies were obliterated in a myriad of fragments by shelling.

A line of humour in cartoons of the period makes jokes about ouija boards and ghostly visions. A popular song of the late 1920s, sung by a ghost watching his own funeral, is entitled 'Ain't it Grand to be Bloomin' Well Dead'. The variety stage, films and plays, released from the serious purposes and pain which drove those left to search for comfort, make great play with supposedly haunted houses and spooks. Often, in comedy, the effects are manipulated by crooks to cover their dastardly deeds.[1] In a play called *The Unknown* (1919) by Somerset Maugham, which is not about the war at all, and which seems to have slipped out of the canon of his works, there is an almost gratuitous exchange of forgiveness in which a mother expresses the pain of her loss when she asks who will give her back the two sons she has lost and who will forgive God? In the same year J. M. Barrie, an older playwright noted largely for *Peter Pan* and who had paid several visits to the front line during the war, wrote *Mary Rose*.

Mary Rose is a strange and haunting play.[2] An Australian soldier visits a house, now old and for sale, where he has lived in the past. The surly housekeeper denies stories that the house is haunted but she is obviously uneasy about one room in particular. Once the soldier is alone the atmosphere changes and the room comes alive just as it was thirty years earlier. Here two middle-class parents are visited by a young sailor, Simon, who wants to marry their eighteen-year-old daughter Mary Rose. The parents tell him a story they have never told anyone before but which they have promised to tell to anyone who wishes to marry their daughter. The story goes that while vacationing on a Scottish island Mary Rose disappeared, only to return twenty days later: she has no idea that time has past. So the story ends and the young man's proposal is accepted. Act II takes place four years later; the couple have a son, Harry, and they are holidaying on the same island as in the story of the first Act. The Scotsman who rows the family to the island tells them that it has a strange reputation; he tells the story of Mary Rose but does not know that he is telling it to her. As they prepare to leave Mary Rose disappears. Act III is set twenty-five years later – Mary Rose has not returned. Simon, who has never remarried, is coming to visit Mary Rose's parents. When he arrives he says he has seen two people walking across the fields. The two people arrive –

they are the boatman, now the island's minister, and Mary Rose, found sleeping on the island.

She is disconcerted as she seems to have no idea of what, if anything, has happened. The scene changes back to the original setting in the first act. The soldier asks about the household ghost and reveals that he is Harry, the son of Simon and Mary Rose. The housekeeper tells him that she has seen Mary Rose, the ghost, roaming round the house looking for something or someone. She leaves and the ghost of Mary Rose appears to Harry – she can't remember where or when she disappeared – she has forgotten the island, forgotten who she is looking for and is tired of being a ghost. But some way, through her contact with Harry, she is released and called – to heaven?

> The magic was still there, and for three hundred and ninety-nine performances . . . audiences wept, sniffed, swallowed and choked without ever being able to explain what had reduced them to this state . . . Some sought a meaning but it was never vouchsafed. For nobody knew it. The players certainly didn't, and the author had told everything by this time and had nothing more to say . . . [he] didn't know where his heroine had been, or why she had been taken, or the reason for her return. He didn't know where ghosts come from, nor the meaning, even for the purposes of this story, of life and death.[3]

J. C. Trewin, in a manner typical of his butterfly approach to surveys, offers us, almost in an aside, '[T]he play . . . trembled at once into success: it had something in it to console many whom the war had bereaved.'[4] The great attraction of *Mary Rose* lay in its loose ends and in its inability to give answers to questions to which no answers could be found. In positing a different concept of time, a limbo we can never know or penetrate, but from which we will nevertheless return and will be redeemed by love, released into ease and rest, Barrie offered some way of coming to terms with the agony of not knowing what had happened during the 1914–1918 War and the desolation of loved ones blown to one knows not where.

Sutton Vane begins a search for a solution to problems in time by having his characters escape from time into a different dimension.

Outward Bound (1923) takes place on a boat ferrying the dead – the captain is Charon. The main thrust of the play gives reassurance that after death we are judged according to our deeds in life, which posits a light form of predestination. This might have given some comfort to those bereaved by the war – their sacrifice was ordained and their reward would come in a future existence and the supreme, heroic sacrifice will guarantee a favourable judgement in the afterlife. The play has many humorous moments and ends lightly as two of intending suicides, who are between life and death, find the courage to carry on and are sent back in hope through the device of their dog breaking the window and letting the gas out and the air in. The audience are given no direct instruction as to what the nature of the boat is – they have to work this out from clues released during the first half of the play. *Outward Bound* had a considerable success, but further plays from Vane in this dimension were much less well received, and whatever *Outward Bound* had to offer to those who were left behind after the war, the other plays did not have it.

In 1921, Lord Dunsany wrote *If*, the story of a 15-minute time-slip when a business man catches the train he usually misses and ends up a despot in some 'place off the map' near Persia. In 1922, Pinero wrote *The Enchanted Cottage*, in which a man broken by the war, and his wife, married only for mutual consolation, find true love under the spell of an enchanted cottage and are promised that time will stand still and they will stay beautiful to each other as long as their love remains constant. It is not difficult to see through the whimsy and view it as a sympathetic response to many such situations arising out of the casual sexual arrangements of the war period. In the same year, a play called *Old Bill*, named after a Bruce Barnfather cartoon character, the epitome of the old soldier, appeared replete with jokes and comic cartoon characters. Trewin perceptively assessed that dramatists had still not summoned up enough courage to tackle the war seriously at this point.[5]

Life in the trenches

The first of the plays depicting war is Harry Wall's *Havoc* (1923). Wall and many of the cast had fought at the Front so the dialogue and action reflected the slang patois of the trenches, and the details of behaviour and conditions had verisimilitude. Ernest Short records that after the great climactic scene of a half-demented young soldier who had just seen hand-to-hand combat for the first time, the curtain rose thirty-five times to take the applause. The play is rather bitter, and the main theme is the love which sustains and betrays the soldiers. One by one their love is shown to be an illusion; some men die without ever having known this, others have to face up to the fact. In 1924 Alan Monkhouse's *Conquering Hero* continued the somewhat simplistic, short anti-war plays of the immediate post-First World War period. The play takes place entirely in England and although it deals with the experiences of war it does not seek to present these directly but from a distance. The central character is a 'conquering hero' in the sense that he has returned from the war which has been won and in which he served with some distinction. The problem is that he refuses to occupy the role and persists in struggling against war. His family expect him to return with glory and soon become alienated by his pacifist stand. His family and friends regard him as a disgrace, a coward, an idealist and dreamer.

> But playgoers who saw [him] with Monkhouse's eyes knew that
> what in the imaginative 'hero' seemed cowardice was really
> high courage, and that it was his uncompromising honesty
> which forbade him to accept the role of 'a conquering hero'.[6]

So when his girlfriend asks to be allowed to be proud of him, he realises that this is the one thing he cannot accept.

Hubert Griffiths' *Tunnel Trench*, acted outside London in 1925 and in London in 1928, returns to realism and is set in France. It is the first play to use a Flying Corps Squadron base as a setting. The second act takes place in the general's headquarters and the third in the front-line trenches – all this before and during an infantry attack near the end of the war. The play examines and contrasts the experiences and emotions of the combatants before and during the battle. The third act maintains high suspense as the soldiers are aware that German sappers are tunnelling beneath their trench with the intention of planting explosive mines. The sound of their digging can be heard throughout the act.[7]

J. R. Ackerley's *The Prisoners of War* (1925) is equally detailed and authentic in language and actions.[8] It draws on Ackerley's own experiences as a prisoner of war, but has a psychological dimension as it examines the stultifying effect of forced inaction. We see the slow and sordid decline of Conrad's mind – a more intelligent prisoner of war than his companions – through the degradation and wearing monotony of servitude and communal life.[9] Nicholas de Jongh quotes James Agate as saying that Conrad's problem is not depression but the repression of his homosexual love for a consumptive fellow-captive. De Jongh attributes the success of the play to the fact that the censor could not see that the play was about homosexuality, and gives such a masterly coverage of *Prisoners* and the cultural social environment into which it was launched that it could not possibly be absorbed here with any sense of justice.[10]

Ackerley should also be noted in other contexts. As he watched his brother prepare to lead a suicidal raid, he writes that only theatrical clichés seemed appropriate: 'Here was a situation which would have appealed to the actor in him, drama indeed, the limelit moment, himself in the leading role, all eyes upon him.' As Ackerley saw his brother off on his mission he noticed that 'it was impossible to speak the most commonplace word or make the most ordinary gesture without it at once acquiring the heavy overemphasis of melodrama'.[11] Paul Fussell, whose work is the major reference point for culture and the First World War, notes and analyses many of the resemblances subsumed under the ironic title, 'Theatre of War'. He gives a number of examples, such as a military historian describing a Canadian Brigadier: 'in real life he was . . .', as though war is a pretence played out in costumes and roles allocated without choice, and the historian and war theorist Liddell offering a corrective to the interpretation given earlier that the theatre was the prelude to the brothel: 'I . . . [f]elt an intense desire to see plays again . . . more intense than ever before or since . . . I went twice a day to the theatre . . .'.[12] Fussell points to the fact that the end of the war is signalled by a German machine-gunner standing up, doffing his helmet and taking a bow; a successful attack or manoeuvre is greeted with 'Good Show'. There are many references to pre-battle nerves being described as stage fright – Sassoon divided his memoires into 'Acts' – and so on. The soldiers' satirical newspaper *The Wipers Times* imports music-hall terminology into its text. Fussell notes too that melodrama and music hall are the modes in which the British have twice memorably recalled the war on stage, once in *Journey's End* and later in *Oh What a Lovely War*.[13]

The melodrama that is *Journey's End* began life in 1928 and reached the West End by 1929. R. C. Sherriff comes on the scene at a special moment when the double standards expressed in Monkhouse's *The Conquering Hero* were becoming generally felt. 'The Age of Confusion', as H. G. Wells described the post-First World War period, was passing and serious questions had to be answered before the memory of war was laid to rest. Sherriff presents, with some melodramatic touches, an accurate picture of life in the trenches opposite Saint Quentin. Stanhope, who commands and leads the unit, conquers his nerves and sustains himself through secret drinking and the thought of his fiancée back home. Raleigh, a former pupil at Stanhope's school, and the brother of his fiancée, has had himself posted to his hero's unit. This gives Stanhope the problem of concealing his drinking, which would, he thinks, diminish him in his fiancée's eyes if she were to find out. Osborne, the second-in-command, in between enemy attacks, discourses of the beauty and joys of the New Forest and the fascination of Roman excavations. After an attack on the German lines for prisoners, during which Osborne is killed, Stanhope goes back to drinking. In the next attack, Raleigh is mortally wounded and tended by Stanhope, who, as his old schoolmate dies, receives orders to withdraw the remainder of the men to the trenches, which will probably lead to the death of all of them. Camillo Pellizzi is critical of the inclusion of the fiancée which had, he thought, a strong, sentimental effect on audiences, especially the women, but who, for him, was not necessary to the plotting.

> The human soul (or should I say the Christian soul), which
> knows no greater torment than internal conflict, is portrayed, in
> these few scenes, and especially in the second act, where the
> play reaches its crisis and could well end, in one of the saddest
> and most widely significant attitudes, torn between duty and

instinct, between dignity and fear . . . Today we think that the real cowards are those who are afraid of courage; the courageous, on the other hand, have the courage of their fear . . . Mr Sherriff has been clever enough to let the war speak.[14]

One of the external factors which brought *Journey's End* its success was the need to establish a dramatic picture of the *reality* of war, so that later playwrights could address the subject more imaginatively and theatrically. Alternatively, it could be said that Sherriff had done his job so well that following him was a grave hazard. Nevertheless Patrick McGill, in *Suspense* (1930), takes the third-act action from Griffiths and sets a whole play in a captured dugout, under which the Germans are mining in order to plant a bomb. However, the style of the play places it more in the category of psychological thriller than that of war realism. Allardyce Nicoll, however, notes the mixture of the actual and the symbolic in Griffiths' *Tunnel Trench* and sees this as a forerunner to a new approach to war plays.

> As the years advanced, playwrights began to think of the war itself in a way different from that which had first been universal; this new way meant that the playwrights were looking upon their themes less in specific terms, that they were frequently turning their gaze from the past to the future, and that, sometimes at least, they were beginning to conceive their subject-matter imaginatively rather than realistically . . . The new mood, however, could not find free scope until the older style had received its complete fulfilment – and that fulfilment came unexpectedly in 1928 with R. C. Sherriff's powerful *Journey's End* . . . The tantalising thought of the future was now dominant- and it is by no means without significance that 1928 which has seen the appearance of *Journey's End* also saw the publication of C. B. Fernald's *Tomorrow* . . .[15]

Fernald's play shows a man building a private air-raid shelter for himself, the coming of a new war and a glimpse of an afterworld. Nicoll admits this play is confused, which is why it received no production, yet values the way it looks towards the future. To take on such a visionary task instinctively draws the playwright towards the dream world, allegory and and other forms of fantasy involving time slips.

Playing with time

In Richard Pryce's *Thunder on the Left*, also performed in 1928, a boy is projected twenty years forward in time. The play gives some thought to the devastation that lies ahead of the devastation which has just ended. The boy decides to return to his own time. There is an anecdote concerning Clemençeau who, leaving Versailles after signing the peace treaty, paused on the steps and said: 'I thought I heard a child crying.' A *Daily Herald* cartoonist drew this into a cartoon, drawing in the figure of a crying child of the future, labelled *Class of 1940*.

The first of the ghosts returning from the Front does so in *Thunder in the Air* (1928) by Robins Millar, after a novel by Christopher Morley. The ghost of a soldier, killed in France on the penultimate day of the war, returns to his family and lovers in the form in which they remembered him best:

> To his mother he was still a small child, to the fiancée and
> mistress who had loved him of totally different facets.
> Gradually the man's life and character dramatically emerged; he
> was a liar, a seducer and a thief, who had not been killed on the
> battlefield. This revelation was made in an appearance to the
> unforgiving father; by a soldier in battledress with bandaged
> mouth, who in a simple dumbshow mimed the revolver shot
> which had ended a worthless life. It was a scene made
> impressive not only by the mute bandaged figure of the youth
> but by the cry of the father in bitter realisation. It was the
> climax of the play, and a dramatic coup de theatre.[16]

The structure of the play is audacious and if the author does not fully pull off the equation between war and corruption the attempt is deserving of meritorious acclaim. The climax of the play does not come with the father's cry, but rather it comes ambiguously on the curtain call, which in turn becomes an integral part of the play. The audience applauds, while in front of them are all the images of the stages in the soldier's life and corruption, from the small boy to the self-destructive man.

At the very end of 1928, the main backer and benefactor of *Journey's End*, Maurice Browne, with Robert Nicols, wrote a prophetic play called *Wings over Europe*. Although produced immediately in New York, it had to wait until 1932 for a very short run in London. The play deals with a young scientist offering his discovery of the process to split the atom to the British government. *Wings* is much too ambitious and speculative, but this might not be what denied it an audience. Its pronouncements and forecasts would hardly be welcome to a country struggling out of one war and looking for some form of peaceful existence, however illusory. The opening act closes with the Foreign Secretary saying:

> Kindly realize that every word that young man said is – I am convinced – literally true . . . Every word! . . . And I solemnly say to you all, it would be better for that poor young man and for the world had he never been born. And the final curtain falls as 'The roar of aeroplanes fills all Europe.'[17]

Another ghost from the Front might have emerged in 1930 and from a most unexpected quarter. On a holiday cruise around the Orient, which reads more like a form of punishment than rest and recuperation, Noël Coward was persuaded to play Stanhope in *Journey's End* to help out a touring company, which included John Mills playing Raleigh. Coward is very critical of his performance, given with insufficient preparation. During the continuation of the cruise, from Ceylon to Marseilles, Coward produced an angry, accusing ghost in *Post-mortem* (1930). Here the ghost of one who died in the war returns to visit his comrades and to question them as to how things have worked out. Have the ideals they all once talked about been realised? Was the sacrifice worth it? There is no comfort as, one after the other, his friends reveal the shallowness of their lives and their cynical attitudes to life. In the process of the play, Coward mounts a savage attack on the jingoistic mass media and on the world of the 1920s, the same world of which he was a glittering ornament and which served as the material for much of his writing. *Post-mortem* is the missing play that was needed to lay the war and its consequences to rest. Needless to say it was never produced or even offered for production. On his return Coward carried with him *Private Lives* (1930) and began work on the ultra-patriotic *Cavalcade* (1931).

> During that voyage, I wrote an angry little vilification of war; my mind was strongly affected by *Journey's End*, and I had read several current war novels one after the other. I wrote *Post-mortem* with the utmost sincerity; this, I think, must be fairly obvious to anyone who reads it. In fact I tore my emotions to shreds over it. The result was similar to my performance as 'Stanhope': confused, underrehearsed and hysterical. Unlike my performance as 'Stanhope', however, it had some very fine moments. There is, I believe, some of the best writing I have ever done in it, also some of the worst. I have no deep regrets over it, as I know my intentions to have been the purest. I passionately believed in the truth of what I was writing; too passionately. The truths I snarled out in that hot, uncomfortable cabin were all too true and mostly too shallow. Through lack of detachment and lack of real experience of my subject, I muddled the issues of the play. I might have done better had I given more time to it and less vehemence. However, it helped to purge my system of certain accumulated acids.[18]

There was an amateur/school performance sometime after the Second World War which aroused interest and which might have lead to a full professional showing but is now lost in the recesses of memory without being recorded. Perhaps the recent revival of Coward might push someone to look at it again.

There are two non-British plays which need to be included here; both had a strong effect on the British public. Paul Raynal's eponym in *The Unknown Warrior* is another soldier destroyed by the absence of love. Parted from him for the duration of the war, the Betrothed finds she no longer has any need or love for the Soldier. When she gave herself to him for a single night – which was to be his last on earth – she could only mimic the passion she would willingly have lavished on him in the fullest measure. In a beautiful passage, the Soldier calls upon the Shades of the comrades who fought at his side in the trenches to justify the tokens of love exchanged that night. But, perhaps, the deepest pathos arose from the Soldier's cry: 'I don't want to be a hero. I want to come back.'[19] In *Miracle at Verdun* by Hans Chlumberg (1932), English adaptation by Edward Crankshaw, the thesis is that there will never be peace among the European nations as long as the sacrificed lie in their graves between them. In a hair-raising scene, the dead rise from the battlefield cemeteries and flood back to their homes. By shrewd perception or good luck, the scene is set in 1939. After brief rejoicing, and delight among the clergy that the doctrine of bodily resurrection is not a fantasy, the results are disastrous: the men's wives have remarried; their jobs are taken by others; there is no food, no home and no money. At curtain-fall the men decide they are not wanted, so return to the tomb, flaunting the very slogans of world betterment which they had borne with them to their first death a quarter of a century earlier. 'A telling example of the changes which the war years had wrought in drama. In its bitter insight, imaginative grip and far-reaching unification, Hans Chlumberg's play was utterly unlike anything which could have arisen in the psychological climate of Victorian times.'[20]

Politics and war

In the same year as *Miracle at Verdun*, another play appeared which spanned the inter-war years. At the opening night of Shaw's *Too True to be Good*, Somerset Maugham was heard to claim that the theme of his new play *For Services Rendered* would be the same as Shaw's. Both plays were presented by Barry Jackson and both were categorical failures. The theme was the muddle politicians had made of the post-war reconstruction – 'They muddle on, muddle on and one day they will muddle us into another war', says the blind, seer-like Sydney in *For Services Rendered*. Failure for Somerset Maugham was a new experience after the great success he had had in the 1920s with his successful formula and pattern of working. In the late 1920s he decided to end his career with four more plays, sensing perhaps that the audience was changing and leaving him behind. His previous play, *Sheppey*, which had failed to find favour, was a sardonic comedy about a barber who wins a lottery and decides to give it all away in a Christ-like fashion – hardly a Maugham theme or setting. *For Services Rendered* (1932) ended Maugham's playwrighting career. The play takes place fifteen years after the war has ended and is set in a small country house outside London. The owner is a solicitor, Leonard Ardsley, and the play deals with the experiences and disillusionment of returning war heroes and the final decay of the middle class under the strains of post-war England. Eva Ardsley has never recovered from the shock of losing her fiancé in the war; being unmarried, she is given the job of companion to her war-blinded brother Sydney. She sees herself playing chess until the end of her days, although she has some romantic interest in Collie Stratton, who bought a garage with his gratuity on being discharged from the Navy and is now, due to the recession, close to bankruptcy. The younger daughter Lois yearns for excitement and is pursued by a wealthy married neighbour, Wilfred Cedar, who wants her to elope with him. Sydney is cynical and bitter and it is through him that Maugham gives the voice of the returned, damaged heroes:

> I know how dead keen we all were when the war started. . . .
> honour did mean something to us and patriotism wasn't just a
> word. And then, when it was all over, we did think that those
> who died hadn't died in vain, and those of us who were broken
> and knew they wouldn't be any good in the world were buoyed
> up by the thought that if they'd given everything they'd given in
> a great cause . . . we were the dupes of incompetent fools who
> ruled nations. I know that we were sacrificed to their vanity,
> their greed and their stupidity. And the worst of it is that as far
> as I can tell they haven't learned a thing . . . They muddle on,
> muddle on and one of these days they'll muddle us all into
> another war. When that happens I'll tell you what I'm going to
> do. I'm going out into the streets and cry: Look at me; don't be a
> lot of damned fools; it's all bunk what they're saying to you,
> about honour and patriotism and glory, bunk, bunk, bunk.[21]

Lois agrees to elope with Wilfred Cedar. Ethel, the third daughter, remains chained to her alcoholic husband. Collie Stratton, faced with prosecution for signing dud cheques, commits suicide, and this is the final blow that sends Eva into a nervous breakdown. The play ends when Ardsley makes a little speech on the satisfaction of being surrounded by one's family in a state of health and happiness: 'The world is turning the corner, and we can all look forward to better times in future. This old England of ours isn't finished yet, and I for one believe in it and all it stands for.'

> As the curtain falls, Eva in a crazy voice begins to sing the National Anthem, and, while the others look at her in horror, Lois runs from the room.[22]

The play is a masterpiece of textured dramaturgy: Maugham creates a picture of this corner of English society which, like a tapestry, cannot be cut into sections without destroying the whole. Supporters of the play in its time felt it would live. The play was revived at the Northcott Theatre, Exeter, in 1974 and later at the National Theatre. Otherwise it seems to have remained a forgotten masterpiece. What cannot be conveyed through textual analysis is the skill with which Maugham constructs what Kean would have called 'hits' and Meyerhold 'attractions'. Theatrical moments which, for Kean, stunned the audience and, for Meyerhold, carried an ideological punch. Maugham's skill lies in taking the audience's attention in one direction, when the punch is coming from a different direction. Just when you least expect it, the traumatic experience of an unconsidered character hits you hard as his/her experience is thrust at you.

> Spectators leaving the Globe in the autumn of 1932
> walked self-consciously down Shaftesbury Avenue. It was not
> long since the economic crisis. Maugham, instead of patting the
> nation on its back for its attempt to recover, was asking what it
> had done for the boys who came marching home . . . For Services
> Rendered is a cutting east wind of our stage. It did not run; the
> playgoers of 1932 sought something more benign; Maugham
> was told that he had assembled too many tragedies in one
> household. But the house in Kent was the tottering post-war
> world in microcosm.[23]

At a time when a critic could say that the most remarkable thing about the year was that there was *nothing* remarkable and Ernest Reynolds could say of the plays that:

> In the course of an evening's acting many a performer has had no gesture to make above the level of cigarette lighting or hand-shaking . . . no walk except from the window to the sofa or from the cocktail cabinet to the radio. Plays have sometimes run in London in which the conversation has been far flatter than that of ordinary life, in which a single setting was more drab than that of many a back-room tenement, in which from curtain to curtain there was not merely never a whisper of poetry but never a spark of wit. Such plays were particularly noticeable between 1930 and 1940.[24]

In such a climate of taste, it is unlikely that a play as passionate and emotional as *For Services Rendered* would ever find favour.

Other writers began to use the device of ghosts appearing for a variety of reasons. In Emlyn Williams' *A Murder has been Arranged* the ghosts become theatricalised (see John Stokes' chapter). In Noël Coward's *Bitter Sweet* (1929) the ghost of Sari's lover, killed earlier in a duel, returns at the end of the play to remind us that a love that lives in the memory can never die; a perfect example, claims Pellizzi, of 'Palm Court Hotel' culture.[25] The appearance of ghosts is a fantasy belief in immortality, a reaction against images of death – the plays that manifest this do not have to be 'serious' to play upon these beliefs.

As the violence and horror of war seems to have been transmuted into horror plays, the pains of absence created by the mass slaughter of the war become vulgarised, perhaps trivialised, but certainly distanced by illusory portrayals of Death as a transport from one area of existence to another. In *Death Takes a Holiday* (1931) adapted by Walter Ferris from the Italian play by Alberto Casella, which had a big success and a prolonged life in repertory and amateur companies, Death proposes a three-day holiday, while he enjoys taking over the body of the Prince, whose life he has just taken. Grazia, who is betrothed to Corrado, becomes infatuated with the Prince. Suffice to say that at the end of three days, Grazia remains with her fiancé and Death departs without her, thereby proving that love is stronger than death.

On Borrowed Time (1938) finds Death trapped up an apple tree by a small dog. No one dies until Grandpa reaches the time he has chosen and he goes – the readiness is all and sentimental whimsy pays. The play enjoyed success and ended up as a Hollywood film shown during the Second World War starring Cedric Hardwicke and Linden Travers as Death and Grandpa respectively. As J. C. Trewin says of 1939, 'Outside Europe was crumbling. But dramatists ignored the war. Audiences preferred to be chilled by mad maidservants.'[26]

More playing with time: J. B. Priestley *et al.*

The middle to late 1930s produced many plays in which the authors played games with time. In a number of these, principally those of J. B. Priestley, there is a sophisticated development of the ghost and immortality plays. Flashbacks, flash forwards and other cinematic techniques are utilised to manipulate our responses to situations by presenting alternative interpretations of what we normally experience as events happening in linear time. As early as 1926 J. L. Balderstone, in *Berkeley Square*, introduced the idea that time does not move in a straight line, but that events of the past, present and future are intermingled. One way of escaping from unpleasant or destructive actions is to latch on to the idea that time is not linear. If we do not live in linear but circular time then disasters can be alleviated by the thought that the moment of their happening will come round again. Our faults can keep returning to haunt us or they can be annulled by us not making the same mistake the second time round. Alternatively, if time is circular, pre-destination removes from us responsibility for our actions. The principal but not the only exponent of this genre was J. B. Priestley, whose dramatic realisation and manipulation of ideas drawn from J. W. Dunne was masterly. Using suspense, poignancy, even pathos, Priestley created compelling theatre.

In *Dangerous Corner* (1932), three couples at a dinner party given by Robert Caplan and his wife are listening to a radio play about a man who insists on knowing the truth, whatever the consequences, however harmful they will be to him. The couples' subsequent conversation brings up the earlier suicide of the host's brother, Martin Caplan, who is supposed to have killed himself to escape the revelation of his stealing a sum of money from the publishing firm that all the people present have an interest in. A chance remark throws doubt on this motive for the suicide and the host embarks on an investigation in which everyone has to tell the truth. This reveals that one of the company present, Charles Stanton, stole the money. Sexual alliances, betrayals and submerged desires among the company are revealed as well as the fact that Robert's wife was in love with Martin, that he was a drug addict who did not commit suicide, but was killed in an obscene struggle by one of the other women party guests. Deprived of all illusions, the host commits suicide. A replay of the situation leads up to the critical moment at which point the radio blurts out cheerful music, the couples throw themselves into the dance, nothing is revealed and the crisis never happens. The play generates tension and excitement in performance, helping to cover up the slickness of the plotting – sharing some features with the later, much more skilful *An Inspector Calls*.

J. B. Priestley's *Time and the Conways* (1937) is a more complex play. The first act is set in 1919 during the coming-of-age party of a young woman from a provincial middle-class family. The picture is idealised, as all look forward to the 1930s when the war will be well behind them. The second act takes place in 1937 and in retrospect we can see this as the viewpoint from which the first scene is being judged. Those who married are not happy, those who remained single have hopes which have not been realised and plans which have not succeeded. The act centres on a duologue between brother and sister quoting William Blake as the central theme. Kay, the birthday girl, sees time as a destroyer, while her brother Alan sees time as a perpetual continuum with specific moments apprehended as just another bit of the total landscape, always present – at the end of this time we will find ourselves in another time, in which all the moments of our lives, good and bad, will be with us. The third act returns to a rerun of the first act, seen from a changed perspective. We now revisit the optimism of the immediate post-First World War world, seen through the eyes of 1937.

Richard Findlater finds a vein of nostalgia running through

Priestley's plays, a poignant sense of lost innocence, lost privilege, lost safety. To paraphrase Findlater, when we reread Priestley's prose works, such as *Lost Empires*, there is a strong nostalgic feeling for the Edwardian days, however critical of those he may be in later works. How often does he present a man or a woman reflecting on the splendour and misery of the past, thinking of a lost spring, the buried love, the wasted opportunity? In these contradictions of internationalism and insularity, the forward look and the backward glance, he may be said to be in some way representative of the English middle classes in the social revolution of the twentieth century. In many of his plays there is the sign of a search for a means of reconciliation – for a pattern of meaning – that will explain to the English middle classes what has been happening to them in the last fifty years and will define for them their own values and position not only in the social hierarchy but in the universe. Findlater sees Priestley's nostalgia as linked with the time philosophy, for this gives the playgoer, 'a warrant to deny the reality of time, to give a meaning to chaos, to put a kindly face upon nothingness'.[27]

J. W. Dunne's influential *An Experiment with Time*[28] builds upon Bergson, Einstein and others to construct a relativist and serialist view of 'time' which would explain certain phenomena which Dunne himself had experienced. He examines dreams and flashes of intuition which bring back the past and predict the future, which confuse the linear dimension of time. He proceeds to a concept of a second dimension which stands behind every linear experiencing of time. This regresses to infinity, a dimension of time outside of measured time in which all that takes place, past, present and future exist together. He was not alone amongst psychologists, philosophers and even theologians in following this line of thought.

Priestley follows Dunne but, being a playwright, is more interested in the dramatic usages of such thinking. His use of Dunne helps him to create poignant dramaturgy when the present can be judged in terms of future outcome, or when characters are troubled and disturbed by echoes and dreams from the past. In *I Have Been Here Before* (1937), Priestley comes dramatically as close as possible to Dunne by introducing Dr Gortler, who is conducting experiments with a theory in which past, present and future are linked together in three- or four-dimensional spirals, and who is able to prevent the reoccurrence of a past tragedy happening among a group of people whose paths to a Yorkshire moorland inn appear to be directed towards a similar conclusion.

Priestley's time-plays are built upon real-life concerns worked out in strong characterisations and are rooted, explicitly or implicitly, in the social movement of the 1930s. It would be over-stretching reason to make some direct causal connection between Priestley's time-plays and his evasion of the coming war as a theme. It would be more appropriate to say that Priestley's great success as a playwright in the 1930s was due to his being in touch with his audience's anxieties and the fact that he supplied what they were looking for, a palliative which diverted attention away from disaster towards hope.

In *Johnson over Jordan*, Priestley's last play before the war, there seems to be a clear example of what Findlater accuses him and his audience of: denying the reality of time, in the broadest sense, and putting a kindly face on nothingness. To do this, Priestley pulls out all the theatrical stops: he employs masks, mime, dance, music, lighting, projections of character outside time and space. It is an 'Everyman' play, the passing over of Johnson, a senior clerk in no way exemplary or in any way to be distinguished from a million others like him. Death appears and Johnson enters a series of fragmentary memories about his past life, mainly pleasant; he sees his mother again; he is introduced to the woman he will later marry; Don Quixote appears to him and there is a very touching exchange, redolent of Scrooge's return to Christmases past. Quixote recalls a small boy reading his story and Johnson recalls the pleasure of reading and Quixote thanks Johnson for giving him the only life he has in the memory and the affection of the reader. Johnson recalls scenes of past holidays and other happy scenes in which he has the chance to express his feelings to his family, who receive them telepathically. Purged of his admittedly minor and imaginary sins and stored with happy memories of the past, Johnson is bidden by the hooded figure of Death, now friendly, the image of a golden Apollo, to move on to the other side. At other times it might be meritorious to raise such a small and rather insignificant man to the level of

Everyman and to find value in his uneventful life, but, in 1939, amid the atrocities of the Civil War in Spain, with Jews, gypsies, homosexuals and others queuing to be driven into the gas chambers, Johnson marches steadfastly away from the coming war and its horrors to another existence in a time outside of sequential time.

Two other dramatists, who took the theoretical aspects of time more seriously than Priestley, also attempted to escape from confronting the approach of war directly. The opening chorus of T. S. Eliot's *Murder in the Cathedral* (1935) lays out the anxieties and worries of a people waiting for undefined destruction while Becket is adamant that his passive submission to martyrdom has no imminent significance.

Equally Charles Morgan, dramatic critic for *The Times*, entered the lists towards the end of the 1930s with *The Flashing Stream* (1938). The play is set upon a remote island in the Atlantic, where a group of naval officers are engaged in the Scorpion project, which seems to presage later developments. The Scorpion is a ground to air missile which locks on to enemy aircraft until, by the proximity of missile and plane, the vibration of the plane's engines triggers off an explosion. During the play, the state of the project rests between success in homing on to the plane and failure to cause an explosion. Despite what might seem to be a very topical subject, there is no indication of the approach of war. The main problem for the Admiralty does not lie in any haste to have the device ready for war but in the amount of money it is costing.

The play begins after a fatal accident which has killed Selby, one of the two mathematicians leading the project. Selby's sister, Karen – an independent and sexually active woman who is also a leading mathematician – arrives at the island. At the end of the first scene, Karen has agreed to join the project and to work with Ferrers, the second mathematician, who heads the project. The rest of the play follows the path of their attempts to solve the problems and to save the project from being cancelled. Morgan's theme is not the coming of war – the project is incidental to the main theme, which is absolutism. What matters to Ferrers is mathematics and most of the action is concerned with his refusal, to the point of a nervous breakdown, to compromise and to accept the possibility of an error in the mathematics, which might be causing the test failures. The core of the play is the relationship between Karen and Ferrers. Both possess a single-mindedness which will allow no intervention. Both have a strong sexual attraction for each other but this has to be suppressed in the interests of the project. There is a remarkable climax to the second act of a passionate scene in which they declare their love and desire for each other, in circumstances in which Ferrers' sense of personal failure threatens to destroy him if the project is cancelled. Ferrers is saved by Karen announcing that the errors are in her calculations and not in his. Whatever faults there are in the play, there are moments of great dramatic skill and J. C. Trewin, as acerbic a critic as always, nevertheless records: '*The Flashing Stream* remains with us today as a shining gift from the 1930s.'

Several themes that ran through the 1920s and 1930s come together in *The Flashing Stream*. The sense of confusion and lack of direction which characterise the 1920s, leading to the fear and uncertainty of the 1930s, make the strong leader a very attractive proposition. If we criticise Morgan and T. S. Eliot for evading the direct political issues of their times, ought we not also to take up the alternative they offer in opposition to this perverse dimension of absolutism and find some merit in their valuing the individual who dares to stand for belief, faith, integrity, self-negation in humility, dedication, in the face of conformity to mass action? Morgan joins Eliot in conceiving of a concern with actions that are justified only by reference to values which exist above the time we live in and if martyrdom be the price of constancy then so be it. But, unlike Eliot, he does not rule out the possibility of armed conflict.

The path of martyrdom leads to action in *Glorious Morning* (1938), by Norman MacOwan, one of the few plays which tackled fascism head on. The basic theme of the play is the right of the individual to believe in the revealed God. Leda lives in a totalitarian state. When a vision appears to her in a dream, she is told, 'God still exists' and that 'people who do not know him are lost'. She begins to preach and is arrested. In her confrontation with the Leader, he says 'we give them food, clothes, houses, playing grounds, what do you give them?' Leda replies 'I give them the truth, God lives.' Leda stands by her faith and goes to her execution by a firing-squad. In retrospect the play looks to have had little to offer in the face of the impending fascist mass destruction of 1938.

There were other attempts to deal directly with the dictators, which were suppressed by the censor in the interests of not offending the heads of other nation-states. Findlater notes: '*What Made the Iron Grow*, an attack on Nazi anti-Semitism; *Lucid Interval*, a satire on the dictator of an unspecified country; and *Follow my Leader*, an anti-Hitler satirical farce set in Moronia and Neurasthenia' – of which the part author was Terence Rattigan.[29] In revue and cabaret, a sketch about 'Hitler and The Wandering Jew' was slipped in to *After Dark* after opening and immediately taken out again by order. A sketch based on *Journey's End*, had the Germans coming out of their trenches in *lederhosen* and Tyrolean hats. The female chorus split in two and staged a campaign to get the audience to join the 'Blue Brassieres' or the 'Pink Knickers'. Such mild numbers, threatening no possible harm to the foreign dictators, were allowed.

There is one other play which attempts to deal with the growth and threat of fascism. But even that draws away from direct confrontation and takes an oblique approach. Stephen Spender's *Trial of a Judge* (1938) is a brave attempt to bring poetry back into the theatre, to use eloquence to direct attention to what was happening in Europe by escaping the trap of naturalism. The play, performed at the Unity Theatre by Rupert Doone's Group Theatre, was protected from the censor by Unity's club status, and aroused a great deal of opposition. Spender wanted to move away from propaganda to explore the dilemma of justice – the crisis of liberalism in the face of the fascist threat. Like other writers on the left, he chose to idealise the action, abstracting time and place and creating characters who are given names like The Judge and The Wife. In the debate after the show, Unity members heckled Spender for what they had considered to be his liberal retreat into symbolism and mysticism.[30]

The political extravaganza

A new genre of drama appeared in the 1930s with little previous notice. This new form, the extravaganza, and its subgenre, the political extravaganza, takes serious themes and subjects and sets them at a distance.

The writer recognises the seriousness of his material, exposes its para-doxes and contradictions, subjects it to trial by wit and intellectual cat-echism and generally has fun. The extravaganza, as the name suggests, holds no obligation to stick to any of the structural conventions of other types of drama. There need be no consistency in time, space or character. Probable impossibility or possible improbability hold no power – anything goes. The main exponent of the political extrava-ganza was, of course, G. B. Shaw, but other writers also took up the chance to have fun in the face of possible obliteration.

H.M. Harwood's *These Mortals* (1939) had, and possibly merited no more than, one Sunday performance, as the war clouds began to hover. The play is in two parts. In the first, Zeus, in Olympus, presides over an enquiry into the Trojan War. The Greeks regard this as a major trade initiative and are proposing to publicise it under the title of 'A war to make the world safe for husbands'. Homer is taken on as the Greeks' PR man. The second half takes place many years later in Hades. Zeus is tired and depressed – he seeks two mortals to sit with him in Olympus. Various contestants state their claims: Napoleon, Wellington, Queen Victoria, Julius Caesar, Lenin, Hitler and Mussolini. Hitler and Mussolini claim to have remade nations but are rejected on Wildean grounds: 'To make a nation may be misplaced enthusiasm. To remake it is sheer lunacy.' In the end, Zeus rejects everyone except Uncle Tom and Helen of Troy: 'A man who has been a slave and it has not degraded him: a woman whose beauty has with-stood the challenge of three thousand years, these are the ones I choose. Well Rome burned while Nero fiddled.'

The career and achievements of G. B. Shaw have been well chronicled elsewhere and create something of a problem here since they are too wide to be covered and too important to be left out. In 1929, *The Apple Cart* represented something of the confusion of what was happening in the world, since its ambiguities found lively support in some quarters and violent antagonism in others, where it was taken as an attack on democracy. There is certainly, in the portrayal of the incompetence of the Socialist cabinet, an attack on the inefficiency of liberal democracy, which, from the viewpoint of today, sits quite easily with other similar evaluations, however much of it is cushioned by being set in the context of the British talent to compromise. The arguments are also cushioned by the form chosen – a 'political extravaganza'. In *Too True to be Good* (1932), the second of the political extravaganzas, Shaw catches the mood of the times again, even if he fails to find the form in which to explore or articulate it. Shaw's drama wanders widely and wildly in cast list and settings, varying from a spoiled girl's bedroom – in which her invading microbe has a speaking part – to a beach in the Middle East. Further bedroom intruders are a burglar–parson, a Cockney ex-thief acting as a nurse, a sergeant who might double for John Bunyan, and a private soldier, said to be based on T. E. Lawrence. The play provides excellent opportunities for preaching sermons, culminating in one of five minutes from the burglar, returned to being a preacher – which wraps up all the ideas strewn around the stage. It is not that Shaw has nothing to say, it is that he has rather too much.

Shaw followed *Too True to be Good* with the prophetically titled *On the Rocks* (1933). Although described as a political comedy, the play is clearly related to the other extravaganzas. The preface is truly monstrous. Important questions are addressed in terms which seem far removed from reality. Shaw discusses genocide, poverty and unemployment without any emotion – they seem to be no more than academic problems. The play reads like a pastiche of Shaw. In the play itself the Prime Minister has bodged everything for years and is persuaded to go on a rest cure, taking with him the works of Karl Marx. He comes back with solutions to the nation's problems – nationalisation of ground rents; nationalisation of banks, mines and transport; municipalisation of urban land and the building trade, and consequent extinction of rates; abolition of tariffs, and substitution of total prohibition of private foreign trade in protected industries; state imports only to be sold at state-regulated prices; compulsory public service for all, irrespective of income; restoration of agriculture, collective farming; doubling of surtax on unearned income, cuts in the Forces' pay to be restored; police force increased by 5,000 men and their pay raised and so on. He finds approval with the broad centre because there is something for everyone. Only the Tory right and the working class oppose him – he retires.

The play ends on a quizzical note. The Unemployed sing

'England Arise' to percussion accompaniment of baton thwacks. The bitter tone of Shaw's personal invective shines through the play. There is little fun in it and Shaw himself is unable to find a solid social basis on which to rest. The play is open-ended and the only bleak and possible conclusion rests with the possibility of the arrival of a strong leader. This leap Shaw is unable to make. The matter does not end there and in the next political extravaganza, *Geneva* (1938), the dictators arrive upon the stage. *Geneva* is subtitled *Another Political Extravaganza*.

Shaw's Preface to the play was written in 1945, when at least he had the benefit of hindsight, but seems to have learned little from the war – Hitler had great ideas but these got mixed up with fancies such as anti-Semitism. He organised industry but the capitalists made him a prophet and hero. Encouraged by spineless attempts to appease him, he attacked Russia, calculating that as a crusader against Soviet Communism he would finally be joined by the whole Capitalist West. But the Capitalist West was much too short-sighted and jealous to do anything so intelligent. It shook hands with Stalin and stabbed Hitler in the back and so on. Shaw seems to presume in the Preface that history runs according to the rules of the well-made play.

Geneva has a heavily contrived plot. Various people come to the office of the Committee for International Co-operation in Geneva. None of the big names ever go there and the office is run by one girl. She forwards complaints to the International Court at The Hague, which, so far, has not had a case to try. Eventually, the Court summons the various European dictators before it to stand trial. They arrive under assumed names. The farce is played out and, at the end, a rumour begins to circulate to the effect that the earth has jumped its orbit and everyone rushes home to order their deaths in various ways.

In 1939, Shaw came out with another extravaganza of a totally non-political type. *Good King Charles's Golden Days* is redolent of Gilbert and Sullivan's *Iolanthe*, in the aria in which the Peerage sing of the achievements of England's aristocracy in building her greatness. The play is subtitled: *A True History that Never Happened.*

Argument continued about both the policy of appeasement and about how much was known in Britain about what was happening elsewhere in Europe. British people in 1937 felt that they were living in a state of emergency and something of the mood caught the least likely of writers. Ivor Novello produced *The Dancing Years* at the Theatre Royal, Drury Lane, six months before war broke out. Unlike his other shows it had no big spectacular central scene – no liners sinking, no trains crashing. The central story is about Vienna before and during the Nazi regime. Novello plays a half-Jewish composer, at first young and lively, then older and in peril. The show begins by introducing the Nazis.

> This was almost the first time, certainly the first time in a musical play, that Nazis had been brought upon the stage . . . This time he had written a play 'about' something, which had a much deeper note than any of his others. He had not merely a story; he had a theme . . . Although Cruelty, as symbolized by the Nazis, could kill a man, it could not kill his achievement . . . In this case the theme he chose was music.[31]

The show is constructed in two halves. The first half has a series of masques, showing Vienna 'in the old days', Vienna under the Nazis and then Vienna ruined, starving and penniless. The second half is standard musical comedy romance. Novello plays Rudi Kleber, a penniless composer who attracts the love of a comic star, Maria Ziegler. Their romance is interrupted by the arrival of a young girl whose presence arouses Maria's jealousy to the point that she leaves Rudi. Thirteen years later they meet again. Novello aged throughout the show from the young, carefree, penniless composer to the older, weary prisoner of the Nazis facing imminent death. The end of the play is a far from happy one but the show is redeemed by a further ballroom scene returning to the romantic love of the two lovers. It seems unlikely that Hitler would have been deeply offended by this, but the show was stopped by enemy action a short way into the war.

As the fantasies, the extravaganzas, the dream plays, the escapes into other time-planes and into the illusory transcending of death comes to ground, the ghosts returned to enforce the inter-war audiences to face up to the reality of what was happening in the world and to rouse them to action. The surprising thing is that the play that does this uses many of the devices employed by other dramatists to *avoid* facing up to the political realities of life. *Thunder Rock* (1939) by an

American writer, Robert Ardrey, is nevertheless a very 'English' play, premiered in London, and the first play to be subsidised by a British Government grant. Charleston, the central character, bears a resemblance to the American journalist John Gunther, who during the 1930s toured the world, interviewing major political figures and writing up his findings in the 'Inside' books. In the face of the coming war, Charleston has chosen to retire to a lighthouse, erected to commemmorate the loss of a ship loaded with exiles from Europe, seeking a new life in the New World, in 1849. He declines all unnecessary contact with the outside world. In isolation he has chosen to people the lighthouse with the ghosts of some of those drowned in the disaster. He lives in the world of their optimism. Gradually his ghosts tell their true stories, which belie any optimism, and he is forced to face up to the fact that they were not travelling in hope but running away from confrontation with oppression, ignorance and prejudice. Unable to hide in his false Utopia any longer, Charleston decides to face up to reality and responsibility and returns to cover the war; the ghosts dematerialise. As Charleston proclaims:

> We've reason to believe that wars will cease one day, but only if
> we stop them ourselves . . . We've got to create a new order out
> of the chaos of the old, and already its shape is becoming clear. A
> new order that will eradicate oppression, unemployment,
> starvation and wars as the old order eradicated plague and
> pestilences. And that is what we've got to fight for; not fighting
> for fighting's sake, but to make a new world of the old. That's
> our job . . . and we can do it.[32]

There is a great deal of idealism in the play but it does confront the reality of what was actually happening in the world. The play was written and had a few performances in 1939. Its main run was in the year 1940, when audiences would feel it easier to follow Charleston's conversion from cynicism to action. After *Thunder Rock*, the ghosts seem to have served their purpose. The next appearance of ghosts comes shortly after and is in an entirely different key and genre. In Coward's *Blithe Spirit* (1940) they are exorcised and banished from the stage.

Notes

1. See, for example, the last act of Ben Travers' *Thark* or Arnold Ridley's *The Ghost Train.*

2. J. M. Barrie, *Mary Rose* (London: Hodder and Stoughton, 1925).

3. Denis Mackail, *The Story of J.M.B.* (London: Peter Davies, 1941).

4. J. C. Trewin, *The Gay Twenties* (London: Macdonald, 1958), p. 19.

5. *Ibid.*, pp. 30–42.

6. Ernest Short, *Theatrical Cavalcade* (London: Eyre and Spottiswoode, 1942), pp. 155–6.

7. Griffiths wrote a few unprovocative plays and then, in 1929, produced *Red Sunday*, with John Gielgud as Trotsky. It covers a broad span of Russian revolutionary history from 1906 to 1920, ending in the assassination of Trotsky. It was given an airing at the Arts Theatre Club and then banned from full public performance. Griffiths prints a spurious letter from the censor (who is called Ping-Pang-Bong and lives on a South Sea Island) suggesting that the reasons were that the Russian Revolution was too recent and the play included a portrayal of the Czar. No other plays from Griffiths are recorded after this.

8. J. R. Ackerley, *The Prisoners of War*, in *Gay Plays III*, ed Michael Wilcox (London: Methuen, 1988).

9. Camillo Pellizzi, *The English Drama: the Last Great Phase* (London: Macmillan, 1935), pp. 154–5.

10. Nicholas de Jongh, *Not in Front of the Audience* (London: Routledge, 1992), pp. 22–30.

11. Quoted from J. R. Ackerley, *My Father and Myself* (London: The Bodley Head, 1968), in Paul Fussell, *The Great War and Modern Memory* (Oxford University Press, 1975), p. 199.

12. Paul Fussell, *The Great War and Modern Memory*, p. 194.

13. *Ibid.*, p. 195. For more detail see Fussell's chapter 'Theatre of War', pp. 191–230.

14. Camillo Pellizzi, *The English Drama: the last great phase*, p. 283.

15. Allardyce Nicoll, *English Drama 1900–1930* (Cambridge University Press, 1973), p. 440.

16. Audrey Williamson, *Theatre of Two Decades* (London: Rockcliff, 1951).

17. Allardyce Nicoll, *English Drama 1900–1930*, p. 446.

18. Noël Coward, *Present Indicative* (London: Heinemann, 1937), pp. 390–1.

19. Ernest Short, *Theatrical Cavalcade*, pp. 154–5.

20 *Ibid.*, pp. 158–9.

21. Somerset Maugham, *For Services Rendered*, in *For Services Rendered and Other Plays* (London: Mandarin, 1996), pp. 67–8.

22. *Ibid.*, p. 83.

23. Raymond Mander and Joe Mitchenson, *Theatrical Companion to Maugham* (London: Rockliff, 1955), p. 14.

24. Ernest Reynolds, *Modern English Drama* (London: George G. Harrap, 1949), p. 54.

25. Camillo Pellizzi, *The English Drama: the Last Great Phase*, p. 189.

26. J. C.Trewin, *The Turbulent Thirties* (London: Macdonald, 1960), p. 127.

27. Richard Findlater, *The Unholy Trade* (London: Gollancz, 1952), p. 185.

28. J.W. Dunne, *An Experiment With Time* (London: Faber and Faber, 1927).

29. Richard Findlater, *Banned* (London: MacGibbon and Kee, 1967), p. 162.

30. Colin Chambers, *The Story of Unity Theatre* (London: Lawrence and Wishart, 1989), p. 147.

31. W. Macqueen-Pope, *Ivor* (London: W.H. Allen, 1951), p. 386.

32. Robert Ardrey, *Thunder Rock* (London: Heinemann Educational, 1966 [1939]), p. 75.

Index

A to Z (Charlot) 102, 105
Abbey Theatre 151
abject, the 58–9
Abraham Lincoln (Drinkwater) 22
access to art 169
Ackerley, J. R. 80, 220
Ackland, Rodney 81
actor-managers 7–8, 17, 90–1
actors
    star 17; typecast 30–1;
        unionisation 16–17
Actors Association 16–17, 126
Actors' Benevolent Fund 17
actress-managers 127
actresses 116
Actresses Franchise League (AFL)
    9–10, 117, 118, 126, 163
Adelphi 104
Adrian, Max 155
Afagr 21
After the Dance (Rattigan) 20
After Dark 236
Agate, James 25, 40–1, 82, 88, 137–8,
    142, 149, 220
Albery, Bronson 141
Aldwych farces 12, 30–1
Alhambra, Leicester 93
Alibi 53
Allen, Clifford 165, 166
Allgood, Sarah 151
amateur theatre 15, 174

Ambassadors 92, 109
American Actors Equity 17
Anatomist, The (Bridie) 29–30
And So to Bed 22
Anderson, Matthew 201, 204
Anthony, C. L. *see* Smith, Dodie
anti-Semitism 151–4, 236
Antony and Cleopatra 147
Apollo Theatre 182
Apple Cart, The (Shaw) 237–8
Arcadians, The 90
Ardrey, Robert 240–1
Aria da Capo (Millay) 166
aristocracy, dissolution of the 4, 5,
    23
Arnold, Matthew 14
'Art and Democracy' (Barlow) 170
As You LIke It (Shakespeare) 142
    (film) 143
Asche, Oscar 13, 89–90, 135
Ashcroft, Peggy 137, 139, 140, 152
Ashton, Frederick 103
Ashwell, Lena 125, 126–7, 128
Astaire, Fred and Adele 97
Atkins, Robert 143–4, 151
Auden, Wystan Hugh 27, 32, 154
audience
    female 25, 71, 114, 119; social
        class 23–8, 71
Augé, Marc 199–200
Ayrton, Randle 149, 153

Baddeley, Hermione 109, 110
Baker, Elizabeth 5, 10, 24, 122
Balalaika (Maschwitz and Posford)
    106
Balanchin, Georges 103
Balderstone, J. L. 230
Baldwin, Stanley 145
Balkan Princess, The 90
ballet 89, 91, 97, 103, 179
Ballets Russes 91
ballroom dancing 96
Ballyhoo (Nesbitt) 107
Bankhead, Tallulah 116
Baring, Edward 201, 204
Barker, Harley Granville *see* Granville
    Barker, Harley
*Barking Historical Pageant and
    Industrial Exhibition*
    (Lascelles) 200, 206–7
Barlow, E. G. 170
Barney, Nathalie 115
Barnfather, Bruce 218
Barretts of Wimpole Street, The 22
Barrie, J. M. 33, 143, 216–17
Bartlett, Neil 38
Battling Butler 99–100
Baylis, Lilian 127, 136, 139, 140, 141,
    147, 148
Beauty Prize, The 98
Bedroom and Bath 12
Bellew, Kyrle 165
Bells, The (Matthias) 41
Benson, Sir Frank R. 201, 203, 210
Bergerac, Bernice de 201
Bergner, Elizabeth 33, 143
Bergson, Henri 232
Berkeley Square (Balderstone) 230
Bernhardt, Sarah 125
Berringer, Vera 120
Best of Both Worlds, The 177
biblical plays 33
Big Drum, The (Holland) 50–1
Bill Smith Explains 181

Bing Boys, The 11, 97
biography plays, historical 22–3
Birmingham 136
Birmingham Repertory Theatre 15
Bitter Sweet (Coward) 26, 31, 103–4,
    229
Black and Blue 110
Black Coffee (Christie) 53
Black 'Ell (Malleson) 165
Black, George 110
Black, Kitty 125–6
Black Velvet 110
Bland, Joyce 64
Blithe Spirit (Coward) 241
Bolitho, William 47, 56
Bolt, Christine 68
Bolton, Guy 97, 98, 99, 104, 203
Bonham Carter, Lady Violet 124
book musicals 88, 97, 100–1, 102–10
Boughton, Rutland 168
Bourchier, Arthur 16, 162, 165, 166,
    170–1
Bowen, Marjorie 203
Boy David, The (Barrie) 33
Bradford 174, 200
Bradford Pioneer 172, 173, 176, 179
Bradstone 201
Brailsford, H. N. 167
Brain, C. Lewton 181
Brain (Sinclair) 183
Brandon, Dorothy 120
Bridges Adams, W. 145, 146, 147, 150,
    152
Bridgwater 201
Bridie, James 29, 33
Briggs, Hedley 107
British Actors Equity Association 16
British Broadcasting Company 96–7,
    145, 150, 155
British Coucil for Cultural Relations
    155
British Drama League 14, 15, 126, 174,
    175, 202, 211

Index

British Theatre Conference 14–15
Britten, Benjamin 144
Brockway, Fenner 162–3, 173
Brontës, The 22
Brontës of Haworth Parsonage, The 22
Brosnan, Alma 181
Brother Copas (Quiller-Couch) 209–10
Brown, Ivor 65, 80, 101
Browne, Maurice 137, 224
Bruckner, Anton 32
Bruiser's Election, The 177
Buchanan, Jack 89, 100, 102, 104
buffoonery 71
Bull-Dog Drummond ('Sapper') 42–6
Burnham, Barbara 74
Burnup, [?] 65
Burton, Peter 79
Bush, Alan 204, 205
Butt, Alfred 91, 101
Buzz Buzz (Charlot) 93–6
Bywaters and Thompson case (1923)
    55

cabaret 20, 96, 103
Cabaret Girl, The 98
Cadell, Rupert 58
Cairo 21
Calder-Marshall, Arthur 26, 27
Calderon, George 165
Cambridge 96, 107, 136
Cambridge Festival Theatre 107
Canarvon, Lord 166
Cannadine, David 199
Captain Youth (Fox) 180
Carlisle 200, 201
Carpenter, Edward 67, 121
Carrick, Edward 139
Carroll, Sydney W. 53
Carter, Huntley 10–11, 12, 90
cartoons 216, 218, 223
Caryll, Ivan 92
Casanova 105
Case, Sue-Ellen 118

Casella, Alberto 229–30
Casino Girl, The 92
Cass, Henry 147, 156
Casson, Lewis 155, 156, 162, 175
Caste 175
Castle, Terry 83
Cavalcade (Coward) 26, 104, 225
Cecil Sharp Folk Dancers 165
Cellini, Benvenuto 173
censorship 11, 22, 32
    and homosexuality 66, 76, 78, 80,
        83–4; see also Lord
        Chamberlain
Central ILP Players, London 168
Century Theatre, Notting Hill 127
Chadwick, Fred 182
Chandragupta (Roy) 166
Chapin, Harold 5
Chappell, William 103
Charles and Mary 22
Charlot, André 16, 93–6, 97, 100, 102,
        104, 107
Chartism 163, 204–5
Chauvre Souris (Russian 'bat theatre')
    101
Chekhov, Anton 142, 174
Chester Historical Pageant 195, 200
Chesterton, A. K. 138
Children in Uniform (Winsloe) 63, 64,
        65, 73–4, 75–6
Children's Hour, The (Hellman) 76–8
Chinese Honeymoon, A 90
Chlumberg, Hans 226
choreography 103
chorus lines 91
Christie, Agatha 53, 55
Chu Chin Chow (Asche) 12–13, 14, 21,
        89–90
Churchill, Sir Winston 150
cinema 4, 141
cinematic techniques 230–6
Clarion movement 163
Clarke, Frank 205, 207

Clarke, John S. 170–1
Class of 1940 (cartoon) 223
Clemençeau, Georges 223
Cliff, Laddie 100
Clive of India 22
Clum, John 79
Clyde Workers' Silver Band 172
Clynes, John H. 166
Clynes, J. R. 166
Co-optimists 92
Cochran, C. B. 16, 17, 92, 96, 101, 103,
     104, 136
Coghlan, Charles 153
Collins, Jose 98
comedies of situation 32–3
comedy 71, 119, 216
Comedy of Errors (Shakespeare) 143
Comedy Playhouse 93
Communist Party 167, 179, 204
Comus (Jonson) 144
Conquering Hero (Monkhouse) 219,
     221
Constant Lover, The (Hankin) 166
contraception 20
Cooper, Gladys 127
Coriolanus (Shakespeare) 150, 151,
     155
'Corpus Christi Cycles', medieval 195
Country Girl, The 92
Coupons, see Buzz Buzz (Charlot)
Courtneidge, Cicely 89, 100
Coward, Noël 26, 31, 32, 65, 71, 72–3,
     89, 103–4, 106, 125, 224–5,
     229, 241
    book musicals 102; influence of
     81–4
Craig, Edith 127, 129, 162, 182
Craig, Edward Gordon 139
Crankshaw, Edward 226
Crazy Gang 107, 110
crime stories 41–2
Crippen, Hawley Harvey 54–5
Crisham, Walter 97, 106

Critics' Circle 13
Cromer, Lord 74
Croyden Repertory 147
Curzon, Frank 127
Cymbeline (Shakespeare) 144
Czinner, Paul 142, 143

Daily Herald 223
Daily Mail 83, 179
Daily Telegraph 150
Daldry, Stephen 6
Daly's 90, 91, 92, 98
dance 20, 92, 103, 165, 168
    American 91; bands 96–7; clubs 20,
     96; crazes 89; halls 20, 96–7;
     musicals 99–100; orchestras
     96–7; tea 20, 97
Dance of Death (Auden) 154
Dancer, The 12
Dancing Years, The (Novello) 106, 240
Dane, Clemence 29, 32, 117, 120, 121
Dangerous Corner (Priestley) 230–1
Daniels, C. W. 180
Darkwater Bridge (Brain) 181
Dartford Historical Pageant
     (Lascelles) 200, 205–6
Davies, Andrew 163
Daviot, Gordon 120
Dawison, Bogumil 153
Day, Edith 101
de Jongh, Nicholas 65, 66, 70–1, 220
de Leon, Beatrice 126, 127, 128
de Mille, Agnes B. 103
Dean, Basil 21, 105, 128
Death Takes a Holiday (Casella)
     229–30
deCourville, Albert 91, 92, 96, 97
Defeat (Galsworthy) 165
Defendamus (Trevilian) 204, 212
Delius, Frederick 21
Desert Song, The 101
Design for Living (Coward) 81, 82
DeSylva 101

detective stories, and thrillers 52–4
Diaghilev ballet 91
Dickson, Dorothy 98, 106
Die Fledermaus (Strauss) 103
directors
    guest 140; women 128–30
Dodds, Hope 182
Dodds, Ruth 181–3
Dominant Sex, The (Egan) 123–4
Donat, Robert 141
Doone, Rupert 32
Dorset 202
drag queens 73
Drake, Fabia 152
dramatic groups 164
Dramatist, The (Reynolds) 175
Drinkwater, John 22, 23, 32, 201
Drury Lane 101
du Maurier, Gerald 17, 38–41, 42–6,
    48, 53, 59
Dublin 126
Duchess Theatre 128
Duff Cooper, Lady (Diana Manners) 10
Duke of York's Theatre 127
Dukes, Ashley 175
Dunne, J. W. 230, 232
Dunsany, Lord 218

'Echoes of the Jazz Age' (Scott
    Fitzgerald) 92
Eden End (Priestley) 6, 128
Edgington, May 120
Edinburgh 164
education 26–7
Edward II (Marlowe) 193
Edwardes, George 91
Egan, Michael 123–4
Einstein, Albert 232
Eliot, T. S. 55, 142, 151, 234, 235
Elizabeth I, Queen 192
Elizabethan chronicle plays 195
Elizalde, Federico 96
Elliott, Madge 100

Ellis, Havelock 67, 121
Ellis, Mary 106
Ellis, Vivian 101, 104
Ellis, Walter W. 12
Elstree studios 129
Embassy Theatre 18
Empire 91
Enchanted Cottage, The (Pinero) 218
English Drama: The Last Great Phase
    (Pellizzi) 4
English Pageantry (Withington) 194–5
English Theatrical Trust 7
Ephraim, Lee 101
Era 13, 115, 126
Errant Nymph, The (Kennedy) 122–3
Ervine, St John 14, 25–6, 71–2, 114–16,
    118
Evans, Edith 143
Evans, Will 30
Evergreen (Rodgers and Hart) 104
Everyman Theatre 164
Ewer, Monica 176
Experiment with Time, An (Dunne)
    232
expressionism 59
extravaganza, political 236–41

Fabian Society 163
Fagan, J. B. 129
Fairbrother, Violet 126
Fanatics, The (Malleson) 123
farce 12–13, 21
    and Grand Guignol 29–33; Latin 31
Farjeon, Herbert 109, 135, 137, 143–4,
    148
Farrell, M. J. *see* Keane, Molly
fascism 235–6
fashion 26, 113
Fasset, Dorothea 126
Faust (Goethe) 144
Fear of the Factor, The 172
femininity 26, 68–9, 121
feminism 118

Fernald, C. B. 222–3
Ferris, Walter 229–30
Festspiel 194
Fiery Cross, The 181
Fight for Freedom, The (Goldring) 180
film 4, 104, 141, 183–4
Findlater, Richard 28–9, 231–2, 233, 236
Findon, B. W. 22
Firebrand, The (Mayer) 173
First a Girl 143
Fitzgerald, Barry 151
flappers 114–16, 121
Flashing Stream, The (Morgan) 234–5
Fleche, Anne 78
Flecker, James Elroy 21
Florodora 90
Flower family 145
Flying Squad, The (Wallace) 50
Foiling the Reds (Yaffle) 165, 178–9
folk-mumming 194
Follies 92
Follow My Leader 236
Fontanne, Lynn 82
For Services Rendered (Maugham) 32, 226, 227–9
Forge, The 177
Fortune, The 128
Founders, The (Lewis) 177
Fountain, The (Calderon) 165
Four Just Men, The (Wallace) 48
Fourth Wall, The (Milne) 52
Fox, Ralph 180
franchise for women 4, 9–10, 20, 121, 125
Franco, Francisco 138
French, Leslie 144
French Without Tears (Rattigan) 81
Freud, Sigmund 67, 142
Freudianism 67–8
Friends of the Players, The 127
Frightened Lady (Wallace) 54, 55
Frohman, Charles 91, 92

Furber, Douglas 100
Fussell, Paul 220–1

Gaiety Girl, A 92
'Gaiety' musical comedies 90–2
Gaiety Theatre 91–2, 99, 106
Gale, Maggie B. 68, 78
'Gallery Girls' 115
Gallows Glorious 22
Galsworthy, John 5, 32, 41, 165, 174, 176
Garrick Theatre 12
Garscube Pageant 203
Gaslight (Hamilton) 30, 58
Gate Revue, The 108, 109
Gate Theatre, Dublin 77
Gate Theatre, London 107–9, 165
Gateshead 164, 181
Gawthorpe Hall Pageant 197
Gay, Maisie 102
Gay, Noël 106
Gay Twenties, The (Trewin) 21
Geisha, The 90
Geneva (Shaw) 239
Genn, Edward P. 201, 204
George, Prince 150, 206
Gershwin, George 98–9, 103
ghost plays 46, 223–4, 229–30, 240–2
Ghost Train (Ridley) 30, 72
Gibbons, Carroll 97
Gielgud, Sir John 41, 136, 139, 140, 141, 151, 154, 156
Gilbert, S. 69
Gilbert and Sullivan 13, 90
amateur companies 15
Gill, Eric 153
Gingold, Hermione 107, 110
'Girls' 92
Glamorous Nights (Novello) 105–6
Glasgow
Shettleston 164, 172–3, 174
Glasier, Bruce 163
Glorious Morning (MacOwen) 235

Gobbo, Launcelot 143
Godfrey, Philip 22
Goebbels, Joseph 151, 153
Goethe, Johann Wolfgang von 144
Goldring, Douglas 180
Good King Charles's Golden Days
    (Shaw) 239
Gower Pageant and Fair (Lascelles) 202
Grand Guignol 21
    and farce 29–33
Grand Theatre, Luton 148
Granite 29
Granville Barker, Harley xx , 5, 24,
    138–43, 146, 154, 156
Grattan, Harry 93
Gray, Eleanor 180
Gray, Terence 136
Great Day, The 177
Great Hucklow Players 208
Green Bay Tree, The (Shairp) 63–4, 65,
    79–80, 124
Green, Johnny 104
Green, Paul 183
Greet, Ben 129
Gregory, Lady 126
Grein, J. T. 16, 128
Grey, Clifford 97, 98, 104
Griffiths, Hubert 219, 222
Grossmith Jr., George 92, 96, 98
Group Theatre 27, 154
Gubar, S. 69
guest-directors 140
Guinness, Alec 148, 155, 156
Gullein, Marjorie 165
Gunner, Helen 126
Gunther, John 241
Guthrie, Tyrone 135, 136, 140, 141–3,
    148, 149, 150, 154, 155, 156

Haarmann, Fritz 56–7
Halifax 164
Hall, Lesley 68, 69
Hamilton, Cicely 5, 10, 116

Hamilton, Patrick 30, 57–8, 80–1
Hamlet (Shakespeare) 136, 141, 142,
    155, 156
Hammersmith Theatre 18
Hammond, Aubrey 147
Hankin, St John 5, 166
Hardie, Keir 162
Hardwick, Cedric 230
Hare, Gilbert 43
Hare, John 41
Harrison, Rex 82
Harrow 200
Harwood, H. M. 237
Hassan (Flecker) 21
Havoc (Wall) 218–19
Hawkins, Jack 144
Hayes, George 142, 152
Heartbreak House (Shaw) 42
Heirs to the Charter (Bush, Slater and
    van Gyseghem) 204–5
Hellman, Lillian 76–8
Helpmann, Robert 144
Henderson 101
Henderson, Charles 204
Henry IV (Shakespeare) 193
Henry V (Shakespeare) 138, 145, 148,
    149, 155, 156, 193
Henry VIII (Shakespeare) 144
Henson, Leslie 98, 99, 100
Hentschel, Irene 117, 128–9
Hepburn, Thomas 181
Her Shop 24
Herbert, A. P. 101, 107
Hertford Pageant 201
Hicks, Sir Seymour 91, 92
Hilltop, The (Dodds) 181–2
Hippodrome Theatre 96
Hirshfield, Claire 127
His First Money 177
His Last Bread 177
His Majesty's Theatre, Haymarket
    89–90
history plays 22–3

Index

Hitchcock, Alfred 129
Hitler, Adolf 138, 150, 236
H. M. Tennent Ltd 126
Hoare, Philip 10–11
Holland, Harold 50–1
Holloway, Baliol 135, 144, 145
homosexuality 20, 57, 63–6, 124, 220
    and the theatre 69–70, 72–3, *see also* lesbianism
Horney, Karen 68, 121
Horniman, Annie 15, 126
Hornung, E. W. 41–2
Horrabin, J. F. 176, 183
horror plays 30
Housman, Laurence 162, 165
How to Make a Pageant (Kelly) 197–8
Howes, Bobby 104
Hudson, Gilbert 196, 212
Hulbert, Jack 89, 100
Hullo, Ragtime! (deCourville) 91
Huxley, Julian 152
Hylton, Jack 96

I Have Been Here Before (Priestley) 232–3
If (Dunsan) 218
Image Breaker, The (Gray) 180
In Abraham's Bosom (Green) 183
In Dahomey 91
In Town 92
independent theatres 32, 120, 126
Innes, Christopher 81–2
Inside Europe (Gunther) 241
Inside Latin America (Gunther) 241
Inspector Calls, An (Priestley) 6
Interference 38–40
International Labour Party (ILP)
    Arts Guild 162–89; and Labour
    Party 167, 184; publishing
    companies 176–7
Ipswich 200
Irving, Sir Henry 153, 154
Isherwood, Christopher 27, 32

Jackson, Barry 15, 136, 226
Jay, Harriet 116
jazz 20, 71, 96
Jeannie (Stuart) 128
Jeans, Ronald 94, 102
Jennings, Gertrude 117, 120, 129, 175
Jew Süss 152
Jewres, S. A. 206, 212
Jews 138, 151–4
John Bull 55
Johnson, Agnes 182
Johnson Over Jordan (Priestley) 233–4
Jones, Ernest 142
Jones, Lewis 169
Jones, Stephen G. 184
Jonson, Ben 144
Journey's End (Sherriff) 31, 80, 137,
    221–2, 224
Joy Bells 96
Julius Caesar (Shakespeare) 135, 144,
    155, 166
Justice (Galsworthy) 41, 165

Kean, Edmund 228
Keane, Molly 118, 120
Kelly, Mary 197–8, 199, 201–2, 203,
    211, 212
Kenilworth Castle Pageant (1939)
    190–3
Kennedy, Margaret 120, 122–3
Kenyon, Irene 197
Kern, Jerome 91, 92, 98
Keys, Nelson (Bunch) 94
King John (Shakespeare) 144, 148
King Lear (Shakespeare) 156
King O' Men (Robertson) 181
King's Rhapsody (Novello) 106
Kirby, Max 107
Kirkcaldy 181
Kismet (Asche) 13
Kissing Time 97
Komisarjevsky, Theodore 28, 140, 143,
    151, 152–4

Krauss, Werner 152
Kristeva, Julia 58–9

Labour Leader 167
Labour Party 163
    and ILP 167, 184
Labour Publishing Company 176–7
Labour's Northern Voice 164
Lady with the Lamp, The 22
Lally, Gwen 203, 204
Lancashire Cotton Pageant (Anderson
    and Genn) 201
Lanchester, Elsa 141
Laneham 192
Langdon, B. N. 177
Lascelles, Frank 194, 200–1, 202, 204,
    205–7
Laughton, Charles 53–4, 141, 142–3
Lawrence, D. H. 180
Lawrence, Gertrude 83, 89, 102, 104
Lee, Auriol 116, 117, 129, 130
Leeds Arts 127
Left Book Club Theatre 27–8
legislation prohibiting Sunday
    performances (1781) 184
Leicester 200
Leigh, Vivien 144
Leigh, Walter 109
Lena Ashwell Players 127, 128
Lenin, Vladimir Ilyich 6
Leopold and Loeb case 57–8
lesbianism 63–5, 68, 69, 73–81, 124
Lewis, Edwin G. 177
Liberty's department store 90
Liddell Hart, Sir Basil 220
Lillie, Beatrice 89, 95, 102
literary agents, female 126
Literature and Revolution (Trotsky)
    171
Little Bit of Fluff, A 12
Little Dog Laughed, The 110
Little Miss Mustard 12
Little Revue, The 109

Little Theatre movement 15–16, 109,
    126, 128, 174, 175
Liverpool 107, 126, 164, 201
Loafer and the Loaf, The 178
London 10, 84, 97, 115, 118
    Central ILP Players 168; theatre
    during First World War 7, 9
London Calling (Charlot) 102
London Club Theatres 16
London Coliseum 73
London Palladium 96
London Public Morality Council 71
London Revue (Charlot) 102
London Wall (Van Druten) 24
Lonsdale, Frederick 32
Lord Chamberlain 66, 70, 71, 74, 78,
    81, 83, 94, 124
Lord of the Harvest (Housman) 165
Lord Mayor's Shows 194
Losch, Tilly 103
Lost Empires (Priestley) 232
Louis, Marguerite 168
Love from a Stranger (Vosper) 55
Love of Women (Stuart, A. & P.) 124–5
Love's Labour's Lost (Shakespeare)
    140
Lucid Interval 236
Lunt, Alfred 82
Lupino, Stanley 106
Lyric Theatre 18, 101

Macbeth (Shakespeare) 139, 141–2,
    152–3
McCallin, Clement 148
McCracken, Esther 120
MacDermott, Norman 164
MacDermott, Robert 109
MacDonald, Ramsay 151
McGill, Patrick 222
Machine Wreckers, The (Töller) 175
McIntosh, Madge 126
McMaster, Anew 150
Macnamara, Margaret 180

MacOwen, Michael 155
MacOwen, Norman 235
Macqueen-Pope, W. 9, 18–19
Mädchen in Uniform (film) 63, 74–5
Maid of the Mountains, The 90, 95
Malleson, Miles 123, 124, 162, 165,
    167, 168, 171, 172, 174–5, 177,
    180
Malone, J. A. E. 96, 98
Malvern Festival 15
management
    during World War I 7–9; and star
        actors 17–18; theatre and
        production 18, 97;
        unionisation 16; women in
        125–30
Manchester 15, 126
Manners, Diana 10
Man's House, A (Drinkwater) 32
Marlowe, Alicia 109
Marlowe, Christopher 193
marriage 26, 122, 125
Married Love (Stopes) 69, 122
Marshall, Norman 7, 77, 89, 107, 211
Mary Rose (Barrie) 216–17
Mary Stuart 22
Maschwitz, Eric 106
masculinity, crisis of 68–9, 121
masques 143–7, 194
Masses and Man (Töller) 165, 175
Masses Stage and Film Guild (MSFG)
    182–4
Massine, Leonide 103
Massingham, Dorothy 120
Matthews, Jessie 104, 105, 143
Matthias, Irving 41
Maude Allen v. Pemberton Billing
    libel case 10
Maugham, Somerset 24, 32, 65, 216,
    226–9
Maxton, James 167
Mayer 173
Mayerl, Billy 106

Me and My Girl (Lupino and Gay) 106,
    110
Measure for Measure (Shakespeare)
    142–3
Melford, Austin 100
Melnotte, Violette 127
melodrama 58–9, 221
Merchant of Venice, The (Shakespeare)
    140, 141, 143, 151–2, 153, 154,
    166
Merry Wives of Windsor, The
    (Shakespeare) 143
Meyerhold, V. 228
middle classes 4–5, 24
Middlesborough 164
Midnight Follies 96, 103
Midsummer Night's Dream
    (Shakespeare) 136, 139, 143–4,
    146
Mikado, The (Gilbert and Sullivan) 13,
    90
Millar, Robins 46, 223–4
Millay, Edna St Vincent 166
Mills, John 224
Milne, A. A. 52, 175
Milton, Ernest 135
Miracle at Verdun (Chlumberg) 226
Miracle of Swanleigh Village, The
    (Brain) 181
Moissi, Alexander 136
Monck, Nugent 154, 200, 204, 221
Monckton, Lionel 92
Monkhouse, Alan 219
Morgan, Charles 234–5
Morgan, Diana 109
Morgan, Joan 117
Morley, Christopher 223
Morning After the Night Before, The
    (Brain) 181
Morning Post 13, 14, 115
Morrell, Beatrice 201
Morris, Margaret 165, 168
Morris, William 162, 169

Morrison, G. E. 13–14
Mosley, Sir Oswald 138
Moss, Horace Edward 91
Motley 140
Mr Cinders 104
Mr Clive and Mr Page (Bartlett) 38
Mr Whittington 104
Mrs Fitzherbert 22
Mrs Hodges (Macnamara) 180
Mrs Jupp Obliges 177
Much Ado About Nothing
      (Shakespeare) 143
Muggeridge, Malcolm 138
Murder in the Cathedral (Eliot) 234
Murder has been Arranged, A
      (Williams) 51–2, 229
Murder for Profit (Bolitho) 47, 56–7
Murder of Roger Ackroyd, The
      (Christie) 53
Murder on the Second Floor (Vosper)
      51
murder trials 47
music 165
music hall 221
musical comedies 9, 90–1, 97
      European 21–2
musical theatre 88–112
musicals
      American 103, 104; dancing 97;
      film 104, 105; 'sporting' 106,
      see also book musicals
Mussolini, Benito 153
My Mimosa Maid 90
Mystery Plays 31

National Administrative Council
      (NAC) 162, 164, 168, 171–2
national theatre 14–15, 127, 149–50,
      228
Naughty Wife, The 12
Nazism 150, 236
Neagle, Anna 143
Neath ILP Orpheus Male Choir 165

Neilson, H. V. 148
Nesbitt, Robert 92, 107, 110
Neville, Margaret 120
New Leader 165, 166, 167, 170, 172,
      175
New London Theatre 98
New Spirit in European Theatre:
      1914–1924, The (Carter) 90
New Statesman 154
Newman, Greatrex 104
Nicholson, Steve 66
Nicoll, Allardyce 18, 22, 74, 222
Nicols, Robert 224
Nielsen-Terry, Phylis 144
Nietzsche, Friedrich 57
Night Must Fall (Williams) 57, 141
Nijinsky, Vaslav 109, 144
Nine Sharp 109
Nine Till Six (Stuart, A. and P.) 24, 130
No, No, Nanette (Youmans) 101
Norris, Herbert 148, 149
Northampton 107, 200, 201
Northcott Theatre, Exeter 228
Northern Democrat 169
Norwich 200, 201
Nottingham 200
novel, influence on plays 22
Novello, Ivor 29, 59, 89, 102, 105–6,
      155, 240
Nymph Errant (Porter) 103

O'Brien, Kate 120
O'Casey, Sean 31, 32, 135, 136, 138
O'Connor, Sean 65, 66
Odds and Ends (Cochran) 92
Oh What a Lovely War 221
Oklahoma 103
Old Bill 218
Old Vic 127, 135, 136, 138–43, 147–8,
      149, 151, 156
Oliver Cromwell 22
Olivier, Laurence 141, 142, 149, 155
On Borrowed Time 230

On the Rocks (Shaw) 238–9
On the Spot (Wallace) 50
On With The Dance (Coward) 103
'Once a Week Players' 127
O'Neill, Eugene 32, 137
Open Air Theatre, Regents Park 143–4
operettas 90
    American 101; German 105
Organized Theatre, The (Ervine) 14
orientalism 13, 21, 89–90
Original Dixieland Jazz Band 96
Othello (Shakespeare) 129, 137–8
Our Miss Gibbs 92
Outward Bound (Vane) 218
Oxford 107
Oxford Union 148–9
Oxfordshire Historical Pageant (1932)
    205

pageant, historical 22, 190–212
    sediment, theme and narrative
        203–5
Pageant of Bradstone (Kelly) 201, 202,
    203, 204
Pageant of Empire (Lascelles and
    Benson) 201
Pageant of England (Lally and Bowen)
    203
Pageant of Labour (Anderson, Genn
    and Bush) 204
Pageant of Launceston (Kelly) 202
Pageant of London (Lascelles) 201
Pageant of Mangel-Wurzelton 208–9
Pageant Masters 200–1
Pageant of Music and the People (Bush
    and Swingler) 205
Pageant Rehearsal, The (Sequira)
    210–11
Pageant of South Wales (Bush, Slater
    and van Gyseghem) 204
Pageant of Transport (Anderson and
    Genn) 201
Pageant of Victory (Bergerac) 201

Pageant of Wroxall Abbey 190
pageantry
    petit-bourgeois carnival 208–12;
        urbanisation and Depression
        205–7
Palaises de Dance 96–7
pantomime 73, 89–90
Paris 10, 151
Parker, Anthony 191, 193, 211
Parker, Louis Napoleon 22, 193, 194,
    195, 196, 197, 199, 200, 203–4,
    211, 212
Parliamentary Labour Club 166
Parlour, The 12
pastorals 143–7
Payne, Ben Iden 147, 148, 150, 152,
    154
Peach, L. du Garde 208–9, 210, 211,
    212
Pearce, Leonard 168
Peg of Old Drury 143
Pelissier, Harry 92
Pellizzi, Camillo 4–5, 9, 22, 23, 24–5,
    28, 30, 31, 221–2, 229
People Like Us (Vosper) 55
People's National Theatre (PNT) 16, 128
Pericles (Shakespeare) 144
Persian Princess, The 90
Peter Pan (Barrie) 41
Phoenix Theatre 124
Pierrot troupe 92
Pinero, Sir Arthur 9, 25, 32, 218
Pirandello, Luigi 32
Pitman's Pay, The (Dodds) 181
Place in the Sun, A 177
play-reading groups 174
Playfair, Nigel 101
Playhouse Theatre 127, 128
plays
    bedroom and pyjama 12; foreign
        32; team-authored 119
'Plays for the People' 176–7
'Plays for a People's Theatre' 180

Playwright at Work (Van Druten) 129

playwrights, female 25–6, 116–18

playwriting
before First World War 4–6; from ILP Dramatic Groups 180–2

Please Get Married 12

Poel, William 8, 11, 147, 151

political extravaganza 236–41

politics, and war 226–30

Pollitt, Harry 205

Ponsonby, Arthur 169

Porter, Cole 103

Portman, Eric 156

Posford, George 106

Postmortem (Coward) 224–5

Powell, Kerry 116

Pressed Man, The (Dodds) 182

Price, Nancy 16, 127–8

Priestley, J. B. 5–6, 24, 128, 230–6

Primrose (Gershwin) 98–9

Prisoners of War, The (Ackerley) 80, 220

Private Lives (Coward) 71, 83–4, 104, 225

production, women in 128–30

professional plays 24–5

Progressive Players, Gateshead 181

'Propaganda in the Theatre' (Scott) 172

Pryce, Richard 223

psychoanalysis, Freudian 67–8, 82–3, 121

Q Theatre 126

Quaker Girl The 92

Quayle, Anthony 156

Queens Theatre 136, 141

queer identity 69–70

Quiller-Couch, Arthur Thomas 209–10

Quinquaginta Dance Club, Cambridge 96

racism 137–8, 154

radio 4, 24, 89, 97

Radio Revue 97

Raffe, W. C. 172, 176

'Raffles' 41–2

ragtime 20, 91

Rambert, Marie 103

Ramsgate 200

Randolph, Elsie 100

Rattigan, Terence 20, 65, 81, 236

Raynal, Paul 225–6

Razzle Dazzle (deCourville) 92

Reading Historical Pageant 201

realist drama 6, 9, 24–5

Red Stage 179

regional companies 107

Reinhardt, Max 144

Rejane, Gabrielle 125

repertory companies, Shakespearean 136

repertory theatre movement 14, 15, 89, 175

revues 12, 21, 71, 72–3, 88–112, 107–10
go-as-you-please 9; intimate 92–3; 'intimate intimate' 109–10; and licensing laws 92; 'non-stop' 107

Reynolds, Ernest 229

Reynolds, Frederick 175

'Rhapsody in Blue' (Gershwin), Tod's choreography 103

Richard of Bordeaux 22

Richard II (Shakespeare) 139, 141, 142

Richard III (Shakespeare) 142, 144

Richardson, Ralph 139, 148–9, 151

Ridley, Arnold 30

Right of Way, The (Brain) 181

Rillington, pageant for 201

Ringer, The (Wallace) 48–50

Rising Sun, The 176, 177

Ritchard, Cyril 100, 109

Riverside Nights (Herbert) 101, 107

Robert Burns 22
Robert E. Lee 22
Robert's Wife (Ervine) 26
Robertson, James 181
Robeson, Paul 129, 137–8
Robey, George 96
Robins, Elizabeth 116
Robson, Flora 141, 142
Rodgers and Hart 101, 104
Romance of King Arthur, The
    (Morrell) 201
Romeo and Juliet (Shakespeare) 138–9,
    146
Roose, Olwen 43
Rope (Hamilton) 30, 57–8, 80–1
Rose Marie 101
Rose without a Thorn 22
Roy, R. L. 166
Royal Academy of Dramatic Art 128
Royal General Theatrical Fund 126
Royal Variety Command Performance
    (1912) 91
Royde-Smith, Naomi 120
Rubens, Paul 92
Rupert Doone's Group Theatre 236
Ruritania 29, 90
Russian 'bat theatre' (Chauvre Souris)
    101

Sadlers Wells theatre 147, 148
Sagan, Leontine 63
St James Theatre 51–2
Sally 98
Salome (Wilde) 10
Samuel, Raphael 163, 171
San Toy 90
'Sapper' 42–6
Sassoon, Siegfried 220–1
Saville, Ian 171, 174
Savoy Orpheans 96–7
Savoy Theatre 90, 104, 137, 139
Sayers, Dorothy L. 155
Schnitzler, Arthur 32

School for Scandal, A (Sheridan) 175
Scotland 181, 203
Scott, Elizabeth 145, 146
Scott Fitzgerald, F. 92, 100
Scott, Harold 172, 182
Scottish Historical Pageant (Benson)
    203
Scrapped (Brosnan) 181
Selyer, Athene 141
Sequira, Horace 210–11
Service (Smith) 24
settings, downgrading of 24
sex, and theatre during WWI 10–14
sexology 67–8, 121
sexuality
    freedom 20, *see also*
      homosexuality
Shairp, Mordaunt 63–4, 79–80, 124
Shakespeare, William 129, 135–61,
    175, 192
Shakespeare Memorial Theatre 15,
    128, 143
Sharp, Evelyn 168, 176
Shaw, George Bernard 5, 6, 32, 41–2,
    163, 165, 174, 226, 237–9
She Passed through Lorraine 22
Sheffield Repertory Theatre 15
Sheppey (Maugham) 32, 226–7
Sherborne Pageant 193, 194, 195
Sherriff, R. C. 31, 80, 137, 221–2
Shop Girl, The 92
Short, Ernest 114, 219
Show Boat 101, 137
Shropshire 201
Shubert Brothers 8, 91
Silver Tassie, The (O'Casey) 31, 136,
    152
Sinclair, Upton 182–3
Sinfield, Alan 69–70, 72–3, 80
Singing Jailbirds, The (Sinclair) 182–3
sketches 93–6
Slater, Montagu 204
Sleepless Night, A 12

Smith, Dodie 24, 117, 118, 119–20, 128
Smith, G. J. 47
Smith-Dorien, Sir H. 12
Smythe, Dame Ethel 152
Snowden, Ethel 169
Snowden, Philip 164, 171
social class, and audiences 23–8, 71
socialism 162–89
Socialist Choir 165
Socialist Review 172
Society of West End Managers 97
songs 105–6, 216
Southern Maid, A 98
Sowerby, Githa 122
spectacle 71
Spender, Stephen 236
spiritualist churches 215
Splinters 73
Sporting Love (Mayerl and Lupino) 106
Squeaker, The (Wallace) 50
Stage Guild 16
Stage Society 175
Stamp, Reginald 165
Stanislavsky (Konstantin Sergeyevich
        Alexeyev) 142
Stern, G. B. 117, 120, 121
Stokes, John 118
Stoll, Oswald 91
Stone, Lew 97
Stop Flirting 97
Stopes, Marie 20, 69, 122
Storm, Lesley 120
Stowell, Sheila 76
Strand Theatre 91, 162, 165–7
Strange Orchestra (Ackland) 81
Stratford Shakespeare Theatre 145–8
Stratford-upon-Avon 14, 140, 142, 143,
        145–7, 149–50, 152
Strauss, Johann 103
Street, The 177
Strindberg, August 32
Stuart, Aimée 24, 120, 121, 124–5, 128,
        130

Stuart, Philip 24, 124–5, 130
Sullivan, Francis 53
Sunday Play Societies 16
Supply and Demand 24
Suspense (McGill) 222
Swaffer, Hannen 137
Sweeney Agonistes (Eliot) 55
Swingler, Randall 205

Tableaux Vivant method 179
Taming of the Shrew, The
        (Shakespeare) 143
Tandy, Jessica 64, 75–6
tea dances 20, 97
Tempest, The (Shakespeare) 146
Temple, Joan 120
Tennant, H. M. 105
Tennyson-Jesse, Fryn 120
Terry, Ellen 125
Thatcher, Heather 98
theatre
        Americanised 90–1; during First
        World War 7–14; feminisation
        of 114; and political change
        28–9; post-First World War
        14–22; response to war 215–43
Theatre Arts 147
*Theatre in a Changing Civilization,
        The* (Komisarjevsky) 28, 153
Theatre Royal, Drury Lane 105, 240
'Theatre of War' (Fussell) 220–1
Theatre World 154
theatres, chains of 91
Theatres of the Left (Samuel) 163
Theilade, Nini 144
These Mortals (Harwood) 237
This Year of Grace (Cochran) 103
This Year Next Year 107–9
Thomas, L. Edith 191–2
Thomas, Tom 179
Thompson, Fred 97, 104
Thorndike, Dame Sybil 17, 29, 116,
        129, 150, 162, 166

thrillers 38–62, 71
  and detective stories 52–4
Thunder in the Air (Millar) 46, 223–4
Thunder on the Left (Pryce) 223
Thunder Rock (Ardrey) 240–1
time, playing with 223–6, 230–6
Time and the Conways (Priestley) 128, 231
Times, The 13, 53, 142, 145, 150, 152, 156, 183
Timon of Athens (Shakespeare) 144, 154
Tod, Quentin 103
Töller, Ernst 32, 175
Tomb, The (Clynes) 166
Tomorrow (Fernald) 222–3
Tonight at 8.30 (Coward) 104
Tons of Money (Evans) 30
Too True to be Good (Shaw) 226, 238
Torquay 201
Touch and Go (Lawrence) 180
touring companies 15
Towards Tomorrow (Bush, Slater and van Gyseghem) 204
Town That Would Have a Pageant, The (Peach) 208–9, 212
trade unions 163, 182
  actors 16–17; management 16
tragedy 71, 119
Travers, Ben 12, 30
Travers, Linden 230
Trevilian, M. F. Cely 204
Trewin, J. C. 14, 21, 29, 31, 217, 218, 230, 235
Trial of a Judge (Spender) 236
Troilus and Cressida (Shakespeare) 154–5
Trojan Women, The 129
Trotsky, Leon 170–1
Trusts 8, 11
'Truth about Sex Murders' (Wallace) 55–6
Tunnel Trench (Griffiths) 219, 222

Twelfth Night (Shakespeare) 143–4
Twenty to One 106
Tyrer, H. M. 71

Unity Theatre 16, 27, 236
Unknown, The (Maugham) 216
Unknown Warrior, The (Raynal) 225–6
Up in Mabel's Room 12
USA, theatre trusts 8

'Valentine' 30
Valk, Frederick 154
Valois, Ninette de 103, 144
Van Druten, John 24, 78–9, 129
van Gyseghem, André 204
Vane, Sutton 217–18
variety 88–9, 91, 95
Variety palaces 91
vaudeville 73
Vaudeville Theatre 93
Verse Speaking Choir 165
Victoria, Queen 199
village drama society 202
Voltaire 75
Vortex, The (Coward) 82–3, 125
Vosper, Frank 51, 55
Vosper, Margery 126

Walbrook, Anton 82
Walkley, A. B. 129
Wall, Harry 218–19
Wallace, Edgar 29, 30, 32, 48–50, 52, 55
Waltzes from Vienna 105
war
  crimes 47–8; and politics 226–30;
    theatrical response to 215–43
Warwick Pageant (1906) 193
Warwickshire Charity Carnival 190
Webster, Margaret 124, 129
Wedekind, Frank 32
Weekly Dispatch 12
Weeks, Jeffrey 66–7, 69

Index

Weiner, Joyce 126
Wellock, Wilfred 175
Wells 201
Wells, H. G. 221
West End 15, 16, 18, 70–1, 72, 81, 88, 91, 92, 96, 120, 175
West End ILP Orchestra 165, 168
West Salford 164, 181
Westminster Theatre 140, 154
What is Wrong with the Theatre (Poel) 11
What Made the Iron Grow 236
What Tommy Fought For 173
Wheel, The 181
White Chrysanthemum, The 90
White Horse Inn 105
White Slave Act (1912) 66–7
white-collar workers 24
Whiteman, Paul 96
Who's Hooper? 97
Widdop, James 164
Widower's Houses (Shaw) 165
Wild Decembers 22
Wild Violets 22
Wilde, Oscar 10, 67
  trials 69–70
Wilkinson, Norman 146
Will Shakespeare 22
Williams, Emlyn 29, 51–2, 53–4, 56–7, 141, 142, 143, 229
Williams, Harcourt 138–9, 140, 141, 142, 148, 151, 156
Williams, Lawrence and Walter 94
Wimperis, Arthur 94
Winchester Pageant (Benson) 210
Windmill Theatre 107
Wingfield-Stratton, Esme 5, 6, 7
Wings Over Europe (Nicols and Browne) 224
Winsloe, Christa 63, 73–4, 76
Winter Garden 98
Wipers Times, The 221

Within the Gates (O'Casey) 32
Withington, Robert 194–5, 196, 199, 201, 209
Wodehouse, P. G. 97, 98, 104
Wolfit, Donald 15, 150
women
  in audience 25, 71, 114, 119;
    economic independence 20,
    113; and interwar theatre
    113–34; playwrights 25–6,
    116–18; as a problem 118,
    120–5; in work force 113–14;
    and World War I theatre 9–10,
    see also franchise for women
Women and Wine 12
Women's Institute 202
women's movement, and Freudian
    psychoanalysis 68
Wonder, Sam 104
Wonder Bar 104
Woods, Michael 212
Woolf, Virginia 115
Workers' Educational Association 14, 15
Workers' Theatre Movement 16, 163, 179, 183, 184
working class 6, 19, 24, 25
Wright, Geoffrey 107
Wyndhams Theatre 42
Wynyard, Diana 82

Yaffle 165, 178
Yeats, W. B. 148, 151
Yesterday and Today (Winsloe) 63
York Pageant 197
Youmans 101
Young Heaven (Malleson) 165
Young Woodley (van Druten) 78–9
Youth Movement 71

Zaire (Voltaire) 75
Ziegfeld, F. 102